Canada's Teens

Today, Yesterday, and Tomorrow

Reginald W. Bibby, Ph.D.

Published in 2001 by Stoddart Publishing Co. Limited
895 Don Mills Road, 400-2 Park Centre, Toronto, Canada M3C 1W3

Distributed by:
General Distribution Services Ltd.
325 Humber College Blvd., Toronto, Ontario M9W 7C3
Tel. (416) 213-1919   Fax (416) 213-1917
Email cservice@genpub.com

05 04 03 02 01 1 2 3 4 5

Canadian Cataloguing in Publication Data

Bibby, Reginald W. (Reginald Wayne)
Canada's teens : today, yesterday, and tomorrow

Includes bibliographical references and index.
ISBN 0-7737-6181-0

1. Teenagers — Canada. 2. Teenagers — Canada — Attitudes. I. Title.

HQ799.C2B518 2001   305.235'0971   C00-932834-3

Cover design: Bill Douglas @ The Bang
Text design: Joseph Gisini/PageWave Graphics Inc.

THE CANADA COUNCIL | LE CONSEIL DES ARTS
FOR THE ARTS | DU CANADA
SINCE 1957 | DEPUIS 1957

We acknowledge for their financial support of our publishing program the Canada Council, the Ontario Arts Council, and the Government of Canada through the Book Publishing Industry Development Program (BPIDP).

Printed and bound in Canada

To my three guys,

Reggie, Dave, and Russ

Sources of great joy
as children,
as teenagers,
as men.

Contents

Preface

FUNNY THAT THIS FIRST PART OF A BOOK IS THE LAST THING WRITTEN. It consequently is often coloured by the weariness and emotion that come from having spent a very long time working on a very demanding project.

Canada's Teens releases extensive new data on Canadian young people and adults produced through two new national surveys carried out in 2000. But it also draws on our previous youth surveys in 1984 and 1992, and our adult surveys carried out every five years dating back to 1975 — a total of seven other surveys in all. This lifetime project of mine has involved a lot of work and a lot of money.

It continues to be anything but a one-man show. The early money came from a variety of generous sources cited in earlier works. In recent years the primary source of funding has been the Lilly Endowment; I cannot adequately express my appreciation to the Endowment for its tremendous support, and the positive and warm encouragement of Craig Dykstra, Jim Lewis, and Chris Coble.

Nine surveys have required nine samples, meaning thousands of Canadians have given of their time. The three youth surveys have involved more than 3,500 high school students each, while the sample average for the six adult surveys has been around 1,600 people. Many thanks to the adults, students, and schools for making it all possible. Large numbers of adults have participated in more than one survey as part of our ongoing "panels"; about two hundred have filled out *all six* of the questionnaires since 1975. The teen participants are as young as 15. Our oldest adult survey participant in 2000 was a 95-year-old man from a small Ontario community; he wrote, "Thank you for letting me answer your questions. I am presently retired and living with my wife of 74 years"! Large numbers of people have shown large amounts of generosity.

And then there has been the workforce. I'm not great at delegation, but in a project of this magnitude, one either delegates or dies. My primary research associate over the years has been my oldest son, Reggie Jr., who has served as project manager since 1990, overseeing the carrying out of five of the surveys, after having provided assistance on two others. His competence and commitment have been key to the successful completion of the surveys. My other two sons, Dave and Russ, have also been part of a number of the surveys and have likewise brought a unique level of commitment and quality to the project. Some other main players need to be acknowledged briefly: Jim Savoy, my tireless computing whiz; research assistants Michelle Burke and Michèle Therrien; translator Diane Erickson; people "on the lines" over the years such as Bob Probe, Heather McCuaig, Lorraine Ogilvie, Tanneya Barclay, and Nicky Bullock; and the input of James Penner and Dave Overholt. I again have enjoyed working closely with Stoddart's Donald G. Bastian, a long-term associate and friend. For a fourth time, Maryan Gibson has provided her valuable copy-editing skills. I also want to thank Don Posterski for his significant contributions to the earlier teen surveys; he continues to be a valued colleague.

The dissemination of such an extensive amount of data is not easy. I have been torn between trying not to overwhelm readers with sheer volume, while at the same time feeling the need to adequately clarify and provide a cultural context for the material presented. Undoubtedly there will be critics who will want less, as well as others who will want more. This volume is just an aerial-photograph start. I hope that other articles and even another book or two will help to fill out the picture, written not only by me but also by others. Overholt and Penner, for example, will be coming out shortly with a Stoddart publication on the implications of the findings for youth ministry.

As usual, my goal has been not only to produce a book that is academically solid, but one that can be both understood and enjoyed by people who are interested in youth and Canadian life. If it disappoints academics who want more theory and practitioners who want more application, I would take a deep breath and suggest, as I have in the past, that I can't do it all. What you have before you, I believe, is one of the richest bodies of data on Canadians that we have ever seen. I hope we can build on it.

And thanks to you the reader for giving this a look. The line between work and play has seldom been clear for me, because of the enjoyment I receive from trying to understand how the world works. An unexpected gift over the years has been the extent to which I have been allowed to share my findings and ideas. That's where you come in.

REGINALD W. BIBBY
Lethbridge, 2001

The Need for Some Conversations

Age-Old Anxiety about Youth

In late October of 2000, respected pollster Alain Giguere told an Ottawa gathering of the Canadian Conference of Catholic Bishops that he was reluctant to bring the bishops the results of surveys carried out by his Montreal-based firm (CROP) because of the shocking findings about today's youth. Giguere reported that today's young people love violence, are sexually permissive, pleasure seeking, get high on risk-taking, are weak on ethics and social concern, and are devaluing both religion and the family. "We are dealing with a generation that has grown up on Hollywood," he said. "They are bombarded with sex and violence, and have no sense of responsibility." And then he added the knockout punch: "I tremble to see what kind of society they are going to produce in 20 to 25 years."[1]

By the time you are through reading this book, you will find it very difficult to agree with Giguere. This will not be a total good-news story. Far from it. But it will hardly leave you trembling when you think of the place young people will have in Canada's future.

Yes, we worry a great deal about young people. We worry about what they are like now and we worry about what they are going to be like later. One expert on youth, Jonathon Epstein, goes as far as to say that confusion and anxiety are so widespread that those interested in young people are inclined to define adolescence itself as a social problem![2] I have no doubt that one of the main reasons there has been such interest in the youth research program we began in the 1980s is that people in each new decade have been worried about each new teen cohort — what exactly their teens have been up to and whether they are going to turn out as well as those of previous decades and generations.

Two quotes are worth resurrecting from our earlier books. The first is a well-worn lament that sounds like a wild-eyed quote from a TV interview last night: "Children today are tyrants. They contradict their parents, gobble their food, and terrorize their teachers." Sound like something you heard recently? Actually, it's a relic, offered by Socrates some four centuries B.C. The second observation also provides some historical perspective on concern about young people. Educator Anthony Kerr has commented, "I have a pretty fair idea of history over the past twenty-five centuries and cannot recall a time when the old were fully satisfied with the young." Fortunately the anxiety is seldom justified. Despite all the hand-wringing, says Kerr, "the world has gone on, apparently getting no worse."[3]

Nonetheless, adult anxiety levels about teenagers have remained high through recent decades. In 1965, 76% of Canadians believed there should be a curfew in their own communities for youths under the age of 16.[4] As of 1995, when people thought youth problems were reaching new highs, the pro-curfew figure was still significant — but actually dropped to 62%.[5]

In short, adults have always worried about young people. They still are worried today.

A Time to Worry

To some extent, of course, the anxiety is certainly warranted. Pronouncements from people like Kerr that previous generations of teens have turned out OK might console us for a moment or two. But the feeling soon passes. There's no guarantee that history is going to repeat itself. Precisely because past adults and their offspring have been living in eras characterized by significant social and cultural change, they have been concerned that those changes may have unprecedented effects on young people and societies as a whole.

At this point in Canadian history, change seems almost overwhelming. The emergence of the computer and the Internet in the past few decades has contributed to massive social, cultural, economic, and technological changes. Such accelerated and extensive changes are often bewildering. Mystique-filled talk about "digital technology" and "cyberspace" and "virtual reality" sometimes makes it seem that we are not all living on the same planet. Or maybe it's just that some aliens landed in Seattle and have been taking over the earth. As if that were not enough, the sense of change undoubtedly has been intensified by the fact that we find ourselves in the first years of a new millennium, complete with daily conjecture, facts, and myths about how this new century is going to be very different from anything in the past. Given all this change, who but the non-reflective would not be concerned about what it will all mean to young people?

Another reason Canadians, especially parents, are worried about young people is that they want to see them get through their teens without making, as one young person told me, "life-altering mistakes." They don't want them to get hurt, run into problems with drugs or the law, get pregnant; on the positive side, they want to see them finish school, be happy, be healthy. In the words of another teen, adults don't want "to see us throw our futures away."

Here, as if change and a new century were not enough, anxiety among parents about the health and safety of their teenagers has been heightened in recent years by highly publicized incidents of violence and youth crime. Then there has been the ongoing reality of drug abuse, including the potential for alcohol to contribute to any number of unwanted problems. The heading of a recent article by Christie Blatchford in the *National Post* summed things up this way: "It's not easy being a teenager today," continuing on with "More drugs, more cliques, more sex, more casual cruelty in today's schools."[6]

As for happiness, Canadian parents want their teens to be happy, but they also want them to behave themselves and stay out of trouble in the process — guidelines with important implications for how they want their daughters and sons to deal with alcohol, sex, and anything else that can mess up life for everybody. In the midst of it all, parents worry about grades and, in some instances, the problem of keeping their kids in school. And when all's said and done, they want them to turn out OK — whatever exactly that means.

In short, virtually all parents want their teenagers to . . .

- be happy.
- be safe.
- get through school.
- be healthy.
- stay out of trouble.
- turn out OK.

> **What Parents Say to Teens as They Leave the House —
> and the Hopes Those Lines Reflect:**
>
> | | |
> |---|---|
> | 1. "Have a good time." | Happiness. |
> | 2. "Take care of yourself." | Good health. |
> | 3. "Drive carefully." | Safety. |
> | 4. "Behave yourself." | Stay out of trouble. |
> | 5. "Did you do your homework?" | Get through school. |

Many worry a great deal when they think such hopes might not be realized.

A Time to Worry More

Beyond immediate concerns, adults invariably express concern about how teenagers are going to turn out. In this regard, it's time we took on two widely held myths.

1. What teens are like today is what they will be like as adults tomorrow.

Obviously, that's a false assumption. We all know that life does not follow some magical straight course; the line on our biographical charts is not linear. Few of us would maintain that the values, attitudes, beliefs, and expectations we had as teenagers are the same as the ones we have today. In the words of a 17-year-old female from Sherbrooke, "My point of view on certain things changes from day to day." We grow, progress, and sometimes regress. But, thank goodness, we don't stay the same. How people start is not necessarily how they will finish — as any class reunion serves to remind us. Where teenagers are today is a poor gauge of where they will be tomorrow. At best, we can only hope to get our sons and daughters and students off to a good start. Teens today are not the adults of tomorrow.

2. Today's teens will control tomorrow's world.

This second common assumption is triumphantly declared from convocation podiums and enthusiastically embraced by young people. In our latest youth survey, one 16-year-old male from North York,

Ontario, comments that "The people in power should listen to the youth of today because we are the ones who will be running our country in the future," while a 15-year-old male from Edmonton tells us, "Teen views on world issues are important because, after all, we are the ones who will be running the world in a few years." Such observations are based on the assumption that when teenagers "graduate" into the adult world, they essentially take over. It's as if they arrive in an *Ally McBeal*–like, one-generational world, where everything is suddenly run by people who are in their 20s and 30s, and where people who are older — save an aging judge or two — are conspicuous by their absence. It's time the news got out: life doesn't work that way.

In reality, of course, young people never take over the world. Nor do old people stay at the controls. More accurately, young women and men are gradually integrated into a world that is "run" by adults of all ages. The adult world is an intergenerational world. That world includes more than a few older people who exert considerable control and power because of their status, for example, as owners, CEOs, investors, directors, board members, consultants, alumni, long-term members, and consumers. To use a simple sports analogy, it seems to me that teenagers enter an adult-dominated world that is more like an NHL team than an *Ally McBeal* set, where, as young adults, they are the unproven rookies surrounded by average players, seasoned vets, an older coaching staff, and even older upper management and owners. It may not be what the rookies want, but that's the reality the rookies get.

Consequently, to shudder about what the world of tomorrow will be like, given today's teenagers, is, frankly, a waste of shudder. That's just not the way the world works. In reality, teens will one day be working alongside people of all ages. Teens today will not control the world tomorrow.

Refocusing Our Anxiety

To recap, yes, we need to clearly understand today's teenagers because we want them to stay alive and live well. In light of accelerated and new forms of change, we need to monitor the nature and quality of their lives, including comparing the latest emerging generation with those of the past. We need a clear and comparative reading of today's young people.

But we also need to do more than make precarious assumptions about how they will turn out and how they will shape our world, based on where they are now. We need to take a careful look at how, in fact, teenagers have been changing over time so that we can get some clues as to what will happen to today's teens, and how they might be expected to contribute to our collective social life.

The Plan of the Book

To get a comprehensive reading of teens today, I engaged in lengthy conversations with some 3,500 young people, aged 15 to 19, in the late spring and early fall of 2000. The conversations took place through the use of a carefully designed, self-administered questionnaire that was filled out by students in more than 150 randomly selected high school classes across the country. This superb sample makes it possible to generalize to Canada's 15-to 19-year-old high school population with a high degree of confidence. The survey allows us to hear directly from today's teenagers — to get an inside look at what they are thinking, how they are living, their values, hopes, and fears, and how in general they are putting the world together.

The limitation of such a survey is that we still are left wondering about the unique impact of social and cultural change on today's youth; we don't know how they compare with their counterparts of yesterday. Fortunately we have additional surveys that make it possible to explore "teens yesterday."

In 1984 and 1992, I also had extensive conversations with similar numbers of teenagers across the country and asked them many of the same questions that were put to teens in 2000. Consequently it's possible for us to take a look at the extent to which teens have been changing in recent decades. A total of about 10,000 young people are involved. But that's not all. Through my complementary adult national surveys, I also have been having conversations with Canadian adults every five years from 1975 through 2000 — close to 7,000 people in all. I've put many items from the youth surveys in the adult surveys, so that we can compare teens and adults. In the 2000 adult survey, I also asked people to reflect on their lives as teenagers, allowing us to get an interesting peek at how parents and grandparents remember life being "back then."

Having explored teens today and yesterday, we will tackle the difficult task of exploring what teens will be like tomorrow. It's a tough assignment, but we will take it on. Here we will try to get some informed ideas by drawing on what adults of various ages have told us about how they have changed since their teenage years. In addition to relying on their perception of how they have changed, we will also carry out a "cohort analysis," a fancy way of saying that we will use our 1980 youth survey and 2000 adult survey to simulate how teenagers in the 1980s "have turned out" as adults who are now in their 30s and 40s. I will explain the specifics later.

The book will start with teens today, move to teens yesterday, and then focus on teens tomorrow. I'll conclude with a general assessment that brings us back to where we started — common anxiety about young people — and, in light of everything we have been finding, address the question, "What's all the fuss about?"

I discuss two generations throughout the book, Generation X and the Millennials. The names of these generations come to us from popular culture, the former from the title of a book by Douglas Coupland, *Generation X*, about those born between 1965 and 1984. The generation that has followed them, then, are those born since 1985, the Millennials. I'll be defining these groups in more detail in chapter 5.

One important point of clarification. A few years ago I was speaking to students at a prestigious Toronto high school. During the question period, a young woman somewhat indignantly protested, "How can you generalize about all of us? We're all individuals. We're all different." Her point is well taken. Obviously we are all individuals. And in a cultural environment where individualism is widespread, all of us want to believe that we are unique. But surely we also have some things in common. Otherwise social life at any level would not be possible.

In a March of 1999, *Maclean's* carried a front-page story on today's nine- to 14-year-olds — "tweens" — and 15- to 19-year-old teens. Sean Saraq, a demographer with the highly regarded Environics Research Group, commented, "The deeper people dig, the more they realize that teens are all over the map." Further, the writer of the article, Andrew Clark, claimed that, because of Canada's cultural diversity, "They are, by far, the most racially diverse generation in

Canada's history." The net result, Clark maintained, "is a teen culture without a single overriding identity."[7]

Depending on the criteria one wants to use, young people can be divided into any number of market segments or "tribes," as Michael Adams and the Environics people like to call them.[8] But diversity — especially when it is magnified in order to market products to specific segments — hardly precludes commonalities. Clark acknowledges that gender, for example, represents a striking and important division in understanding the market demands of young people. And Saraq humorously acknowledges, "They are trying to be different just like everyone else."[9]

So, beyond impressions, assumptions, and marketing agendas, let's let the data speak for themselves. In what follows, I will be bending over backwards to respect individuality, while at the same time keeping an eye out for patterns that also point to commonality.

There's an important story in all this that needs to be told. Let's get started.

Part I

Teens Today

Chapter One

What's Important

IF I WANTED TO GET TO KNOW YOU, WHAT YOU ARE REALLY LIKE, AT some point I would want to know what you care deeply about. I'd want to know your values, what you want out of life, and what you think is important in the course of pursuing your goals. That's our starting point with teenagers.

Values

We gave teens a list of 27 characteristics and asked them to indicate how important they *personally* consider each characteristic to be. The four response options were "very important" through "not important at all."

What we found is that there is nothing teenagers value more highly than *friendship* and *freedom*. Close to nine in ten place high levels of importance on being linked to friends while simultaneously having the freedom to live life as they see fit. Not surprisingly, the related traits of *being loved* and *having choices* are also among the characteristics teens value the most. *Friendship* and *being loved* are particularly important to females, but they are just as likely as males to place importance on freedom and choices. These seemingly paradoxical values are ones that are common to all of us. Most of us find we deeply value good ties with the people we care about. At the same time, we don't want to sacrifice our individuality and autonomy. The trick is finding out how to get it all. It's a delicate balance. By the time young people have reached their teens, they already are experiencing that tension. Friends are great, but so is freedom.

Next in importance to Canada's young people are *a comfortable life* and *success*. Some seven in ten say they want to succeed at what they do, and also live well materially. No surprises here. Who doesn't want to be good at what they do? Besides, while onlookers may be extremely tolerant — or at least indifferent — towards what interests people, no one particularly applauds those who fail at what they choose to pursue. Implicit in the attitude of "just do it" is the expectation that winners "do it well." Just think of the pervasiveness among young people of the term "loser." Winning is much more fun and much more valued. And teens, like the rest of us, want to continue to experience the comfortable life to which many of them have grown accustomed, coming out of the reasonably comfortable homes of Baby Boomer parents. If they have not been so fortunate, our consumption-oriented society constantly reminds them what they are missing and makes consumption a matter of conformity.

One stereotype that is reasonably accurate is that young people want to have fun. Approximately six in ten teens say that *excitement* is "very important" to them. What troubles adults, of course, is what goes into having fun. As one Hamilton-area 18-year-old put it, "My parents want me to have fun. But in the next breath, they're worried about how I have it." Here those concerns about things like music, friends, sex, drugs, safety, and staying out of trouble all begin to kick in. A 16-year-old female from southern Alberta offers this view: "Most teenagers are quite responsible. It's just that they want to have fun while they can before life gets too hectic. Everyone needs to experience life a little bit."

Liking excitement doesn't mean that young people are self-absorbed, happy little hedonists who are indifferent to other people. *Concern for others* and *family life* are also highly valued by six in ten, including some 70% of females and 50% of males. "The world around us could get much better," suggests a 15-year-old female from Toronto, "if we cared about our neighbours and less about ourselves." She adds, "Life is good when you are good to life." Another female, a 16-year-old who lives in the Yukon, commented somewhat playfully, "I'm not a typical teenager. I contribute to my community and I do tip. I smile at strangers and say hello to those who look a little blue."

Just under one in two young people indicate that *what their parents think of them* is extremely important, with the figure for females (50%) higher than that of males (38%). Basic social psychology confirms what teens are willing to acknowledge. When children value their parents, the views that their mothers and fathers have of them are fundamental to how they see themselves. As parents come to be devalued and are replaced by other "significant others," their views of their children cease to carry as much psychological and emotional weight. For some teens, the alleged devaluation at this point may be temporary, reflecting their growing dependence on friends for their sense of who they are. For others, the minimizing of parents' views of them may indicate that a father or a mother no longer is playing a key role in their lives, often because of divorce or separation.

Table 1.1. **Valued Goals of Teenagers**

% Viewing as "Very Important"

	Nationally	**Males**	**Females**
Friendship	85%	80	90
Freedom	85	84	85
Being loved	77	65	87
Having choices	76	73	79
A comfortable life	73	71	74
Success in what you do	71	70	73
Concern for others	62	51	73
Family life	59	51	66
Excitement	57	58	55
What your parents think of you	44	38	50
Your looks	39	40	39
Recognition	32	34	31
Spirituality	29	23	35
Having power	24	32	16
Being popular	16	21	11
Religious group involvement	10	9	10

During this time of physical emergence, when teens literally are trying to figure out what they look like, four in ten males and females admit that *their looks* are "very important" to them. Stay tuned to this topic: as we will see shortly, while many males and females place high value on their looks, young women are less likely to feel good about their appearance and to worry a lot more about their weight. *Recognition* is valued highly by around three in ten teens, exceeding the proportion of young people who place high levels of importance on *having power* or *being popular;* levels for males slightly exceed those of females in all three instances. While many teens want people to recognize their accomplishments, being a part of one's valued group of friends is clearly more important to them than having power or popularity more generally.

Spirituality is very important to close to one in three teenagers, including about 35% of females and 25% of males. Teens have been living at a time when spirituality has been "in," given extensive and positive media treatment, including being associated with high profile celebrities. In contrast, *religious group involvement* is highly valued by only about one in ten young people. Unlike spirituality, to borrow the recent headline of respected *Vancouver Sun* columnist Douglas Todd, "'Religion' just doesn't seem hip."[1]

So far we have been looking at the kinds of things that teenagers want out of life — what well-known social psychologist Milton Rokeach referred to as "terminal values." **It's also important to get a sense of some of the traits young people value in the course of pursuing the things they want** — what Rokeach dubbed "instrumental values."[2] After all, many adults are not so much concerned about teens' goals as they are with how they are living life in the course of pursuing the things they want.

This is where considerable consternation sets in. Speaking at a luncheon in May of 2000 in South Bend, Indiana, the home of the University of Notre Dame, former NFL player and coach Mike Ditka told his audience that the traits needed to be successful instilled in him by his father are becoming increasingly hard to find. "He taught me about discipline, sacrifice, hard work.[3] But the chief thing he taught me was respect, something we're losing in our society."

The same kind of lament is frequently heard on this side of the border as well. In June of 2000, *Globe and Mail* columnist Egle Procuta asked the question, "Is rude and ruder the new face of the polite Canadian?" His sources maintained that there has been an alarming upswing in rudeness in cities like Toronto. Incivility, wrote Procuta, can be found in such diverse areas as bus-riding, aggressive driving, complaints about bad service, curt voice-mails, and snarky e-mails. An expert on civility from Johns Hopkins University, Professor P.M. Forni, offers this observation: "People are becoming ruder and ruder as they run faster toward their professional goals. We see no point in slowing down for the sole purpose of being civil." Edmonton high school guidance counsellor Maureen Yates-Millions is quoted in the article saying that young people don't even notice when they're swearing and have no notion of basic good manners, like holding doors open. "We perceive it as rudeness," she says, "but they haven't been taught it at home."[4]

There's no lack of conjecture. But how, in fact, are teens looking when it comes to interpersonal values? Well, for starters, their top-rated "means" values are *honesty* and *humour*. They place high value on integrity and they also like to be able to laugh. It's worth noting that young females are considerably more likely than males to indicate honesty is "very important" to them (83% versus 62%). In filling out their questionnaires, many teens offered humorous comments, jokes, and drawings with playful captions. One apparently well-balanced 16-year-old male from the Prairies quipped, "My friends call me 'Flake' and they think it bothers me. I kinda like it." Rounding out the top three instrumental values is *cleanliness,* highly valued by seven in ten females and six in ten males. There might be few rules about appearance. But don't be fooled; a majority of teens have a very clear rule that a person has to be clean. The jeans can be ripped and the hair can be orange. But both have to be clean. Anything less is gross.

Politeness is highly valued by about six in ten young people. One 15-year-old female from Prince Edward Island comments, "People should be treated with respect for who they are, not what they are." *Forgiveness* is also seen as "very important" by about six in ten teens, *generosity* by just over four in ten. Here there are noteworthy differences between females and males. These findings undoubtedly clarify why many adults think teens, especially males, are rude and self-centred. No, it's not their imagination. Truth is, some one in two aren't placing high value on either politeness or generosity. And while they're at it, almost half are not particularly forgiving of things they don't like — such as being cut off when they are driving or being told their music is only so much noise . . .

Around six in ten teens say they regard *intelligence* as "very important," while five in ten feel the same about *working hard.* Again, the stereotype people like Ditka paint — that hard work is not prized — is in part probably based on experiences with the other five in ten. Observers who think young people are eagerly embracing high tech and a rational world should note that, on the negative side, 40% do not place high value on intelligence. Perhaps more disturbing, given the ongoing need for innovation where people take chances, only four in ten teenagers indicate that *creativity* is "very important" to them — far fewer than the number who give a top rating, for example, to cleanliness. Alas and woe, for many, being clean seems to be more important than thinking pretty thoughts.

Table 1.2. **Valued Means of Teenagers**

% Viewing as "Very Important"

	Nationally	**Males**	**Females**
Honesty	73%	62	83
Humour	73	71	74
Cleanliness	64	61	68
Intelligence	59	59	60
Politeness	58	51	65
Forgiveness	58	47	67
Working hard	52	49	54
Generosity	42	37	47
Creativity	42	42	41

A Closer Look at Politeness and Honesty

Beyond looking at the importance teens place on general traits like politeness and honesty, we explored both characteristics by posing some common situations and responses and asking teenagers for their personal reactions. In one set of questions, we asked them if they "approve," "disapprove," or "don't care either way" when people

• say "sorry" when they accidentally bump into someone;
• come to a four-way stop and proceed out of turn;

- say "please" when they order food at a restaurant drive-through;
- walk on a red light and make traffic wait;
- go through a door and hold it for the person behind them;
- park in a handicapped stall when they are not handicapped.

Overall, approval of courteous responses is fairly high, although in each instance the level of approval is higher for females than males. Approximately nine in ten teens approve of people holding doors and apologizing for bumping into someone. About eight in ten disapprove of people proceeding out of turn at a four-way stop, or parking in a handicapped parking space when they are not supposed to. A 17-year-old from a small town near Guelph adds some insight into the rationale of some who do approve of slipping into a handicapped space: she says she approves "if there are lots of stalls."

Walking on a red light at the expense of traffic and not saying "please" at a drive-through receive the disapproval of about eight in ten females and seven in ten males. Among those giving thumbs-up to a "please" is a grade 11 student from a small Ontario community who says, "I work at a drive-through and I totally appreciate it." Conversely, in these two instances, about 30% of males and 20% of females are not bothered by people walking on a red light (moan — I hate it when people do that!) or not saying "please" when they order food.

Table 1.3. **Courtesy-Related Attitudes**

*"Do you tend to APPROVE or DISAPPROVE of people who . . ." ***

		Nationally	**Males**	**Females**
Go through a door and hold it for the person behind them	Approve	89%	86	92
Say "sorry" when they accidentally bump into someone	Approve	86	84	88
Park in a handicapped stall when they are not handicapped	Disapprove	80	76	85
Come to a four-way stop and proceed out of turn	Disapprove	79	77	81
Walk on a red light and make traffic wait	Disapprove	75	72	78
Say "please" when they order food at a restaurant drive-through	Approve	73	69	77

* Options: "Approve," "Disapprove," "Don't Care Either Way."

As for honesty, a situation was posed in which teens find that a clerk has accidentally given them an extra $10 in change. They were asked whether they would be inclined to return the $10, keep walking, or make a decision based on situational factors, such as the store's size, the salesperson involved, or whether they would be shopping there again. In such situations, clerks are clearly in trouble. Just one in three young people, led by females, say they would return the $10. About two-thirds would either keep walking (34%) or base their decision on factors other than sheer honesty (31%). The walkers include this grade 12 female from a small town near Calgary, who says with what sounds like a shrug, "They made the mistake. It's their loss." Another twelfth grader, a male who lives near Thunder Bay, is among those who take a situational posture: "It depends on what kind of mood I'm in, how badly I need the money, and how nice the salesperson is."

Is such an apparent lack of honesty very pervasive, touching other areas of teens' lives? For what it's worth, in a recent poll of 3,123 top students in the United States by *Who's Who Among American High School Students*, 80% admitted to having cheated as students; further, 53% of those who had cheated brushed it off as "no big deal."[5] A New Jersey study using focus groups to get a closer look at the perception of cheating has found that cheating does not weigh heavily on the conscience of high school students. Researcher Donald McCabe says some students believe cheating is a normal part of life, and further feel there is little that can or should be done about it.[6] Things may be different in Canada; maybe not.

A Peek at Honesty in Action

"A person gives you change for what you have bought. As you walk away, you realize he/she has given you $10 more than you were supposed to receive. Do you think you would be inclined to . . ."

	Nationally	Females	Males
1. Keep the $10 and keep walking.	34%	27	41
2. Go back and return the extra $10.	35	42	28
3. It would depend on factors such as the size of the store, whether you expected to shop there again, and whether or not you knew the salesperson involved.	31	31	31

Such findings about the valuing and selective application of honesty, even among females, raise significant questions about honesty and emerging technology. The ability to be able to download information of virtually any kind means, for example, that students can readily borrow other people's work and claim it as their own. In a recent article, journalist Stanley A. Miller II wrote, "The Internet can be a powerful research tool, but it can also be a cheater's paradise, where students can point, click and copy their way to completed assignments in minutes." As many readers are well aware, a large number of "paper mills" are available that offer free essays, book reports, and term papers for students of all ages, opportunities to request specific assignments, and even advice on how to cheat on exams. Miller noted that one site boasts, "We'll be around for as long as students have homework to do," while another touts the slogan, "Download your workload."[7]

Resource possibilities have always been available for students to "cheat" on papers. In my first semester as a graduate student teacher I discovered the ease with which university students would swap old book reviews and term papers. Many didn't even attempt to be subtle, simply "sandwiching" an old, yellowish draft between new white cover pages. In other instances, the type (font hadn't yet arrived) on cover pages was different from that of the inserted paper. What is different today is both the enhanced accessibility of "alien resources" and the ability to package those resources in a form that can totally disguise its origins. Given such technological resources, along with what appears to be a situational approach to honesty, teachers and professors can be expected to experience a considerable increase in what we might politely call "deviant submissions."

Does Region or Community Size Make a Difference?
An examination of a sampling of values — such as friendship, success, honesty, and concern for others — by region and community size shows very little variation either across the country or between the size of the communities in which teenagers live. Similarly, there is considerable uniformity in the response of teens to a situation such as people saying "please" at a food drive-through, or their inclination to return money given to them in error.

Table 1.4. **Select Values, Politeness, and Honesty**

By Region and Community Size

% Viewing Values as Important, Approving of Saying "Please" at a Drive-Through, and Indicating They Would Return the $10 if It Were Given to Them in Error

	Friendship	Honesty	Success	Concern for others	"Please" at drive-thru	Would return the $10
Nationally	85%	73	71	62	73	35
B.C.	86	73	74	69	73	35
Prairies	86	71	76	66	74	31
Ontario	86	74	78	65	72	33
Quebec	81	73	58	51	72	37
Atlantic	90	75	74	63	78	33
North	90	69	66	59	70	35
>400,000	85	72	77	62	73	33
399,999–100,000	85	76	73	65	71	37
99,999–30,000	83	74	69	64	74	37
Town/city <30,000	85	73	69	63	74	36
Rural non-farm	85	75	63	60	69	35
Farm	84	71	74	59	76	34

Enjoyment

The two most important sources of enjoyment for both male and female teens are *friends* and *music*. The finding on the role of friends is consistent with the high value they place on friendship. And when they are with their friends or by themselves, they love their *music*. We'll come back to the topic of friends very shortly. As for music, it's worth noting that almost 90% of teenagers listen to music every day. One 16-year-old Edmonton male who gets a "great deal" of enjoyment from music tells us, "Music is my life." A 15-year-old female from rural Nova Scotia says, "I think music plays a big part in teenagers' lives. The words tell a lot, and send out messages to us. Sometimes good, sometimes bad."

More than a few adults are inclined to agree with the latter, often giving pretty negative reviews of the music that teens enjoy. A book edited by Jonathon Epstein in the mid-1990s entitled *Adolescents and Their Music* carried the telling subtitle *If It's Too Loud, You're Too Old.*[8] But there's no question that music has important functions for people of all ages. Exposure to music, of course, starts early, with mothers and fathers singing lullabies to their babies. Music is virtually everywhere, filling everything from cars through elevators to dental offices. Heavens, it was recently reported that harp music is being played to premature newborn babies at one leading U.S. medical centre, muffling sounds for the babies and alleviating stress for their parents.[9]

The pervasiveness of music is such that the question is not "Do people listen to music?" but rather "What do they listen to?" A 1998 Statistics Canada survey found that the so-called contemporary music format is particularly popular among teenagers, while interest in both talk format and the CBC increases with age, peaking among Canadians who are 65 and older.[10] In the case of Canadian teens, our current survey has found that their three top favourite kinds of music are rap/hip-hop, alternative, and pop. Their three top favourite performers are the Backstreet Boys, Blink-182, and DMX. Undoubtedly most readers are muttering, "I knew that . . ."

Despite the vast number of entertainment choices available, teenagers are showing no sign of losing interest in music. Between March and May of 2000, three albums sold more copies in their first week of release than any albums since accurate records have been kept — and possibly in music history: those of 'N Sync (2.4 million), Eminem (1.7 million), and Britney Spears (1.3 million). Prior to 2000, the one-week record was held by the Backstreet Boys (1.1 million). One industry executive, Danny Goldberg, the president of Artemis Records, summed up developments this way: "It's a great sign that a new generation is bonding to music."[11] But today's young people, say observers, see rock as a retro style compared with their pop, R and B, and hip-hop tastes. The consequent casualties have included the Smashing Pumpkins, one of the most popular bands of the '90s, which announced in May of 2000 that it was calling it quits, tired of "fighting the good fight against the Britneys of the world." A number of established Canadian acts, such as the Jeff Healey Band, Ashley MacIsaac, Our Lady Peace, Amanda Marshall, and Moist have all been experiencing recent declines in album sales, squeezed out by what some in the rock fraternity view as "disposable, lightweight pop."[12] A reminder that music tastes are diverse and not always predictable, however, was served up in November of 2000 when the Beatles' collection "Beatles 1" sold 3.6 million in its first week of release, easily topping the previous sales record of 'N Sync. Sales passed 12 million after three weeks.[13]

Rapper beats rap

TORONTO (CP), October 26, 2000 — *The little rapper with the big mouth was in the house Thursday night, despite the Ontario attorney general's plan to slam the door in his face. An attempt by the province's top legal watchdog to have Eminem stopped at the border failed, leaving the controversial musician free to perform at a scheduled concert at SkyDome.*

On Wednesday, Attorney General Jim Flaherty said the federal government should try to stop Eminem from entering Canada because his lyrics promote violence against women. But an Immigration Department spokesman said it could do nothing to prevent his crossing the border. "If all people who made bad music were kept out of Canada we could have stopped disco," said Derik Hodgson. "If you listen to his lyrics or read them, they're abhorrent. But having said that, if somebody's seeking entry into Canada and they're convicted of a crime, including hate crimes, we can deny them entry. He hasn't been convicted of anything and that's the bottom line."

The furor over the immensely popular rapper's visit has drawn an international media bull's-eye over the city and has prompted comment from politicians and others. "I hope we can get this guy off the stage and get him the hell out of Toronto," flamboyant Toronto Mayor Mel Lastman said Thursday. "Because we don't need hate against women or hate against anybody. This is not entertainment. People of Toronto, be ashamed if you go — and you should not go."

Eminen fans waiting to see him perform couldn't believe the fuss. "It's stupid," said Stacy Park, 14, of Mississauga, adding she didn't believe his lyrics would incite violence against women.

After friends and music, males and females differ somewhat in what they see as major sources of enjoyment. For young males, *sports* is number three; for females, that rank is given to the enjoyment of one's *own room*. Enjoying one's room is common to both females and males; enjoyment of sports is not. One 17-year-old from a small southwestern Ontario community sums up her sentiments this way: "I hate sports." The gender difference here that is typically taken for granted is worth a closer look.

The sports finding may well reflect the kinds of sports a male-dominated media tend to make available, rather than women's lack of interest in sports. One in four young females, for example, follow figure skating — similar to the proportion of men who follow Major League Baseball. Such interest is hardly reflected in the coverage of the two sports. CBC's first female head of sports, Nancy Lee, recently raised and answered an important question: "Where is our growth going to be? Women. Getting more sports on the air that appeal to women makes a lot of sense."

In addition, Lee noted that "the big challenge now is getting women on TV where they'll be seen. . . . The sad thing is that [women in sports] is still a story. It's my job to make sure that in 10, 15, 20 years' time that it's still not as much of a story."[14] In the meantime, women who are involved in the sports industry continue to be treated by many as attractive anomalies. In December of 2000, *Playboy* launched an on-line poll to choose "the hottest sports babe" in television journalism. Fox female reporter Sam Marchiano commented, "I'm not a sex symbol. I'm a reporter." Canadian Martine Gaillard, an anchor at Headline Sports, didn't feel that way: "Some say, 'Oh my god, it's so degrading.' It's *Playboy*. Like, give me a break. Who doesn't want to be told you're attractive? You're dealing with sports and a lot of guys watching sports. And you're being naive to say, if you're an attractive woman doing sports, the guys aren't going to notice that." CTV-Sportsnet's Jody Vance advised ESPN she would welcome the opportunity to be included in the poll, but said she would not consider posing nude; *Playboy* is offering the winner $1 million to pose nude.[15]

Additional key sources of enjoyment are relationships — *dating, mothers, fathers, siblings, grandparents*, and, yes, *pets* — all important to about 50% to 60% of young people. At the same time, some 50% note that they also thoroughly enjoy being able to spend time by themselves. Here again we see the desire for balance between wanting people and wanting time with oneself, friendship on the one hand and freedom on the other.

Table 1.5. **Sources of Enjoyment**

% Receiving "A Great Deal" or "Quite a Bit"

	Nationally	**Males**	**Females**
Friends	94%	93	95
Music	90	87	92
Your own room	75	67	82
Your mother	71	65	76
Dating	69	70	68
Sports	66	77	57
Your father	62	58	66
Your boyfriend or girlfriend	62	62	62
Television	60	65	55
Brother(s) or sister(s)	58	53	61
Your grandparent(s)	54	50	58
Your pet(s)	51	46	56
Being by yourself	50	47	52
Your computer	47	56	39
The Internet	42	48	37
School	41	36	46
Your VCR	40	43	38
Youth groups generally	39	37	40
Your job	36	39	33
E-mail	33	28	38
Video/computer games	32	51	14
Your car	32	38	27
Your religious group specifically	21	19	23

For all the publicity given the increasing importance of the computer and Internet in the lives of Canadians young and old, the survey has found that, as of the year 2000, *television* (60%) still holds a wide lead over *computers* (47%) and the *Internet* (42%) and *e-mail* more specifically (33%) as sources of enjoyment for teenagers. Perhaps the finding is not surprising. Television is an established and user-friendly medium; the Internet specifically is still in its infancy as an entertainment medium with its possibilities yet to be demonstrated. A few years back, Bill Gates appeared on *David Letterman* and announced with enthusiasm, "For the first time in history a World Series game was shown on the Internet." In typical satirical fashion, Letterman scowled and said, "But didn't people know it was on television?" Ultimately, the greater popularity of one over the other in terms of entertainment will depend primarily on what they can deliver with what level of ease.

In the meantime, what seems to be happening is that the Internet is complementing rather than reducing the place of other media more generally, including films, music, books, and newspapers. With regard to electronic books, for example, the publisher of *Harper's* magazine, John R. MacArthur, wrote recently, "I suspect that e-books will function something like videos, which have failed to supplant the pleasures of going to a movie theatre and watching a film on a big screen with a lot of other people."[16]

In a stimulating article that appeared in August of 2000, journalist Ann Oldenburg wrote, "The Web has become the great enabler, particularly for entertainment. Chat rooms for TV shows have meant vocal viewers can steer plot lines, and movie Web sites and message boards generate buzz — negative or positive — about films. Self-proclaimed critics offer opinions on the latest songs, novels, actors." But, while adding an important interactive component to media, the Internet hasn't taken away from the original products made available through older forms. Instead, she says, it has been driving more people to those products. For example, Internet ratings reports show that many of the most popular sites are media sites. Oldenburg concludes that the Internet will increasingly converge with other media. And with that evolution, television, movies, books, and computers will not be competing for our time. The products will be available; we "will just choose the delivery system and format" we want. Consistent with such a position, sociologist John Robinson of the University of Maryland comments, "From a variety of different angles, it does appear that the Internet is simply leading to enhanced information media use, rather than adversely affecting it."[17]

Such observations are consistent with the growing trend of media conglomerates such as Rogers Communications and BCE to pursue control of a wide variety of media forms, and hence control of the diverse delivery systems that Canadians are choosing both now and in the future. As of late 2000, the umbrella of Montreal-based BCE, for example, extended over Bell Canada telephones, Bell ExpressVu satellite TV, international telecom service provider Teleglobe, the CTV network, the TSN cable channel, and Sympatico-Lycos, Canada's largest Internet service provider. It also had just formed a partnership with the *Globe and Mail*, and was eyeing sports properties, including the CFL.[18]

Returning to Gates, in a recent interview with Larry King, he put the more general complementary role of the Internet into perspective. Asked if the Internet will replace mail and courier services, he responded, "Quite a bit of the shopping we do in person today will be done over the Internet in the future, and whenever we buy a physical object, it will have to be delivered."[19] The heralded notion of "convergence" will include the new with the old.

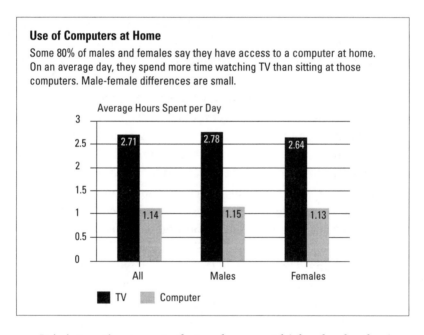

Use of Computers at Home

Some 80% of males and females say they have access to a computer at home. On an average day, they spend more time watching TV than sitting at those computers. Male-female differences are small.

Average Hours Spent per Day

It is interesting to note that males report higher levels of enjoyment from computers and the Internet than females; however, more females than males say they receive enjoyment from using e-mail. Observers maintain that part of the reason for greater enjoyment on the part of males has been the appeal of computer games, often featuring competition and violence. A recent study of junior and senior high school teachers and students in the U.S. by the American Association of University Women concluded that girls certainly have the ability to learn and use computers, but are turned off by technical careers that they view as "full of geeky guys in windowless offices who toil at keyboards for hours." Since the 1980s, the proportion of women obtaining degrees in computer science has actually been declining in both the U.S. and Canada.[20]

Values, music, and the Internet

TORONTO, *Globe and Mail*, Matthew Ingram, September 9, 2000 — *The lawsuits flying through cyberspace over the issue of digital music might lead you to think that the titans of the entertainment industry are winning the war against the twenty-something Internet pirates and dot-com upstarts. In fact, nothing could be further from the truth.*

The legal challenges against Napster and MP3.com are nothing more than angry lashing out by an entrenched industry when it doesn't really know how to fix the mess it has gotten itself into. Something has gone wrong with the way the world is supposed to work, but record companies can't figure out what it is, exactly, or how to get things back to the way they were before the Internet came.

What's happening to the entertainment industry is the same thing that happened to the brokerage business when on-line stock trading appeared: An industry built on one business model feels fear when something new appears that threatens that way of doing business. Just as brokers had to come up with new revenue models, record companies are being forced to come to terms with the changing reality of their industry.

So do people — musicians or music lovers — still need record companies at all? In the end, that's up to the record companies themselves to decide. As Softbank CEO Masayoshi Son put it, the Internet means "you must cannibalize [your business] before someone cannibalizes it for you."

School, youth groups, and *jobs* are each enjoyed "a great deal" or "quite a bit" by about four in ten teens, *religious groups* by just over two in ten. If young women are slightly more inclined than young men to report enjoyment from school, the reverse holds for enjoyment received from *VCRs, jobs, cars,* and especially *video/computer games.* In the case of school, about 50% of females as well as males feel their teachers "are genuinely interested in me," while the same proportion maintains that "most of my school courses are fairly interesting." We'll continue to look at school, groups, and jobs as we examine further survey findings.

Table 1.6. **Daily Activities**

	Nationally	**Males**	**Females**
Watch television	92%	93	91
Listen to music	86	84	88
Spend time with friends	60	59	62
Do homework	44	34	54
Use a computer	41	48	34
Use e-mail	27	27	26
Access web sites	24	31	18
Follow sports	21	37	7
Keep up with the news	16	19	14

Consistent with what teens say they enjoy, on a *daily basis* a majority are watching TV, listening to music, and spending time with friends. Fewer numbers are doing homework, using computers, following sports, and keeping up with the news, with gender differences what you might expect in light of the enjoyment findings.

On a *daily to weekly* basis, more than one in two young people are watching videos at home and some 70% of males are playing video/computer games; about three in ten males are reading books they want to read, compared to some four in ten females. One 16-year-old "reader" from a small community in northern B.C. suspects she is an exception: "I don't know if many teens would say this, but I love books. I love to read them and write them too. That is what I spend a lot of my time doing, writing stories and poems. Some of us teens are deeper than we appear."

About 80% of teenagers go to a movie *at least once a month,* while 40% — led by males — attend a sports event. Teens don't just listen to music; although 20% attend a music concert "monthly or more," in the same period 40% jam or work on music. It's not all fun and games. As one 16-year-old from the Prairies who works on her music every day reminded us, "I do it because I have to." Gambling is far more common among males (35%) than females (9%). Close to 20% of teens say they go to a rave at least once a month, with the level for males higher than that of females. More about raves later.

Table 1.7. **Other Common Activities**

	Nationally	Males	Females
Daily to Weekly			
Watch videos at home	60%	64	57
Play video/computer games	47	69	26
Read books you want to read	33	29	37
Monthly or More Often			
Go to a movie	78	77	79
Jam/work on music	42	42	42
Attend a sports event	41	49	34
Go to a music concert	21	21	19
Gamble with money	21	35	9
Go to a rave	18	21	15

The Myth of the Canadian Sports Fan

"Hello, hockey fans in Canada!" Sports media in Canada give us the impression that Canadians are avid fans of hockey, baseball, football, basketball, and, increasingly, pro wrestling as well. The survey shows such an assumption holds for young males but not females. Only about one in five teenage women closely follow any of the major pro sports, with their top three favourites being basketball, hockey, and figure skating. Relatively few are interested in wrestling, baseball, or football.

% Indicating Follow "Very Closely" or "Fairly Closely"

	Nationally	Males	Females
National Hockey League	34%	51	9
National Basketball Association	30	40	20
National Football League	21	34	8
Professional wrestling	20	32	10
Major League Baseball	17	25	9
Canadian Football League	16	26	6
Figure skating	11	3	18

Sources of Influence

Sociologists are among those observers of life who make a living working from the assumption that the key to understanding people is to understand the social environments from which they come. While we may like to think we are wonderfully creative and individualistic, a prosaic peek into our lives typically reveals a more humbling reality: who we are can be traced back with embarrassing ease to the cultures, communities, families, friendships, and other social settings from which we have come. That's not to say we never relate to others as creative individuals. But it is to say we are the recipients of considerable social influence. As one sociological sage from yesteryear, Charles Horton Cooley, once put it, "In the give and take process, we typically take much more than we give."[21]

In reflecting on what influences their lives, today's teenagers recognize the importance of how they were raised. But they also believe that they themselves have a dominant place in determining what happens to them. They see the primary influences on their lives as their *upbringing* and their *own willpower*. A 15-year-old female from Oshawa sums up the combination of the two factors this way: "My parents have raised me to make my own decisions." Another 15-year-old, a male from a small Manitoba town who was raised by his mother and grandparents, emphasizes willpower: "You control your future," he says. "You determine your life."

As young people are getting into their teens, they are acknowledging the growing influence of *friends* and a high, but decreasing, level of influence of their *mothers* and especially their *fathers*. In more than one in two instances, teens note that other adults they respect have a noteworthy influence on them. The decrease in parental influence is due not only to the emergence of other sources but also to changes in parental input. One young woman from the small community of Okotoks near Calgary says, "I really believe that strong family life is the base for a good person. But family life has just been thrown out the window. Parents seem to be too busy to spend time with their children and children never seem to be interested in spending time with their family." Another female, a 15-year-old from rural Nova Scotia, comments, "I think family life influences the way we behave and treat others. A lot of teenagers have it rough at home, and that makes things hard to deal with."

While they put tremendous stock in their own willpower, most young people recognize that what they are able to do is influenced by the *characteristics with which they were born*. They exhibit far less consensus, however, about other potential sources of influence, including *music,* what they *read, God, teachers,* and *television.* The downplaying of the influence of television is somewhat amazing, given that a Canadian child by the age of 12 has spent more time in front of a television set than in a school — and, in English Canada, more hours watching American programs than spent in a Canadian school.[22] An articulate 17-year-old female from Saskatoon is among those who believe that the impact of media is powerful: "One of the greatest problems affecting the world is public ignorance. This usually results from consumer advertising, publicity-seeking media, lack of available information, and even plain apathy."

As for gender differences, females are more likely than males to see reading and God as influencing their lives. Conversely, males assign a bit more importance than females to the impact of television.

Table 1.8. **Perceived Sources of Influence**

% Seeing as Influencing Their Lives "A Great Deal" or "Quite a Bit"

	Nationally	**Males**	**Females**
The way you were brought up	91%	90	93
Your own willpower	89	89	88
Your mother specifically	81	79	84
Your friend(s)	78	77	79
The characteristics you were born with	71	69	73
Your father specifically	70	70	70
Another adult(s) whom you respect	58	58	58
Music	53	54	53
What you read	43	37	47
God or some other supernatural force	40	35	43
Your teacher(s)	36	35	37
Television	34	38	29
Luck	31	34	28
What people in power decide	25	29	21
The Internet	15	20	11

Presumably reflecting their belief in their own willpower, only about one in four young people think their lives are influenced significantly by *what people in power decide* — less than the proportion who think that *luck* plays a key role. Needless to say, such perception makes sociologists cringe, providing pretty damning evidence of our inability to get our message across concerning the importance of social environment. But we are joined by at least one titan. For all the incredible day-to-day media hype about the Internet, at this point, at least, a mere 15% of teenagers think the *Internet* has a noteworthy influence on their lives. This finding is consistent with an April 1999 U.S. poll of 13- to 17-year-olds conducted for *Time* magazine, which found just 13% put "a great deal" of trust in the information they get from the Internet, compared to 83% for information they receive, for example, via their parents.[23]

When teenagers face a serious problem, their key resources are friends and family. Almost four in ten say they are inclined to turn to their *friends*, including boyfriends and girlfriends specifically. Just over two in ten maintain their number one resource is *family members*, usually their parents but sometimes their brothers and sisters. Another two in ten indicate they look equally to *friends and family* members. A further one in ten teens report they turn to other sources, including a small minority who admit they resort to drugs and alcohol. One Alberta 16-year-old is pointed in her expectations of parents generally: "I think adults should pay more attention to their kids when it comes to depression, drugs, gangs, violence, sex, etc. They should be a little more caring and involved in order to help their children make it through life."

Approximately one in ten Canadian young people report that, when faced with a serious problem, they typically *do not turn to anyone*. They rely on their own resources. Among them is a 17-year-old female from Hamilton who says, "Life is hard to deal with — too many choices, too many things to think about, and no one to talk to." Some find solace in music, reminiscent of singer Christina Aguilera's recollection of dealing with domestic abuse by gravitating to music: "It was my way," she says, "of releasing all that energy and kind of escaping into my own world."[24] Similarly, Shania Twain has been open about the way that music functioned to provide her with an escape into an imaginary world. There are other teens in the survey, like a 15-year-old from Moose Jaw, who tends to bypass her friends and parents, preferring "my journal. I write down how I feel." Still others simply try to give their attention to other things. A grade 11 male who lives on a reservation says, "I turn to sports," while an 18-year-old female from Winnipeg says, "I just block out my problems."

Table 1.9. **Resources When Facing Problems**

"When I face a serious problem, I turn to . . ."

	Nationally	Males	Females
Friends	35%	31	39
Boyfriend/girlfriend specifically	5	5	5
Family members	21	21	21
Parents specifically	18	18	18
Brothers/sisters	3	3	3
Friends and family members	22	18	26
Myself/no one	12	17	7
Other	10	13	7
Drugs, alcohol	1	2	<1
Totals	**100**	**100**	**100**

Given the prevalence of personal concerns among young males and females, some who rely strictly on themselves are finding life extra tough. They include a 15-year-old from North York, Ontario, who speaks frankly: "Today's youths are dealing with more problems than before. Take me as an example — I've been suicidal and thought of abusing my body. We suffer a lot. We need support and respect."

"When I face a serious problem, I turn to . . ."

sleep . . . my sister or my close best friend . . . my friends . . . nobody . . . my girlfriend and listening to music . . . my father . . . my mom . . . my friends and God . . . my friend or brother . . . my girlfriend . . . counselors . . . alcohol . . . my friends and my family . . . the police . . . my bed and sleep . . . my sisters . . . my older brother . . . my best friend . . . my closest friends . . . my grandmother . . . God . . . friends or drugs . . . my knowledge . . . humour . . . my inner soul . . . music . . . a friend . . . drugs and cigarettes . . . a few of my closest friends . . . friends or music . . . my mom or friends . . . God, parents, friends . . .

Concerns

Personal Concerns

Maybe it's because we are overly self-absorbed; maybe it's because of our selective memories. **But a good many adults think of the teen years as years of fun and freedom, a time when young people don't have much to worry about. They're wrong.**

This is how one grade 12 female who lives in a Vancouver suburb sums things up:

> *Adults do not realize the stressfulness of being 18, and that it's not just one big party. I find that I don't have time to worry about things like the federal deficit while worrying about obtaining a job, school, boyfriend, social life, and dealing with all my emotions, problems, and pressures in everyday life.*

To be a teenager is to experience multidimensional emergence — simply put, emergence on all fronts. Teens are sort of like "embryonic adults," emerging physically, socially, sexually, intellectually, spiritually, vocationally, and so on. It all adds up to a lot of adjustments for adolescents and everyone else in their world. Of course they have lots of laughs. But that's only half of the story.

The two primary personal concerns of teenagers pertain to life at school and life after school. Almost seven in ten say they feel *pressure to do well at school* and are concerned about *what they are going to do when they finish school.* Females are somewhat more inclined than males to acknowledge that both these issues trouble them. Queen's University researcher Alan King and his associates, who have been monitoring the health of Canadian youth since the late 1980s, report that the pressure students feel to do well increases steadily as they move from elementary school through junior high to high school.[25] We are seeing students who speak of this pressure.

As all of us who have been in school know well, the name of the game, ultimately, is to succeed by way of getting diplomas. In the course of facing such a reality, it's good to know that 50% of students get a fair amount of enjoyment from the experience. But people have to graduate. And to varying degrees, students are expected to do more than just graduate; they are expected to pull solid grades.

A 17-year-old from St. John's notes that much of the pressure surrounding school comes from parents: "In some situations, parents are trying to get their kids to do things they don't want to do. That's a lot of pressure on children. I find that young people today are feeling the pressure to be better than others when, actually, being themselves should be enough." What's more, since a majority of teens plan to go to university, what they have to look forward to is more school, followed by the uncertainty of what exactly they are going to do when their school years run out. It all adds up to a fair amount of anxiety — especially if one shares the conclusion of a grade 12 student from Vancouver that "given the disappearance of pensions and medicare, pollution errors, and government money problems, my future in Canada looks bleak."

The next two dominant concerns involve *time* **and** *money*. About five in ten young people maintain that they don't have enough of either. Such findings are hardly surprising. School time and travel takes up perhaps seven to eight hours a day, and then there's homework. Half report that they are working at jobs averaging 15 hours a week, and many are involved in sports and other forms of extracurricular activities. They do have to have a little time to eat, want time to hang out, need time to relax, maybe get on the computer — and, of course, get a good night's sleep. That doesn't leave an awful lot of hours in a day. A 16-year-old from Alberta said she feels "a lot of pressure to do good, but I have a very tight schedule and often it's hard to do everything." A Brampton, Ontario, teen reminded us that we needed to put something into our survey about how much sleep teenagers get, adding, "Trust me, it's not very much."

As for money, teens typically rely on (1) income from part-time work and (2) parents. David Foot has called teens "six-pocket kids" who get money from mom, dad, grandparents, and sometimes step-parents.[26] They obviously represent a rich market that is aggressively targeted by advertisers. More than 70% are believed to have ATM cards. It all sounds perfect, and billions of dollars are being spent. But more than a few teens find that those parental resources are not necessarily easy to come by, especially when half of them feel their parents do not understand them particularly well. And this will come as a shocker: they discover like the rest of us that ATM cards are only as good as the bucks in the account. More credit help may be on the way — well, sort of. In the late summer of 2000, VISA announced that it is coming up with a new card aimed at teenagers, beginning in the U.S. The new card is known as "Visa Buxx." Parents will set a spending limit and prepay that amount into a special account and can "reload" the card as needed. Teens will be able to use the Buxx card to make purchases and download cash.[27] Obviously parents will still be in control.

Table 1.10. **Primary Personal Concerns**

% Indicating Bothered "A Great Deal" or "Quite a Bit"

	Nationally	Males	Females
Pressure to do well at school	67%	64	69
What going to do when finish school	66	63	70
Never seem to have enough time	57	52	61
Lack of money	53	52	54
Losing friends	47	39	53
Not being understood by my parents	45	41	48
My looks	45	38	51
Wondering about the purpose of life	43	38	46
Boredom	42	44	41
So many things changing	38	35	40
Feeling not as good as others	36	27	43
My weight	34	21	45
Not having a girlfriend/boyfriend	34	36	32
Loneliness	30	26	33
Depression	29	25	33
Parents' marriage	27	24	29
Sex	26	30	22
My height	20	19	21

- Some four in ten teens say that a number of other issues trouble them "a great deal" or "quite a bit." They include *losing friends, not being understood by parents, their looks, wondering about the purpose of life,* and *boredom.* As we have noted earlier, boredom undoubtedly is associated with the place where they have to spend time — school — rather than being tied to having time on their hands where they are at a loss as to what to do.

- Around three in ten indicate they are concerned about *so many things changing, feelings of inferiority,* their *weight, not having a boyfriend or girlfriend,* and *loneliness.*
- About two in ten are troubled by *depression,* their *parents' marriage, sex,* or their *height.*

We'll revisit a number of these issues shortly. **Overall, young females are more inclined than males to acknowledge a number of personal concerns, particularly regarding looks, weight, and feelings of inferiority.** It is clear from such findings that the basic feminist concern — going back to the latest major women's movement of the '60s and '70s — about women being excessively valued on the basis of their appearance has not been resolved in Canada. For all the talk about gender equality, young women simply are feeling much more pressure than men to be attractive, including the pressure not to be overweight. In early 1999, Toronto writer Aliza Libman, penned these words as a 15-year-old:

> *Just when did having an average weight become the eighth deadly sin? Why exactly is it so important to drop a few pounds and then a few more? When will this obsession end? Lose 30 pounds in 30 days, say the diet gurus. Their approach is to cultivate feelings of inadequacy, eating disorders and the decline of self-esteem in a whole segment of society. In today's world, it appears that looking good is more important than loving yourself for who you are. And social workers are wondering why more and more girls are committing suicide.*[28]

The issue here is not the cultural value placed on physical attractiveness. Rather, the issue is the ongoing double standard lamented by the likes of Susan Sontag 30 years ago, whereby men are valued primarily for their accomplishments while women are valued primarily for their looks.[29] If that sounds too strong, then let's rephrase the cultural allegation this way: looks play a more prominent role in the measure of a woman than they do in the measure of a man. That's why more young females than males are concerned about their appearance.

Sometimes, in certain domains dominated by males, the reality is not exactly subtle. On the eve of the summer 2000 French Open tennis championships, the widely read *Sports Illustrated* magazine featured glamorous tennis star Anna Kournikova on its cover, a player ranked fifteenth in the world who had never won a major tournament, yet was generating $10 million annually in endorsements. A prominent woman star, golfer Karrie Webb, has failed to generate anything close to that kind of enthusiasm. A writer summed up the difference this way: "One is the hottest female athlete in the world. The other — in the eyes of Madison Avenue and the mainstream media — is simply hot."[30] And then there has been the outbreak of female athletes, posing in the near nude for any number of fund-raising and consciousness-raising causes. They have included Waneek Horn-Miller of Canada's water polo on the cover of a pre-Olympic *Time* magazine in the summer of 2000 "wearing" only a polo ball; and Canada's national cross-country ski team, posing, as one Montreal editorial writer put it, "in the clothes God gave them (along with some strategically placed skis) for a pricey calendar."[31] While some athletes and many others are quick to defend such practices for any number of reasons,[32] the fact remains that the appeal is primarily to males and is certainly sexist; few men find it necessary to shed their clothes to raise either money or the profile of their sports. It also needs to be noted that the women doing the posing are not just athletes; they are extremely attractive athletes — consistent with the allegation that looks continue to play a more prominent role in the measure of women than they do in the measure of men.

As long as that message continues to be sent, more women than men are going to be worrying about their looks. Eating disorders such as anorexia and bulimia will continue to be more prevalent among them. Body-image businesses will boom, and remedies that include cigarettes will be pursued. One grade 12 Fredericton student interviewed recently by Canadian Press noted, "A lot of girls are smoking because they think it'll help them lose weight. They think they have to look a certain way to be accepted."[33] Males may want to be attractive. But few appear to be feeling the pressure to go through the acrobatics common to females to get there.

The weight problems of teenagers, both female and male, are not about to go away, according to an important new national study by University of New Brunswick researchers Mark Tremblay and Douglas Willms, published by the Canadian Medical Association. They found that the rate of obesity among girls seven to 13 more than doubled between 1981 and 1996, from 5% to about 12%. But the level almost tripled for boys, from 5% to close to 14%. The rates of overweight children also rose dramatically, with some 30% of boys and 25% of girls considered overweight, including those deemed obese. The researchers put the blame squarely on the increasing lack of exercise.[34] The computer generation is going to have to find more ways of getting on its feet.

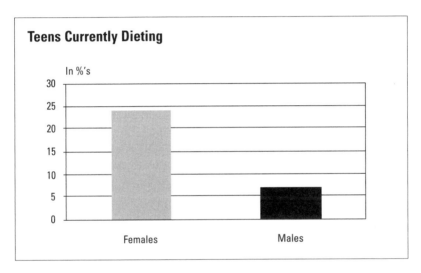

Obviously there are young people who have very poor self-images, a reality that needs to be taken very seriously. Yet the good news is that the majority of Canadian teenagers hold views of themselves that point to positive self-images. Asked to respond to six statements regarding their self-esteem, more than nine in ten maintain that they are good people, have a number of good qualities, and are well liked. A majority also see themselves as competent, good-looking, and having lots of confidence. These findings are consistent with Alan King's previously mentioned 1998 survey on the health of Canadian youth, which included students in grade 10. King found that only a minority of these high schoolers expressed unhappiness, low self-esteem, depression, or loneliness.

However, King also found that females were less likely than males to feel self-confident.[35] We have found the same thing. About four in ten females versus two in ten males do not see themselves as *"having lots of confidence."* Further, one in four females, compared with only one in ten males, do not think the competence statement *"I can do most things very well"* accurately describes them. And finally, about 30% of females do not describe themselves as *"good-looking,"* versus some 20% of males. So it is that a 17-year-old female from a small Ontario town tells us, "We need to have more programs for teens about self-confidence, because if teens felt better about themselves, so much of this shit that goes on wouldn't, like drugs and alcohol abuse. Did you know there are more girls suffering from eating disorders than there are people living with AIDs? That sucks."

Young males are more inclined than young females to say each of these six positive self-esteem items describes them "very well" versus

Table 1.11. **Self-Images of Teenagers**

% Indicating How Well These Statements Describe Them

	Very well	Fairly well	Not very/ not at all	Totals
I am a good person.				
Females	50%	46	4	100
Males	53	43	4	100
I have a number of good qualities.				
Females	39	51	10	100
Males	50	43	7	100
I am well liked.				
Females	34	60	6	100
Males	36	56	8	100
I have lots of confidence.				
Females	20	43	37	100
Males	32	47	21	100
I can do most things very well.				
Females	16	61	23	100
Males	29	58	13	100
I am good-looking.				
Females	14	58	28	100
Males	22	57	21	100

"fairly well." Does this mean they believe what they say? Perhaps that is irrelevant. At minimum, young males *think* they are supposed to have positive views of themselves. That finding speaks volumes about how we are socializing men versus women.

Personal Problems of Young People

Is it true that grownups have a more difficult time here than we do? No. I know it isn't. Older people have formed their opinions about everything, and don't waver before they act. It's twice as hard for us young ones to hold our ground, and maintain our opinions, in a time when all ideals are being shattered and destroyed, when people are showing their worst side, and do not know whether to believe in truth and right and God.

Anyone who claims that the older ones have a more difficult time here certainly doesn't realize to what extent our problems weigh down on us, problems for which we are probably much too young, but which thrust themselves upon us continually, until, after a long time, we think we've found a solution, but the solution doesn't seem able to resist the facts which reduce it to nothing again.

— Anne Frank at 15, about a month before her family was discovered.[36]

Still, we do not want to be simplistic here. Harvard psychologist William Pollack maintains that we need to be conscious of the common "mask of masculinity," where boys feign "self-confidence and bravado," hiding their "feelings of vulnerability, powerlessness, and isolation." Pollack says that the mask is worn very well and often even unconsciously, making it difficult to detect when males are having problems. What makes the situation potentially serious, writes Pollack, is that boys are "not expected to reach out for help, comfort, understanding, and support," and consequently are not as close as they could be to the people who could add to their lives. He calls for parents, teachers, and others to become sensitive to such a masking of feelings.[37]

Social Concerns

Canadian young people tend to be fairly buoyant about the quality of life in the country. One Kelowna 17-year-old tells us that she believes that many social problems "apply less to Canada than to other countries," adding, "I believe we live in an incredibly peaceful place in comparison to others." But another female, 16, who attends a francophone school in a small Ontario community, expresses concern about social indifference: "Society today is becoming increasingly bad, and most people don't do anything about problems such as violence against women, abuse, depression, and poverty." A 15-year-old from Newfoundland who describes herself as an "African-Canadian" offers this personal observation that helps to remind us that some people are experiencing a Canada that is far from perfect: "I live in a city and go to a school with very few people of my own race. Most people feel that racism is not a problem. But I experience it almost every day."

We asked young people about their social concerns. **The two issues seen by the largest number — some 55% — as "very serious" today are** *child abuse* **and** *AIDS.*

- About 50% maintain that *violence in schools, teenage suicide, drugs,* and *racial discrimination* are extremely serious problems, while around 40% say the same about the *environment, violence against women, poverty,* and *crime.*
- Issues seen by fewer teens as "very serious" include *youth gangs, the unequal treatment of women, American influence,* and *the lack of Canadian unity.*

What is striking is the general tendency for far more females than males to see any "person-related" issue as serious. For example, violence in schools is seen as "very serious" by almost 60% of females but just 40% of males. Similar large differences are found in the case of such issues as AIDS, child abuse, drugs, suicide, crime, discrimination, violence against women, poverty, and youth gangs.

However, differences between males and females are minor when "institutional-related" issues are involved, such as the environment, nuclear war, American influence, the economy, intergroup relations, and unity.

Obviously a number of these social concerns of young people are also areas of great concern for Canadian adults. We will take an

Table 1.12. **Primary Social Concerns**

% Viewing as "Very Serious"

	Nationally	Males	Females
Child abuse	56%	44	66
AIDS	55	46	62
Violence in schools	50	40	59
Teenage suicide	49	36	60
Drugs	48	41	55
Racial discrimination	47	40	53
The environment	42	41	44
Violence against women	42	33	51
Poverty	41	34	47
Crime	40	29	49
Youth gangs	32	28	34
Unequal treatment of women	32	23	39
American influence	25	27	22
Economy	25	27	23
The threat of nuclear war	24	22	24
Lack of Canadian unity	21	22	21
Native-white relations	21	20	21
French-English relations	20	20	20

Teens' Top Ten Social Issues

Teens were asked what they see as Canada's single most serious problem. Here is a ranking of what they said:

1. Crime
2. The economy
3. Racial discrimination
4. Drugs
5. Violence generally
6. The environment
7. Poverty
8. Violence in schools
9. Unity
10. American influence

---

in-depth look at some of the most prominent issues very shortly, including violence in schools, abuse, sexuality, and drugs.

Three in four teens admit that they are not very interested in politics; in fact, 37% say politics doesn't interest them at all. One 16-year-old francophone from Montreal speaks for many when he says, "I am personally not very involved in politics as I am much more involved with my life — school, extracurricular activities." The remaining one in four who are interested in politics consist of 4% who say they take an active part and 23% who are interested but not actively involved. Exceptions don't necessarily appear in predictable places. One feisty respondent from the North, who calls former U.S. president Bill Clinton "a loser," says she is both interested in politics and takes an active part, adding, "Me and my dad argue all the time about politics." Her father is a lawyer.

Even if the majority of Canadian young people are not especially interested in politics as such, this is not to say they lack opinions on a wide variety of social issues.

LAW • Almost three in four feel the *Young Offenders Act* needs to be toughened, with females leading the way. Among those who are not in favour of such toughening of the act is an 18-year-old from the Okanagan who writes, "I believe that if you make the *Young Offenders Act* harsher, there is more chance of having repeat offenders. If you throw the kids in jail, they will rebel more than if you had given them a slap on the wrists." Over half favour the use of the *death penalty*, but here males outnumber females. Young women, in the face of their greater concern about violence, are more likely to want tougher laws, but they are not as likely to call for people to be executed. A solid majority of young people say they think that *law enforcement* is being applied evenly, but only one in four feel people who commit crimes are *almost always caught*. Gender differences are small.

EQUALITY AND RIGHTS • A three-quarters majority (led by females) feel that *homosexuals are entitled to the same rights* as other Canadians and about 70% feel *euthanasia* is sometimes justified. Around 60% feel that *women* are encountering little discrimination in Canada, while only 30% feel that *retirement should be mandatory* at age 65. Females are inclined to be more pro-rights and more concerned about gender inequality than males.

GLOBAL ISSUES • Males and females differ considerably on global concern and war. Close to half of young men but just one-third of young women feel our focus should be our own country rather than the world. A grade 11 female from Kamloops comments, "Third World countries need our help. Canada and the USA need to come together to help those Third World countries. We are all one." A 15-year-old who lives in Edmonton but was born in Poland suggests that "Canadians and particularly youth need to travel more around the world and gain a perspective on how other societies function and the beliefs of other cultures. Many people in Canada," she says, "are way too isolated from the rest of the world." If females are inclined to take such a benevolent position toward other countries in need, males are considerably more likely to attack them, if necessary; about 40% of males feel war is sometimes justified, compared to less than 20% of females.

Table 1.13. **Select Social Attitudes**

% Agreeing

	Nationally	Males	Females
Law and Enforcement			
The *Young Offenders Act* needs to be toughened.	71%	67	75
Law enforcement is applied evenly to all those who break the law.	68	67	69
The death penalty should sometimes be used to punish criminals.	59	65	54
People who break the law are almost always caught.	26	29	24
Equality and Personal Rights			
Homosexuals are entitled to the same rights as other Canadians.	74	62	86
There are circumstances in which a doctor would be justified in helping end a patient's life.	69	71	67
Women in this country now encounter very little discrimination.	62	71	53
A person should retire at 65, regardless of health.	30	33	28
International Matters			
We need to worry about our own country and let the rest of the world take care of itself.	38	46	31
War is justified when other ways of settling internal disputes fail.	29	42	18

Assessment

When it comes to values, Canada's teens place primary importance on relationships and freedom, along with success and a comfortable life. Relationships and being loved tend to be valued by more females than males, a finding that is consistent with females' also being more inclined to place high value on interpersonal traits such as honesty, forgiveness, generosity, and politeness. They also give evidence of being somewhat more courteous and honest in real-life situations.

Friends and music are the key sources of enjoyment for teenagers, with sports an important third source for males but not for females. Television currently outdistances the computer when it comes to enjoyment. However, e-mail undoubtedly contributes to the enhancing of friendships, and the Internet to the enjoyment of music as well as sports — thereby illustrating the computer's complementary-versus-independent role in young people's lives.

When they reflect on what influences their lives, teens recognize the influence of their upbringing, but also emphasize the role they themselves play. They exhibit limited cognizance of the importance of social and political factors, including television and the Internet. Their primary resources in times of need are friends and family.

The personal concerns of teens start with life at school and life after graduation. On a daily basis, many feel strain over the lack of both time and money, as well as not being understood by their parents. Females in particular express concern about their looks generally and their weight more specifically. They also are more likely than males to express feelings of inferiority and less likely to exhibit positive self-esteem. Social concerns centre around the two classic universal concerns of "staying alive" and "living well." These days the primary threats to such basic goals are AIDS, abuse, violence in schools, and drugs. Other important issues that directly affect teens to various degrees include suicide, crime, violence against women, and discrimination.

Three recurring themes appear in this exploration of what's important to young people. The first is **gender differences**. More females than males value relationships and general civility. They have limited interest in violence whether it is found in sports and video games, capital punishment, or war. They are more likely to approach social issues with compassion. Yet, while females are more likely to exhibit values and attitudes that most of us would applaud, they are also more likely than males to worry about their looks and to express low self-esteem. I would emphasize that we are talking about patterns, not absolute differences. Yet the patterns are ones that persist across a number of areas. That's something that should trouble us.

Second, young people tend to express a fairly high level of **individualism**. It is particularly evident in the importance they are placing on freedom and having choices, as well as in their belief that they themselves play a central role in determining their life outcomes — with limited awareness of or respect for the reality of social constraints. It is also suggested in their situational approach to honesty. Individualism, if it represents a healthy emphasis on individuality, obviously is a good thing. But if individualism takes the form of emphasizing the individual at the expense of the group, it can make social life difficult at any number of levels.[38] It is a finding worth watching.

Third, thinkers going back to people such as historian Arnold Toynbee and sociologist William Ogburn have warned about the social impact of values and norms failing to keep up with technological advances. Some 80 years ago, Ogburn, an American sociologist, coined the term "cultural lag" to describe such disparity.[39] These days, we can at a minimum expect to experience a period of value adjustment, as we sort out such basic issues as e-mail etiquette, cellphone courtesy, and an array of ethical, moral, and criminal issues relating to the Internet — ranging from basic concerns about the loss of privacy and access to previously illegal material, through the downloading and dissemination of other people's property, to exploitive scams and downright theft. The survey, as expected, finds teenagers sharing in what seems like a technological explosion. But it also is suggesting that some young people, notably males, may be a shade short on the kind of civility and altruism that will help get us through a particular tough time of cultural lag. We need to keep an eye on this precarious balance between technology and values as we move through the survey findings.

Chapter Two

The People in Their Lives

SOCIOLOGISTS HAVE BEEN AMONG THOSE WHO HAVE LONG MAINtained that social ties are indispensable to human development. Some readers may remember professors drawing on the likes of Charles Horton Cooley and George Herbert Mead in arguing that our ability to emerge as healthy human beings depends on other people, starting with the primary groups of family and friends — or hearing or reading psychiatrist William Glasser's oft-cited line that "at all times in our lives we must have at least one person who cares about us and whom we care for ourselves."[1]

The point continues to be made by academics. Highly regarded family expert James Garbarino of Cornell University writes, "Children need stable positive emotional relationships with at least one parent or other reference person." For emphasis he adds, "This is the single most important resource you can have to promote resilience in childhood: having someone who is crazy about you."[2] An article on asthma published in the summer of 2000 in *The New England Journal of Medicine* reported that children who are exposed to the germs of other children may develop healthier immune systems than children who have less exposure. Lead author Thomas Ball of the University of Arizona commented, "Clearly infants depend on their environment for proper development," adding, "They need to hear their native tongue to speak it, they need love to develop a healthy psyche, and it looks as if they need exposure to infections to help direct their immune systems."[3] Harvard professor Robert Putnam, in his recent provocative book,

Bowling Alone, has gone further. He maintains that social life generates "social capital," resulting in healthier and happier individuals: "social connectedness is one of the most powerful determinants of our well-being."[4]

People need people. That clearly includes teens. One 16-year-old female from Alberta expresses things this way: "All kids need love and support from someone or something." But it's also clear they are drawing on some sources more than others.

Friends

It would be difficult to overestimate the role of friends in teenage lives. As we have seen, friendship and freedom are the supreme values of young people. When they think of enjoyment, friends and music stand out. On a daily basis, they are listening to music and spending time with friends. When they think of what influences how they live, friends are among the key sources that come to mind. And when they have problems, friends — followed by family — are where they look

Table 2.1. **Importance of Friends**

	Nationally	Males	Females
Very Important			
Friendship	85%	80	90
Freedom	85	84	85
High Level of Enjoyment			
Friends	94	93	95
Music	90	87	92
Daily Activities			
Listen to music	86	84	88
Spend time with friends	60	59	62
Sources of Influence			
The way you were brought up	91	90	93
Your own willpower	89	89	88
Your friend(s)	78	77	79
Sources of Support			
Friends	35	31	39
Friends and family members	22	18	26
Family members	21	21	21

for support. One 15-year-old from a small town in Prince Edward Island comments that "the only people who can understand teens are teens themselves," but cautions, "And sometimes teens don't understand teens." He adds, "It's very hard for teens to understand parents." Friends would seem to be the key, if not perfect, resource for many young people.

Males are slightly less likely than females to say that friendship is "very important" to them. But, here again, psychologist William Pollack would tell us to be cautious about male masking. He emphasizes that young males "experience deep subliminal yearnings for connection — *a hidden yearning for relationship* — that makes them long to be close to parents, teachers, coaches, friends, and family."[5] His argument is consistent with the finding that 91% of males match 91% of females in reporting that they have at least two close friends. Only three in a hundred males and two in a hundred females indicate they don't have a least one close friend.

As we have seen, the permanence of one's ties with friends is not taken for granted. Some 53% of females and 39% of males admit that the possibility of losing friends is something that concerns them "a great deal" or "quite a bit." Friendships, as intense as they may be, are often transitory for all of us at the best of times for any number of reasons, including the fact that we all don't stay in one place, geographically and otherwise. Commonalities change. As we glance back over our biographies, we all can recall some great friendships. But they frequently were and are limited to space and time. During the teen years, adolescents are sorting out who they want to be and whom they want to be with. It can make for a lot of movement. At this point in time, friendships are particularly short-lived.

Number of Close Friends

	None	1	2	3	4+
Males	3%	6	17	22	52
Females	2	7	16	23	52

A number of observers maintain that, while friends have undoubtedly always been important in the lives of young people, they have become all the more important in recent decades. In large part, their enhanced significance is seen as associated with the changing roles of family members. With two parents frequently employed outside the home and the post-1960s increase in divorces resulting in a large number of single-parent families, friends are seen as filling part of the ensuing relational void. American youth expert Jimmy Long, for example, writes that with Generation X, a new form of extended family began to emerge. Within this new family, he says, are close friends, step-parents, adopted siblings, half-siblings, spouses, and live-in lovers. He notes that in the '50s young people were immersed in family TV shows like *Father Knows Best, Ozzie and Harriet,* and *Leave It to Beaver.* In the 1990s the most popular and most copied TV program was *Friends.* "These communities of friends," Long argues, were "trying to re-establish the trust that went out of the family during the [previous] fifteen to twenty years." He believes that this relational drive is partly a result of Gen Xers' parents failing to provide safe and stable family units for the nurturing of their children.[6] Long might be overstating the situation, but his observations seem consistent with the very central role that friendship has in the lives of today's teens.

These patterns that characterized Generation Xers, it is argued, have carried over to the current generation of Millennials. Patricia Hersch, the author of the 1998 book, *A Tribe Apart,* maintains that teens "are not a tribe apart because *they* left *us,* as most people assume. We left them. This generation of kids has spent more time on their own than any other in recent history." Consequently they particularly need and value friends. In calling for the increase in social capital, Robert Putnam, in *Bowling Alone,* has pointed to the increasing tendency of Americans to be disconnected from family, friends, neighbours, organizations, and institutions.[7] Respected youth-culture analyst William Strauss comments that in sharp contrast to adults, this newest generation of young people is much more group-oriented. "Boomers might be bowling alone," he says, "but Millennials are playing soccer in teams."[8]

Beavis and Butthead: A Social Hieroglyphic

The popular MTV series Beavis and Butthead, *while "only" a "cartoon," provides all-too-real indications of how many contemporary white youth think and feel as they vegetate in front of television, unprepared for the challenges of the new high-tech economy, and how their frustration drives them to extreme behaviour.*

Beavis and Butthead seem to have no family, living alone day and night in a shabby house and being encultured solely by television and media culture. The world of Ward Cleaver and Ozzie and Harriet is nowhere in sight. Thus the series presents a world without parents, contemporary youth who are home alone, fending for themselves, with mass media their prime source of socialization.

Where some 1960s youth dropped out of mainstream culture to drop into a new world of peace and love, or pursued activist projects to transform society, Beavis and Butthead flout these values as wimpy, underscoring the huge gulf between two generations of youth and the alienation today's youth frequently feel toward their 1960s generation parents.

Interestingly, Beavis and Butthead reject all authority except white male bands. The word "rules" accurately portrays their subordination to their white male idols. Thus it is that male rock stars are the role models and the purveyors of capitalist values for the current generation.

Contrary to popular opinion and the show's opening disclaimer that it's only a cartoon, every educator, from kindergarten to the universities, has them in his or her classroom, and many talk just like them! This would be the case even if the series never existed, for Beavis and Butthead is an effect, not the cause, of contemporary youth culture.

Source: Excerpted from Steven Best and Douglas Kellner, "Beavis and Butthead: No Future for Postmodern Youth," in Jonathon S. Epstein (ed.), *Youth Culture: Identity in a Postmodern World.* Oxford: Blackwell, 1998, pp. 74–99.

Family

Dramatic changes in relationships among adults have resulted in today's "emerging generation" coming from a wide variety of family structures and living arrangements. Some 68% of teens have biological parents who are married to each other, while the parents of 25% are no longer married to each another. The remaining 7% of young people come from homes where one or more of their biological parents are deceased, have not married, or something else.

As a result of these parental marital variations:

- 71% of teenagers are living with their *mothers and fathers*;
- 22% are living with their *mothers* only, their mothers and stepfathers, or their mothers and their mothers' male partners;
- 6% are living with their *fathers*, who are either by themselves, have remarried, or have female partners;
- 1% of teens are living in homes that have *other* combinations of parents and guardians; in some instances, teens are living alone.

The extensive changes in family structure should not lead anyone to underestimate the ongoing importance that the family has to teenagers. A grade 11 student from Alberta comments, "Goodness

Table 2.2. **Family Variations**

Biological Parents	
Married to each other	68%
No longer married to each other	25
One parent deceased	3
Never married	3
Was adopted	1
Other	<1
Currently Living With	
Mother and father	71
Mother only	12
Mother and stepfather	8
Mother and her male partner	2
Father only	3
Father and stepmother	2
Father and his female partner	1
Other	1

starts in a home where kids are loved and respected for who they are. If there is a healthy and happy environment at home kids will want to be there!" During this time in their lives when conflict with parents is widely regarded as both inevitable and pervasive, a majority of young people nonetheless say that *family life* is "very important to them" and that they are receiving a high level of *enjoyment* from their mothers and fathers, siblings and grandparents. In the words of one 16-year-old female from Montreal, "My parents understand me. I am fortunate." A male, 18, from a rural Manitoba community pays his parents this tribute when asked the one thing he would like to accomplish in his lifetime: "I would like to be as good to my kids as my parents were to me."

The proportion of teens who say they receive high levels of enjoyment from their mothers (71%) is somewhat higher than the proportion who say the same things for dads (62%). One reason may be the limited time many fathers spend "doing things" with their sons and daughters. Statistics Canada found that in 1998 mothers who were employed full-time outside the home were spending 6.4 hours a day with their children under the age of five, compared to 4.3 hours for dads. By the time kids hit their teens, dads were giving an average of one hour a day to leisure activities with their teenagers — and three hours to such activities without them. Moms working full-time outside the home were finding about one hour of leisure time a day for their teens, and about two hours for themselves.[9] One 17-year-old from a small central Alberta community is among those concerned about the limited time that parents are spending with their children. "Family values are a big problem," she says. "Children would be better off if they were raised by their parents instead of daycares, TV, and the Internet."

As noted earlier, the vast majority acknowledge that how they live life has been *influenced* by how they were brought up, and a clear majority note that their mothers and their fathers more specifically continue to have an impact on their daily lives. One 17-year-old who lives with her mother and her partner in a small Manitoba community reminds us that the influence of parents, while strong, is not always positive: "My dad does influence my life," she says, "but he has a relatively bad influence."

Table 2.3. **Importance of Family**

	Nationally	Males	Females
Very Important			
Friendship	85%	80	90
Freedom	85	84	85
Family life	59	51	66
What your parents think of you	44	38	50
High Level of Enjoyment			
Friends	94	93	95
Your mother	71	65	76
Your father	62	58	66
Brother(s) or sister(s)	58	53	61
Your grandparent(s)	54	50	58
Sources of Influence			
The way you were brought up	91	90	93
Your own willpower	89	89	88
Your mother specifically	81	79	84
Your friend(s)	78	77	79
Your father specifically	70	70	70
Sources of Support			
Friends	35	31	39
Friends and family members	22	18	26
Family members	21	21	21

It is noteworthy that more than half of all teen females and males indicate they are receiving a high level of enjoyment from grandparents, in good and not-so-good family times. When asked who he considers the greatest Canadian of all time, one 16-year-old who attends school on a reserve in Western Canada gave the award jointly to "my grandma and grandpa." North American society is not always so generous in its outlook toward older adults. Sixty-nine-year-old actress Doris Roberts, the co-star of *Everybody Loves Raymond*, recently described older people as "the last group it's still OK to ridicule."[10] Yet the contribution of older people, for example, to children and teenagers in the midst of family upheaval may be significantly underestimated. Robert Glossop, director of the Vanier Institute of the Family, reminds us that grandparents help to sustain a sense of family history that is essential to a child's identity. McMaster University social work professor, Jim Gladstone, notes that when "parents can't provide the time, attention, and emotional support for their kids, grandparents can stay constant figures in their grandchildren's lives."[11] Vancouver is one place where this potential contribution is being recognized. Grandparents are volunteering their services in some ten elementary schools, helping out in classrooms and providing older-generation figures for children whose grandparents are far away.[12]

The impact of separation, divorce, and remarriage on children has been the subject of considerable conjecture and research. Because the question touches so many lives, it continues to receive a great deal of media attention. *Maclean's*, for example, ran a cover story entitled "After Divorce" in its April 20, 1998, edition, while *Time* gave the topic similar front-cover treatment in its September 25, 2000, issue that carried the cover headline "What Divorce Does to Kids."

Frequently, the interpretations of the impact of "marital breakdown" on children are polarized. Some observers see utter doom while others argue that children are incredibly resilient. These diverse positions are highlighted, for example, in the recent *Time* story. The writer of the lead article, Walter Kirn, notes, "A cluster of new books is fueling a backlash, not against divorce itself but against the notion that kids somehow coast through it." Among them is a work by retired University of California, Berkeley, lecturer, Judith Wallerstein, who maintains the harm caused by divorce is graver and longer lasting than we had suspected. However, other experts such as Paul Amato, a sociologist from Penn State University, maintain that large-scale scientific research shows that growing up in a divorced family elevates the risk of certain kinds of problems, but by no means dooms children to having terrible lives. "The fact of the matter," says Amato, "is that most kids from divorced families do manage to overcome their problems and do have good lives."[13]

Similarly, syndicated Canadian columnist Bogdan Kipling, who is based in Washington, recently summed up the findings of a new paper, "The Effects of Divorce on America," written by transplanted Canadian family therapist Patrick F. Fagan and Robert Rector for the conservative Heritage Foundation in Washington. The paper maintains that research over the past 15 years points to what they call "the downward spiral of the family." Children of divorced parents and never-married single parents know higher levels of domestic violence, delinquency, economic deprivation, academic failure, and poor health. Kipling notes that other observers such as Dr. Holly Price of the Toronto public school system maintain that divorce is often bad for kids. But, says Price, in some situations children are better off after parents separate, providing their ability to communicate about their children improves after they split.[14]

Highly regarded sociologist Margrit Eichler of the Ontario Institute for Studies in Education at the University of Toronto makes the point

---

"Brady Bunch" ideal simply unrealistic

TRAIL, B.C. (CP), February 17, 2000 — *When does a blended family not resemble the Brady Bunch? Most of the time, according to Sherri Slater, who knows of what she speaks. She has a 16-year-old son and a partner who has a boy the same age. Slater leads a group program called Blended Families, Blended Lives.*

"We want to dispel the myth of either the Brady Bunch or the totally strange family," says Slater, referring to the 1960s television series about a large, idyllic blended family. "It is becoming more common and accepted for kids to have more than one mom or dad, and yet there is not a lot of support for some of the unique challenges that these families face," said Slater.

Contentious issues can include everything from discipline to who to spend the holidays with. "Children have step-uncles, aunts and grandparents. How do you keep all these relationships straight? Are granddad and grandma accepting of the new kids or not, and what does that mean for the family? Often in blended families, one set of kids lives with the family and the other set comes to visit. How do you make that a positive experience?"

Skater says good communication is the key to successfully mixing families. Doing away with the Brady myth involves realizing that all families have problems, and bringing two families together is likely to create added stresses.

---

that low finances and a lack of social support can cripple the health of the single-parent family. She maintains that children of divorces might best be helped by ensuring that fathers support their children and by governments and community groups taking responsibility for the way single mothers with children are forced to live in Canada.[15]

Our survey allows us to get some good snapshots of teenagers who come from an array of family situations, and we will look at a number of those "family photos" in the course of examining our diverse survey findings.

It's interesting to note that teens living with both biological parents are only slightly more likely than others to say they place *high value on family life.* However, the acknowledged *influence of a parent or new parent* depends a great deal on their being physically present at home. Reported influence of both parents is highest when teens live with both natural parents. The influence of "the other parent" progressively decreases as the natural parent with whom a teen resides (1) remarries or cohabits, and (2) lives without a partner.

Perceived influence of parents consequently appears to be related to a combination of (1) parents being together and (2) providing a positive atmosphere for their offspring. One 18-year-old from the B.C. Interior whose parents are divorced and lives with her father sums things up this way: "I think that children whose parents are not divorced and rarely fight with each other have children who are responsive." Presumably the next most influential setting would be

Table 2.4. **Importance of the Family by Residence**

Living With . . .	Highly value family life	Influence high: Mother	Father
Both parents	60%	82	77
Mother only	57	84	44
Mother and stepfather	56	87	52
Mother and partner	55	82	50
Father only	48	63	71
Father and stepmother*	65	69	77
Father and partner	**	**	**
Other	56	84	82

* N = 48; percentages unstable.
** N = 23; insufficient for stable percentaging.

one in which the biological parents are not together but where the environment in which one is living is nonetheless positive. A Toronto 16-year-old who lives with her mother offers this blunt comment about her parents: "They are divorced and I don't care. I prefer it, actually. I hardly ever fight with my mother — once a year at most."

Although enjoyment of parents — biological and otherwise — is more common when both are physically present, noteworthy numbers of teens with "absentee" dads and moms also say that they are receiving high levels of enjoyment from each parent. Such a claim seems to be particularly important during the preteen and teen years. As we will see, it is not necessarily the case as young people move into their 20s and 30s.

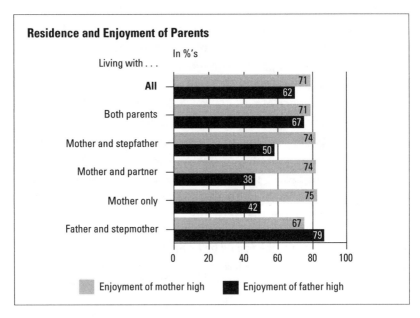

These findings are consistent with an important summary of research on the impact of divorce that family expert F. Philip Rice offered some two decades ago, around the time most of today's teens were born. There is little reason to believe that what he had found through 1980 is any different today. Rice offered this synopsis: the overall effect on children depends on the conditions of the divorce and on events before and after it. When there is little fighting between parents during and after the divorce, and when the children have free access to both parents and support from parents, siblings, and friends, the disruption is kept to a minimum. In cases where divorces are bitter and children are used as pawns, scapegoats, allies, and spies, a wide range of emotional problems results. Rice concludes that the literature indicates that "other things being equal, a happy unbroken home is better for adolescents than a happy broken home, and that both are better than an unhappy, unbroken home, or an unhappy, broken home."[16] Consequently the irony is that, by stereotyping teens from "broken homes" as different, society itself, rather than family structure as such, may be making it more difficult for young people to feel as good about themselves and their lives as other people their age.[17] We'll continue to monitor this important issue throughout the book.

A Quick Footnote on Two Possible Relational Surrogates — Pets and Cyberspace

We saw earlier that some 51% of teens say they are receiving a high level of enjoyment from their pets, including 46% of males and 56% of females. High though these figures may seem, they underestimate the companionship role of pets in the lives of teenagers. The 51% figure refers to enjoyment of pets for all teens. *Among those who actually have pets*, the enjoyment levels rise to 70% overall — 76% for females and 63% for males. In case no one noticed, those levels essentially match those reported for Mom and are slightly ahead of those reported for Dad.

We also have seen that 47% of teens are reporting that they are receiving a high level of enjoyment from their computers, 42% from the Internet, and 33% from e-mail. In addition, large numbers of young people say they are on their computers on a pretty regular basis. One obvious question arises: Is computer use generally and Internet and e-mail activity specifically inversely related to enjoyment received from friends, parents, and others? Put bluntly, are teens who are socially deprived more likely to seek solace at the keyboard? It could, of course, work the other way; maybe those who spend too much time looking at their computer screens find themselves having to hang out alone. While we are at it, we can also check out the same kind of possibilities concerning the role of pets.

Such examinations show that there is no support for the idea that computer-related activities are associated with lower levels of relational enjoyment. If anything, the two are slightly positively related. There also is no indication that people who enjoy the computer are more likely to enjoy spending time by themselves. Clearly, some teens who enjoy the computer are accessing e-mail and chat possibilities to enhance social ties, not because they don't have them in the first place. However, others who aren't particularly excited about things like e-mail are just as likely to be finding other ways of enjoying the people in their lives. As for pets, there's no indication teens who enjoy pets are any less likely than others to be getting a lot of enjoyment from real live humans as well; on the contrary, here, too, the enjoyment of pets and people is positively related.

So much for the myths about lonely computer geeks and socially starved pet owners! (Excuse me a moment; I'll be back to my beloved keyboard as soon as I feed my beloved dog. . . .)

Table 2.5. **Relational Correlates of Computer Activity and Pets**

% Receiving High Level of Enjoyment From . . .

| | ENJOYMENT LEVELS | | | | | | | |
| | Computers | | Internet | | E-mail | | Pets | |
	High	Low	High	Low	High	Low	High	Low
Friends	93%	94	93	94	95	94	95	91
Dating	70	68	70	68	70	69	73	68
Boyfriend/girlfriend	63	61	63	62	63	62	66	63
Mother	72	69	73	69	75	68	77	59
Father	64	60	65	60	67	60	68	54
Siblings	57	58	56	58	61	55	61	49
Self	53	49	50	51	53	50	53	44

While the majority of teenagers value and enjoy their parents, and are influenced by them and turn to them when they have problems, most nonetheless experience a fair amount of conflict with them. About 15% say they have arguments with parents every day, while another 40% or so report that arguments take place at least once a week. Only about 20% of teens maintain that they rarely (17%) or never (5%) have arguments with Mom or Dad. In the straightforward words of one 16-year-old from a small community in northern Ontario, "The family adds a lot of stress to teenagers' lives."

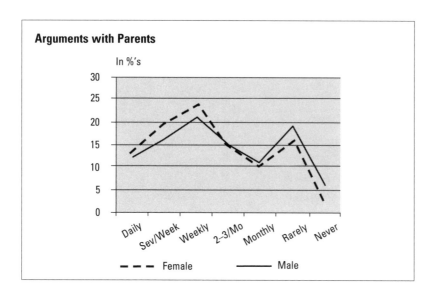

Arguments with Parents

In %'s

| | Daily | Sev/Week | Weekly | 2–3/Mo | Monthly | Rarely | Never |

- - - Female ——— Male

And what do teens and parents tend to argue about? Well, for females the number-one area of conflict appears to be *jobs around the house.* For males, number one is *school.* Other prime areas of contention noted by around five in ten teens include parents' reactions to *the way teens talk* to them, concern about *safety,* and the questioning of their *authority.* Safety as it relates to driving is no small issue for parents; auto deaths are the number-one cause of death for teenagers, and about 40% of teenage drivers who are killed have been drinking.[18] Recent Canadian research by sociologist Robert Wood and his associates indicates teenage drinking and driving is particularly a problem in rural areas where "driving around" is more frequently a leisure activity.[19] As for conflict with parents in the areas of talking or authority, one 17-year-old male from Saskatoon illustrates the potential for problems if he — and others — are verbalizing this kind of concern: "A significant problem for many young people is that parents are set in their ways and are too old to experience significant change. Obviously the key is to educate future parents and anybody else who is involved with youth and children."

About 40% of teenagers say that some of the disagreements centre on such issues as the *time they come in* at night, *money,* and *staying out of trouble.* Some 20% to 30% point to conflict over their *choice of friends,* and concern parents have about things like *drinking* and *drugs* (higher for males), *who they are dating,* and their *appearance.*

Table 2.6. **Areas of Conflict with Parents**

Disagreements "Very Often" or "Fairly Often" Involve . . .

	Nationally	Males	Females
Jobs around the house	58%	56	60
School	55	61	49
Their reaction to the way you talk to them	52	49	54
Concern about safety (e.g., driving, violence)	49	52	46
Your questioning their authority	44	45	43
The time you come in at night	40	39	40
Money	39	41	37
Concern that you stay out of trouble	36	40	32
Your choice of friends	25	25	25
Concern about drinking	23	26	20
Who you are dating	21	17	25
Concern about drugs	20	24	16
Your appearance (e.g., clothes, hair)	20	20	20
Concern about sex	18	19	17

Perhaps surprisingly, only about 20% indicate that disagreements frequently involve explicit concern about *sex* — although disagreements about who one is dating (higher for females) may implicitly reflect similar apprehension, raising the level of actual concern about sex considerably. The potential for conflict can be seen in this poignant statement made by a 15-year-old female from a small town in Nova Scotia: "Parents should be more aware that times are changing and it is OK for teens to *try* things, such as sex when love is involved." Hearing that over the dinner table would make a few moms and dads a little tense, especially if, in the middle of things, she let it slip that — as she confided in us — she has engaged in sex "very recently."

An age-old area of controversy has been how parents and other adults should respond when they're not happy with young people's behaviour. Increasingly, of course, our society has moved away from endorsing the use of physical force in favour of other methods of discipline. Yet we still disagree on the issue of whether or not anything of a physical nature is appropriate.

Take, for example, the recent spanking controversy. Section 43 of the Criminal Code says that "every school teacher, parent, or person standing in place of a parent is justified in using force by way of correction . . . if the force does not exceed what is reasonable under the circumstances." Wow! Doesn't exactly sound in touch with the times, does it? In July of 2000, Ontario Superior Court Justice David McCombs, in response to a petition from a children's rights group, refused to strike down Section 43 as a violation of the Charter of Rights and Freedoms. Corinne Robertshaw, a retired lawyer and founder of the Repeal 43 committee, maintained in an opinion piece in the *Globe and Mail* that the removal of the section would ensure "the rights and protection of children," with "parents and teachers given a clear message that hitting is no longer an acceptable method of correction.[20] An editorial in the paper the same day offered the alternative view that making spanking illegal would be extremely problematic:

> *Nowhere is it stated that people have free rein to beat children or that a court can't decide . . . that harsh disciplining is illegal. What the law does do is recognize a few facts of life. Children often don't listen to words. Having tried everything else, adults sometimes find themselves forced to communicate disapproval in a non-verbal, physical way.*

The editorial closed by noting that the interpretation and application of the law has been changing, and will continue to do so.[21]

The debate continues. Shortly after the Ontario court's ruling, a youth-run advocacy organization known as the National Youth in Care Network came to Ottawa to express their concern over the law's existence. Prior to their news conference, they held a mock debate about the merits of spanking adults who act inappropriately toward young people.[22] In November of 2000, a mother of five near Windsor, Ontario, was found guilty of assault after she spanked her four-year-old son with a wooden stick for not doing his math homework; he was being home-schooled. The woman's 17-year-old daughter, apparently upset with the history of corporal punishment, had complained to authorities.[23]

For what it's worth, elsewhere, the American Academy of Pediatrics has taken a firm stand against spanking, saying the practice teaches children that "aggressive behaviour is a solution to conflict." The association notes that 90% of American families spank their children, and also acknowledges that their membership is divided — close to half of pediatricians approve of spanking. Sweden, Finland, Denmark, Norway, Austria, and Cyprus have passed laws against spanking. But some jurisdictions are going in the other direction. In 1999 Oklahoma and Nevada, for example, passed laws giving parents the right to spank their children.[24]

For their part, today's youth do not generally question the need for discipline. In fact, 56% agree with the statement "Discipline in most homes today is not strict enough." Males and females both maintain that the three most appropriate and effective ways for parents specifically to discipline their teenage sons and daughters are to give them *a good talking to*, *take away privileges*, or *have a discussion without discipline*.

Females are particularly unsupportive of physical discipline. One such young woman, a 15-year-old who attends a private school in a small B.C. community, suggests that the most effective kind of discipline involves "showing a child how much you have been let down. Yelling and freaking out," she adds, "can make your child lose respect for you, and that's the worst thing that could happen." A grade 12 student from Saskatoon, who has professional parents, is somewhat shrill in exclaiming, "There should be none. Discipline is misused in our society," she says. "People need power and control so they take it away from their children. WE ARE EQUALS!!" A 15-year-old female who lives in Kitchener thinks the most effective method of dealing with teens is a discussion with discipline, but adds, "Parents and teens need to have good communication to make things work." Males tend to have similar views, but 8% do endorse physical discipline and another 6% approve of groundings. A 16-year-old male from a small northern rural community on the Prairies maintains age should make a difference: "Being grounded should be applied until 15, then there should be discussions without discipline after that." His parents are no longer together and he lives with his uncle. He offers some provocative thoughts:

> Parents today say they care, yet always take the easy way of "No." There are many discomforts people need to feel. Parents

need to listen and stop talking and lying. I laugh inside all the time when adults try to make up their own truths to benefit their explanations. The brain depreciates at the age of 18 on average. There are people under 18 who can do a lot with a piece of knowledge, followed by other gifts of empathy and creativity. Parents use their opinions and values and unless they can handle being wrong never back down. There should be a book on how to raise Canadian youth over 15 written by teens.

Table 2.7. How Parents Should Respond to Their Teenagers
When They Feel Teens Have Done Something Wrong

	Nationally	Males	Females
Give them "a good talking to"	29%	29	29
Take away privileges	25	25	25
A discussion without discipline	23	22	23
Ground them	5	6	4
A discussion with discipline	5	3	7
Discipline them physically	4	8	2
Combination of responses	8	6	10
Other	1	1	<1

To a large extent, of course, parents and teachers are in a no-win situation when it comes to discipline. If they are seen to be using inappropriate means of discipline, they are assailed. If their children or students act up, they often receive much of the blame. In May of 2000, for example, Ontario passed the *Parental Responsibility Act,* which allows victims of property damage to sue the parents of youthful perpetrators for up to $6,000 in small claims court — with or without the young person being found guilty in a youth court. "Strengthening parental responsibility will help ensure that there is accountability for property crimes committed by young people," said Attorney General Jim Flaherty. The act took effect August 15, 2000.[25] Adults are walking a fine line when it comes to appropriate and effective discipline.

For societies, it's an age-old problem: What do we do when people don't do what they are supposed to do? For parents and teachers, it's a current daily reality. The answer? You know the answer to that question as well as I do: There isn't one answer. We try many options, and

"I want a home like the one I grew up in"	
All	71%
Males	71
Females	70
Living with . . .	
Both parents	76
Mother and stepfather	61
Mother only	61
Father and stepmother	55
Mother and partner	53

sometimes, if we're lucky, we find a few that work. That's not what frustrated adults want to hear. But, as my mother has told me for decades when unveiling things that sounded incredible, "It's the truth." That doesn't mean that as societies and individuals we give up. We keep on trying, and are happy when we occasionally can enjoy a little win.

Other People

Teenagers value good relationships, being loved, and concern for other people. However, in relating to Canadians in general, they frequently have a measure of distrust and apprehension. Many teens are inclined to think that other Canadians do not value what they value — that people place less importance than they do on characteristics such as honesty, concern for others, family life, and spirituality.

For example, some 90% of females say that honesty is "very important" to them, but only about 40% think honesty is that important to Canadians in general. The corresponding "me"/"they" figures in the case of "concern for others" are 79% and 33% for females, and 54% and 33% for males.

The inclination to be suspicious of strangers is widespread. Asked to respond to the statement *"A stranger who shows a person attention is probably up to something,"* 37% agree, including 39% of males and 36% of females. Variations by community size and region of the country are small, suggesting such apprehension is fairly pervasive across the country.

Table 2.8. **Values: Mine versus Canadians Generally**

% Indicating "Very Important"

| | FEMALES | | MALES | |
	Me	Others	Me	Others
Honesty	83%	37	62	34
A comfortable life	74	59	71	59
Concern for others	73	28	51	26
Family life	66	45	51	41
Being a Canadian	41	37	49	43
Spirituality	35	14	23	12

Beyond anxiety and suspicion, many of Canada's teens also feel they are not taken seriously by adults. Only 29% agree with the assertion *"Generally speaking, adults respect young people's opinions,"* with little difference between males (33%) and females (26%). A Kamloops 16-year-old says, "I think the survey is an awesome idea. I think it's important to ask teens for their opinions because many teens have much to give but they don't get the chance." Another 16-year-old who lives in North York, Ontario, puts things this way: "I think it's about time that Canada cares what its young people think and say." She adds this note of skepticism and hope: "It's a shame that this survey won't matter and that it won't influence governments at all. Nice attempt, though. Out of curiosity, will any action be taken after the results are found?" A 15-year-old Toronto male is a self-conscious cynic: "You aren't going to give a damn about the comments I made. I don't even know why I wrote them. It doesn't change anything. Excuse my cynicism. Thanks."

Teens also feel that they are unfairly stereotyped. Survey participants were particularly vocal about this topic. One 17-year-old female from London, Ontario, comments, "Today's adults don't understand us. Although some teenagers give us a bad name, not all of us are like that." A playful 15-year-old male who lives in Hamilton ends his questionnaire by saying, "Toronto will win the Stanley Cup and Hamilton is going to win the Grey Cup again. Not all teenagers are bad but people don't hear about them; they only hear about the bad ones." From Burnaby, a 15-year-old female notes, "Some of us, like me, can know a lot of 'bad' things but do not act bad. Most adults I know mistake me for being something I'm not." An Ottawa-area female, 16, poetically writes, "People may think teens are criminals, but we just want to have fun — rebel but not regret." From Grande Prairie, Alberta, comes this plea for greater respect:

An important issue is how adults treat me just because I'm a teenager. Sure there are bad ones out there but I'm not one of them and it doesn't just hurt but it's disrespectful when security figures follow me around like I'm some kind of loser or criminal. I'm 17 years old and I hope you'll consider my opinions.

And an articulate 15-year-old from Montreal has this to say:

Today's youths are intelligent but some adults don't seem to think so. We are people too. Youths are discriminated against and that's not right. To get through to young people, you have to listen to them, trust them, and respect them. The way I look and the music I listen to does not make me a "bad" person. I am my own person.

It is hard to dispute the legitimacy of such complaints. A cursory glance at daily media reports on virtually any subject involving young people makes it abundantly clear that political correctness has not yet been applied to the use of the word "teen." The term continues to be tossed about recklessly with little regard for the human implications of such stereotyping. If any other group reference — such as "black" or "Jew" or "homosexual" — were substituted for "teen" in a headline or a story reference to undesirable behaviour, people would be threatening lawsuits, asking for retractions, and appealing to human rights commissions. Yet the media routinely not only use the term but also magnify it when reporting on any number of negative acts, ranging from crime through incivility to, well, how about the stealing of the Olympic torch in Sydney! Such age-related reporting does little to enhance interpersonal relations between young people and adults. A Calgary 18-year-old offers this advice on how things might be different: "The one thing that needs to happen is for open communication, trust, and respect to take place between teens and adults." In the immediate future, it sounds about as elusive as winning an Olympic gold medal.

Teen tries to steal torch

SYDNEY, Australia (AP), August 25, 2000 — *The Olympic torch relay survived another sabotage attempt Friday after a teenager tried to steal it from a torchbearer, the second major incident in as many days on the torch's 100-day tour of Australia.*

On Thursday, a teenager tried to douse it with white powder from a fire extinguisher. Police said a 17-year-old tried to grab the torch Friday from a female torchbearer as she ran along the Pacific Highway. After failing in his attempt, the youth fled the scene but was caught by security officers a short distance from the highway.

The runner was uninjured and the relay was not interrupted. The torch is on a 16,700-mile tour of Australia.

A Much Rarer Story

CALGARY (CP), November 19, 2000 — *A Calgary teen who died trying to save a life has been honoured by Scouts Canada with its highest award for bravery. Gov. Gen. Adrienne Clarkson posthumously awarded David Elton the Gold Cross for gallantry with special heroism and extraordinary risk.*

Elton, 17, was with a group of students, teachers and parents from a Calgary high school when he died last March during a hiking trip in northern California. A rogue wave swept parent chaperone Barbara Clement into the Pacific Ocean. Elton and schoolmate Brodie McDonald, also 17, threw themselves into the surf to help. All three drowned.

Two popular teen practices that are associated with considerable stereotyping are tattoos and body piercings. Permanent tattoos and piercings that appear virtually anywhere on bodies have become commonplace among young people, much to the consternation of many adults. In early September of 2000, 16-year-old Jonathan Ibay made national news when his school, St. Thomas More Catholic Secondary in Hamilton, laid down a dress code forbidding more than one piece of face-piercing jewellery for grade 10 to grade 12 (OAC) students. The school intends to eventually forbid the practice entirely. Ibay, who had two studs in his nose and two in his eyebrow, had to remove three of his studs if he wanted to return to his school. His mother acknowledged that she didn't particularly like the piercings and expected "he'll probably get over it when he gets older." She had tried to persuade school officials not to enforce their ban and said that her son has "never been in any trouble in school. He's not the type to get into any fights."[26] This is not a debate that is going to go away either quickly or quietly.

Our survey has found that 9% of Canadian teens have permanent tattoos and 13% have body piercings other than ear piercings. As for overlap, it's more common for those with tattoos to also have piercings (56%), than for those with piercings to have tattoos (43%). Both are slightly more prevalent among females. This, of course, is just the current snapshot. One 15-year-old from a very small Saskatchewan community reminds us that the camera's still running: "I haven't got a tattoo yet," she says with a tone of enthusiasm, "but I am getting one."

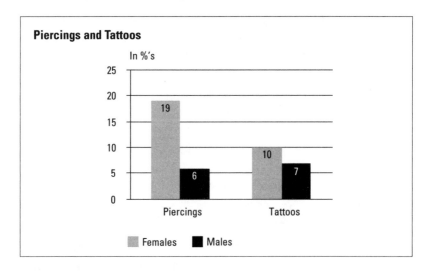

Further to the issue of stereotypes, the survey findings reveal that teens with body piercings or tattoos differ little from other teens with respect to their self-images, as well as the value they place on concern for other people. However, those who have piercings in particular, as well as those with tattoos, are somewhat more likely than other young people both to engage in sex and use marijuana. Teens with tattoos and piercings are also somewhat less inclined to indicate that they would return $10 given to them by mistake by a store clerk.

However, lest people see these findings as confirmation of their stereotypes, they need to be reminded that these relationships are far from "perfect"; large numbers of teens with piercings and tattoos are *not* having sex or smoking pot, while significant numbers of teens with neither a piercing nor a tattoo are in fact sexually active and using marijuana. Similarly, it's true that some 70% to 80% of young people with piercings and tattoos would not return the $10, but neither would more than 60% of other teens.

In short, the self-images of teens with tattoos and piercings are generally very similar to those of other teens. But any attempt to attribute sexual activity, drug use, and dishonesty to all such teenagers is an unfair exaggeration. A 16-year-old female from Kamloops makes this plea to adults: "Please do not judge someone because of their race, hair, style of clothing, piercings, or tattoos. Although there will always be people we don't like, we need to learn to be kind to everyone!" All right, I know that sounds a bit melodramatic and overly idealistic. But it nonetheless is a plea in a life-giving direction that needs to be taken seriously.

Table 2.9. **Correlates of Piercings and Tattoos**

	PIERCINGS		TATTOOS	
	Yes	No	Yes	No
Self-image				
I am well liked.	94%	93	94	93
I am a good person.	93	96	92	96
I am good-looking.	79	76	80	76
I can do most things very well.	78	83	82	83
I have lots of confidence.	67	71	69	71
Behaviour/Values				
Engage in sex	71	45	82	45
Highly value concern for others	68	62	61	62
Use marijuana	61	33	65	33
Would return the $10	29	37	23	37
Attend services weekly-plus	12	23	10	23

Apart from what adults may think of them, teenagers do not lack in respect for adults who are heading up the country's major institutions. More than six in ten say they have "a great deal" or "quite a bit" of confidence in people in charge of *schools* as well as the *police*. That's quite remarkable, given many of us adults assume those are two parts of society that are tough on teens and are probably generating a fair amount of antagonism.

- Around six in ten also express confidence in leadership in the *newspaper* and *movie* industries.
- Just over half say they have a high level confidence in the *music* and *computer* industries, as well as the *court system*.
- Some 45% express confidence in people in charge of *major business*, *radio*, and *television*.
- The confidence level for the leaders of *provincial* and *federal governments*, along with *religious organizations*, stands at about 40%.

In most of these institutional instances, more females than males indicate high levels of confidence in leadership, one notable exception being the higher expression of confidence that males say they have in leaders in the computer industry. An illustration of a balanced view of

Table 2.10. **Confidence in Leaders**

"How much confidence do you have in the people in charge of . . ."

% Indicating "A Great Deal" or "Quite a Bit"

	Nationally	Male	Female
Schools	63%	58	68
Police	62	59	65
Newspapers	60	57	63
Movie industry	60	57	63
Music industry	54	53	54
Court system	52	50	54
Computer industry	51	56	46
Major business	48	50	47
Radio	48	46	49
Television	44	46	40
Provincial government	41	41	40
Federal government	41	40	41
Religious organizations	40	38	41

the media comes from this 17-year-old who lives in the Okanagan: "I have confidence in the movie, music, and TV industries. I realize their downfalls, particularly their overuse of sex and violence. But they are excellent as creative sources, and I am confident in their ability to inspire ideas."

Obviously every institution has its detractors, including the confidence-leading schools and police. One 17-year-old female from a small community in Ontario offers the view that the "police should worry about people getting shot on the streets, not about kids drinking or smoking weed," and a 15-year-old from Toronto charges that "the police are racists who do nothing to help the community." Schools also are frequently berated. One upset 17-year-old male from Saskatchewan comments, "Schools should not hire vice-principals that hate kids." A Toronto 16-year-old says, "I really think that we need *new* teachers," continuing on to say, "My teachers are so grouchy; they've been working in the same field for too long now. I'm starting to think they no longer like their jobs." A grade 11 student from a small town in southern Ontario offers this sensitive observation: "I think teens should feel comfortable in school. I do, but I see some students with their heads down all the time. I don't think that it's right. I wouldn't want to live like that." And a 16-year-old from a small town in Alberta offers this short comment: "I feel that you should be able to talk to your teacher more."

Undoubtedly school personnel are particularly vulnerable to criticism by students because of the stakes involved. As we saw earlier, a major source of stress for students is the pressure they feel to do well

---

Some Thoughts on Teachers and Courses

Teens are divided down the middle when it comes to interested teachers and interesting courses.

% Agreeing

	Nationally	Males	Females
All in all, my teachers are genuinely interested in me.	51%	52	50
Most of my school courses are fairly interesting.	54	52	55

in school. Research presented in Montreal at the annual meeting of the American Headache Society in June of 2000 involving teenagers who are prone to migraines found that 20% got them on Mondays, compared to 9% on Saturdays, leading the researchers to conclude the migraines are associated with the anxiety of beginning another week at school.[27] Unfortunately, the researchers didn't also produce results on the "head state" of teachers, as well as parents who had to make sure those kids showed up on Mondays. At times life isn't easy for anyone.

A 16-year-old female who lives near the U.S. border in Alberta provides us with these closing thoughts on teens and adults:

> *Teens shape their values from what they see around them, like media, political leaders, and teachers. If you want teenagers to make the right decisions, then set the right examples for them. Let them know it's not OK to use drugs (like a few Olympians), it's not OK to have sex with someone other than your wife (like Bill Clinton), and it's not OK to break the law (like so many famous actors and actresses are doing).*

Teens want respect; they also want adults they can respect.

Assessment

Teens, like the rest of us, need people. The question is, where do they find the most gratifying social ties? The answer today is **friends**. As obvious as that may seem, observers have been inclined to see the role of friends in young people's lives as having become increasingly important because of the changes in the form and functions of family life. Simply put, more and more young people have been spending more and more time without their parents.

Teens these days come from homes with a variety of structures and living arrangements. Yet the majority continue to place value on their **families**, find enjoyment from them and turn to them for support. Conflict with parents is common and tends to centre on jobs around the house, communication, and parents' concerns about school, safety, and their kids' staying out of trouble. Teens recognize the need for discipline, but most feel it should be in the form of taking away privileges or parents' discussing their concerns.

Although most teens value good relationships and express concern for others, they often feel distrust and apprehension in dealing with **adults in general.** They also feel they frequently are not taken seriously and are unfairly stereotyped. However, they express fairly high levels of confidence in major institutions, particularly led by law enforcement and schools.

Two quick points. A typical response to the findings on the **preference teens have for friends** is "What's new about that? That's just the way people are at that point in their lives." I know that response well; I have been hearing it from the outset of our surveys in the 1980s. I also have only become more militant in my response. It's great that teens can turn to friends. But there's nothing written in the stars that says they should not simultaneously be enjoying both their mothers and fathers. In an ideal world, they should be enjoying friends *and* parents. It's time parents dropped the "that's inevitable" position and took more responsibility for why they too frequently are being left out.

Second, the **suspicion** that teens have of adults is ironic, in view of the fact adults are also so suspicious of teenagers. Teens are widely stereotyped, yet obviously teens are commonly stereotyping adults. It points to a great need for our major institutions, perhaps led by the media in its diverse forms, to play a major role in finding ways for adults and teenagers to better understand one another and, ideally, interact more. Undoubtedly many teens label adults based on contacts with relatively few, starting with their parents and teachers. The same is true of adults, who begin with their own teens and may move only short distances from there. Things need to change. They could.

Chapter Three

Five Areas of Particular Concern

Violence

During the past few years, adults have been increasingly concerned about teenage violence, stimulated in large part by a series of violent acts in Canada and the United States. On April 20, 1999, 12 students and a teacher were killed at Columbine High in Littleton, Colorado, followed on April 28 by the shooting of two students, one fatally, in Taber, Alberta. Ever since, threats of violence in schools across Canada have been seen as abounding.[1] A knife attack on the one-year anniversary of Columbine in April 2000 resulted in the wounding of four students and one staff member at Cairine Wilson High School in the Ottawa suburb of Orléans. In November 2000 a Toronto teen admitted he had shown classmates a list of fourteen students he planned to kill and had attempted to buy an assault rifle over the Internet to carry out his plan.[2] The same month a student was stabbed to death at Calgary's Lester B. Pearson High School.[3]

Parents are among those feeling new pressures. *National Post* columnist Jane Christmas described the ambivalence she felt when her 14-year-old wanted to stay away from his Hamilton school on the day of the Columbine anniversary. In the end, she decided to let him. But it required the confirmation of her mother, her doctor, and word of what happened in Ottawa — what she describes as three votes of confidence. "Did I overreact?" she asks, and then answers her own question: "I don't believe anything you do in the interest of protecting your child is an over-reaction."[4] The headline of her article referred to the times as "the age of Columbine."

> ## Dale Lang prays for peace
>
> TABER (CP), May 2, 1999 — *Tears of anguish and celebration mingled Sunday as Rev. Dale Lang led his congregation through a rollicking revival-style service calling for peace and healing of the world's "damaged humanity."*
>
> *The Anglican priest's 17-year-old son Jason was shot dead Wednesday in the hallway of W.R. Meyers high school in this southern Alberta town of 7,200 people. A 14-year-old boy — said to be a target of incessant physical and verbal abuse by other teens — is also accused of seriously wounding another 17-year-old. The Alberta shooting came just a week after two teens gunned down 12 fellow students and a teacher at a high school in Littleton, Colorado, before killing themselves.*
>
> *Lang — with his other children looking on from the wooden pews — offered healing prayers to all involved in the tragedy, including the boy accused of the shootings. "Before I became a Christian 25 years ago, I would have wanted revenge. God has done a lot of work in my heart," Lang told the flock. "He has continued to soften my heart."*

Violence among young people has not been limited to schools. On November 14, 1997, Victoria teenager Reena Virk was beaten by a group of girls she'd sought to befriend, then drowned by one of the girls and a teenage male companion.[5] Eight young people, seven of them girls between the ages of 14 and 16, were charged, and one of the girls was subsequently convicted of second-degree murder and sentenced to five years in prison before she can apply for parole. Virk's mother told the presiding judge, "My dream to raise and love my child is shattered like a vase."[6] In November of 1999, 15-year-old Dmitri Baranovski was punched and kicked to death in a Toronto park by eight to ten males wearing balaclavas and blue bandanas who demanded cigarettes, drugs, and money from the victim and his friends.[7] Just two days later, a 14-year-old Toronto girl was found bruised and bleeding with cigarette burns on her back; she'd been tortured for two hours by four older teenage girls.[8] In November of 2000, a 14-year-old

Edmonton boy was taken off life support two weeks after being brutally beaten beyond recognition by two older teens behind a junior high school.[9] And youth violence was further highlighted when an eight-year-old boy in Lytton, Quebec, used his father's high-powered rifle to shoot and critically wound a 64-year-old man, claiming he was shooting at a tree to scare the man.[10]

In the light of these and other forms of violent acts — including child abuse, sexual assault, and suicide — it's important to hear what young people have to say.

Violence in schools **is seen as a "very serious" problem by significant numbers of teenagers. But the difference by gender is fairly dramatic.** Some 65% of females see the issue as extremely serious, compared to just 40% of males. Nonetheless, out of 18 issues posed, violence in schools is among those most widely cited by males as being particularly serious.

One 17-year-old male from a small northern Alberta city expresses his concern this way: "We have had threats and it makes me scared to come here and learn. I mean, just the other day there was a fight in our hallways." A 15-year-old who lives in a small community in northern Ontario says she doesn't feel safe at school, adding, "I could at any time be shot." But another female, 16, from Regina warns against stereotyping teens: "In reaction to the recent school shootings, I would like to say it isn't all kids in black who listen to Marilyn Manson, have black trench coats, and get beat up at school who do these kinds of things. I would never do anything that stupid and I am a goth, black trench–owning, Marilyn Manson–loving freak who gets picked on."

Table 3.1. **Perception of Seriousness of Violence, Crime, and Suicide**

% Viewing as "Very Serious"

	Nationally	Females	Males
Child abuse	56%	66	44
Violence in schools	50	59	40
Teenage suicide	49	60	36
Violence against women	42	51	33
Crime	40	49	29
Youth gangs	31	34	28

In addition to violence in schools, some 50% to 65% of females and 30% to 45% of males view *child abuse, teenage suicide, violence against women,* and *crime* as "very serious" problems. In each instance, the concern levels for females are significantly higher than those of males. About 35% of females and 30% of males see **youth gangs** as "very serious."

Beyond perception of the seriousness of these various issues, teens were asked if they have *a close friend* who personally has encountered violence or has had depression or suicide-related experiences.

- Some five in ten, led by females, say they have had a close friend who has been *severely depressed,* while four in ten indicate that they have a close friend who has *attempted suicide.* In both cases the levels for females exceed those for males.
- Almost 40% of males and 25% of females report that they have had a close friend who has been *physically attacked at school;* conversely, around 40% of females and 25% of males say a close friend has been *physically abused at home.*
- Three in ten females and just under two in ten males confide that they have a close friend who has been *sexually abused.*
- About 30% of males and 20% of females say a close friend has been a victim of *gang violence.*

Some caution needs to be used in interpreting such findings; one's close friend may also be the close friend of others. To find that three in ten females has a close friend who has been sexually abused, for example, does not mean that three in ten females have been sexually abused; obviously the figure, based on such an item, is somewhat lower.

Table 3.2. **Extent to Which Problems Have Been Experienced by a Close Friend**

	Nationally	Females	Males
Has been severely depressed	48%	57	39
Has attempted suicide	41	50	31
Physically attacked at school	32	25	39
Physically abused at home	31	37	25
Has been sexually abused	26	32	18
A victim of gang violence	24	21	28

Still, these findings suggest that the incidence of depression and suicide attempts, physical attacks and abuse is startlingly high. What is disconcerting is that the violence is frequently found not only at school but also at home.

A final note on bullying. Alan King's 1998 national health survey found that just under 30% of males and females in grade 10 reported that they had been bullied during the school term. Such physical, verbal, or psychological intimidation has few clear-cut correlates, other than being disproportionately directed at males who feel isolated. Bullying tends to be cyclical: those who are bullied bully, and in turn receive similar treatment.[11]

DIFFERENCES ACROSS THE COUNTRY • Overall there are few distinct differences in the perception and incidence of school and home violence among regions and communities, regardless of size. Simply put, perception and behaviour are distributed fairly evenly across Canada.

Concern about violence in schools is somewhat less in Quebec than elsewhere, despite the fact that students there are marginally more likely than others to say they do not feel safe at school; presumably such concern has been normalized. Contrary to what I suspect is widely believed, teens in cities of over 400,000 are slightly *less* inclined than young people living elsewhere to view school violence as "very serious," and no more likely than others to say they do *not* feel safe at school. Teens living on farms are the least likely to report that they have close friends who either have been attacked at school or physically abused at home.

There is little difference in concern about violence at school and at home between young people born in Canada and those born outside the country. There is, however, a slightly greater tendency for teens who have come to Canada to say both that (1) they have a close friend who has been attacked at school and (2) they themselves don't feel safe at school. As might be expected, as teens from outside Canada share in Canadian life, their inclination to engage in offences comes to resemble those of teens born here — a pattern noted, for example, by Brandon sociologist Siu Kwong Wong in a recent study of Winnipeg teens of Chinese descent.[12]

Table 3.3. **Concern about Violence by Region, Community Size, and Birthplace**

	School violence a very serious problem	Close friend attacked at school	Not safe at school	Not safe at home	Close friend physically abused at home
Nationally	50%	32	22	7	31
B.C.	51	30	19	7	30
Prairies	49	32	17	5	30
Ontario	53	32	22	7	32
Quebec	43	33	27	7	33
Atlantic	54	30	21	8	27
North	53	34	19	2	31
>400,000	44	35	21	5	32
399,999–100,000	51	32	21	7	34
99,999–30,000	56	36	28	7	31
Cities/towns <30,000	53	29	21	8	33
Rural non-farm	52	32	18	7	27
Farm	50	24	19	6	25
Born in Canada	50	31	21	7	32
Born outside Canada	47	35	26	6	28

Concern about youth violence has led to proactive measures in cities such as Toronto. In June of 2000, a Youth Violence Task Force comprising Toronto police, Catholic and public school boards, and the transit commission recommended that:

- police officers be assigned to schools, recreational centres, and subway stations during lunchtime and after-school hours;
- police disclose conditions of release for young offenders to schools as permissible under the *Young Offenders Act*; and
- a young offender program be implemented to target high-risk, repeat offenders.

A member of the task force, 17-year-old Krista Lopes, noted the need to work together "to combat the ever-increasing problem of youth violent crimes," while Toronto Police Chief Julian Fantino noted that "the ol' thing is no longer adequate," adding, "We need to do things that are more strategic and we need to count on parents, politicians, educators, and certainly the police community and all others, but especially the youth, to turn things around."[13]

In order to understand current youth violence in relation to the past, it is important to first ask, what constitutes violence? By way of illustration, a 1999 survey of 2,000 grades 7 to 12 students in Alberta by the Canadian Research Institute for Law and the Family found violence to be highest among grades 8 and 9 students. Some 40% of grade 9 students, for example, admitted to slapping, punching, or kicking someone in the past year, compared to 32% of grade 12 students. About 16% of students acknowledged they had brought weapons to school, with the most common being illegal knives, replica weapons — mostly plastic guns, clubs, and bats. The least common were pellet guns and handguns. In addition, more than half the students surveyed said they had been victimized at least once during the past year at school; perhaps significantly, almost the same percentage said they had been victimized while they were *not* at school. The most frequent forms of victimization — similar in all Alberta communities — included being slapped, punched, or kicked, having something stolen, being threatened with bodily harm, and having property damaged. The least frequent included being attacked by a group or gang and being threatened by a weapon. Such survey findings prompted the Calgary police chief at the time, Christine Silverberg, to call for an expansion of school resource programs in junior high schools.[14]

It is clear from such research that "violence" is being applied to an extremely wide range of activities beyond beatings, stabbings, and shootings. Such a broad application of "violence" undoubtedly is associated with a "zero tolerance" response to any physically aggressive act toward another person. *Hear me clearly:* this is in no way to minimize the gravity of such acts today. But it is to say the bar that defines violence has been raised considerably over where it has been in the past. Adults also may be placing the bar at a higher level than where many teens — especially males, but also some females — are placing it. Among them is a 16-year-old female from a small town near Calgary who comments, "School violence has been around since schools came about. Let kids be kids," she says. "Don't punish them for wrestling. Punish them for guns and severe fighting."

A Reality Check

It is worthwhile to compare our survey perceptions and reports with additional information on young people. A victimization analysis released in December of 1995 by Statistics Canada using data from police departments indicated that teenagers are certainly vulnerable when it comes to violent crime. In fact, they are at greater risk of violent crime than either adults or children. Young people between the ages of 12 and 19 made up 20% of the victims of violent crime in the mid-'90s, even though they represented just 11% of the population. About 80% of violent incidents against teenagers were assaults, some 15% being of a sexual nature; most of the others involved robbery. Victims of violent crime were equally likely to be males and females; however, a large majority of victimized females were victims of sexual offences, whereas males were more likely to be victims of assault and robbery. Police statistics also revealed that about five in ten violent incidents against teenagers involved acquaintances, and three in ten strangers, while two in ten were committed by family members, with parents implicated in half of those incidents.[15] Further, Statistics Canada survey data for 1999 show that young people 15 to 24 are reporting the highest rate of personal victimization, more than twice the national average. Seniors 65 and over, by the way, are reporting the lowest rates of victimization.[16]

In July of 2000, Statistics Canada released a new report, also based on police records, revealing that the national crime rate in 1999 fell to its lowest level in two decades. Young people under the age of 20 were more likely than people in other age groups to commit both violent and property crimes. Youth crime, however, was down more than 7% from 1998 and was 21% lower than in 1989. The rate of youths charged with violent crime fell 5%, the largest year-to-year drop since the *Young Offenders Act* was introduced in 1984. While the 1990s saw an increase in violent crimes among females, the female rate as of 1999 was still only one-third of the male rate. The report reminded readers that many non-violent young offenders are diverted from the formal justice system, but also said that available statistics indicate the number of youths being diverted has also been decreasing in recent years.[17] Coincidentally, the same day the report was released, Britain released crime statistics for England and Wales, which showed a large jump in violent crime in those two countries over the past year.[18]

A third Statistics Canada report, made available in August of 2000, is also worth acknowledging. An analysis of sentences given to young offenders (12 to 17) who were convicted in youth court during 1998–99 reveals that one-third were put in some form of custody. Males were more likely to be sentenced to custody than females. A comparison of the sentencing of adults and youths for the most common offences for nine of the most frequent offences — such as common assault, breaking and entering, and possession of stolen property — showed that young people were less likely to be placed in custody. But when they were jailed, they were more likely to receive longer sentences than the adults. For example, in the case of common assault, the report found that 65% of young offenders were sentenced to more than one month in jail, compared to 43% of adults.[19] Commenting on the report, Robert Gordon, the director of the Department of Criminology at Simon Fraser University, suggested the sentencing differences reflect public calls for stiffer penalties for offences involving young people.[20]

Taken together, these three reports indicate that (1) a disproportionate number of teens are victims of violent crime, (2) the rate of violent crime committed by young people has been decreasing in recent years, and (3) young offenders who are placed in custody tend to be punished to a greater degree than adult offenders. **These findings document that teen violence is a serious problem. But contrary to widely held perception, teen violence has actually been declining. In addition, reaction to young offenders in recent years, in some instances at least, has been harsher than that shown adults.**

Even in the face of the Calgary school homicide in November of 2000, Dennis Eastcott, the founder of the Alberta Association of School Resource Officers and the officer in charge of Edmonton's youth and crime prevention services, maintained that statistics do not support the notion that kids are becoming more violent or are getting "out of whack." As for school violence, Staff Sgt. Eastcott commented, "Studies based on where kids are victimized show one of the safest places for them is at school."[21] Obviously not everyone agrees.

It therefore is not surprising that it's difficult to obtain a consensus on how to respond to so-called youth crime. At a conference of victims'-rights advocates held in Hamilton in October of 1999, Justice

Minister Anne McLellan said that Ottawa would do what it thinks is right to deal with young offenders, regardless of pressure from the provinces. "Quebec is telling me: 'Your legislation is too tough.' Ontario is telling me: 'It's not tough enough.' Well, you know what that tells me? Canadians are generally right in the middle and I think our legislation reflects that balanced approach."[22]

Safety at School and at Home

Although teens are aware of friends who have been attacked and abused, 19 in 20 say they feel safe at home, 16 in 20 feel safe at school.

% Indicating Feel Safe

	At home	At school
Nationally	93%	78
Males	94	79
Females	94	78

A national survey of 400 American teenagers, 14 to 17, conducted in April of 2000 for *Time* magazine found 86% felt either "very safe" or "somewhat safe" from violence at school.[23]

Sexuality

Our sexually liberated society is characterized by considerable openness about sex, led by the media. If Pierre Trudeau took the government out of the bedrooms of the nation, the media takes us into the bedrooms of the nation on a daily if not hourly basis. TV programs such as *Sex and the City*, the *Sunday Night Sex Show*, and *The Sex Files* lead the way explicitly. But sex is everywhere to be found, spanning sitcoms, movies, stand-up comedy, and, for reasons well known to all of us, even nightly newscasts in the U.S. and Canada on a regular basis during 1999.

Craig Colby, the Toronto producer of *The Sex Files* that airs on the Discovery Channel, recently commented, "There's definitely a lot more permissiveness in society." Colby says that two events have been new groundbreakers — the Monica Lewinsky affair, which made oral sex and phone-sex discussion topics, and the memorable "Master of His Domain" episode on *Seinfeld*, that "completely destigmatized" masturbation.[24] Yes, these are days of sexual freedom and openness.

And with the morning-after pill becoming more accessible to women, making it possible to prevent pregnancy within three days of intercourse,[25] some would argue that the incidence and enjoyment of sexual activity, marital and otherwise, will only increase.

In the midst of all this, adults worry a great deal about teenagers and sex for any number of reasons. And they should, if the words of this 17-year-old female from Hamilton are accurate: "Sex is like an everyday thing for teens now."

The survey shows that Canada's youth are divided almost evenly when it comes to sexual attitudes and behaviour, although males typically hold more liberal attitudes than females and are more sexually active.

- Approximately six in ten teens, led by males, maintain that *consenting adults* should be able to do whatever they want sexually. Moreover, the same proportion of males and a smaller proportion of females feel that *consenting teens* between the ages of 15 and 17 also should be able to do whatever they want sexually. One 17-year-old from the B.C. Interior sums things up this way: "I believe in people's right to do whatever they want sexually, as long as it doesn't hurt any other living thing. In the case of teenagers, however, more thought has to go into it because they are less able to deal with accidental pregnancy than adults."

- Some 80% of young people approve of sex before marriage *when people love each other*, with little disagreement between males and females. In addition, close to 60% think that sex before marriage is all right *when people like each other*. Here there is a significant difference in opinion between males (68%) and females (48%). A Burnaby, B.C., 16-year-old says, "I'm worried about diseases in Canada; more people are having unprotected sex." The issues of birth control and pregnancy are expressed starkly by a 17-year-old from Alberta: "Teens should have more information about protection if they are going to have sex. People should be told how to take birth control properly, along with the fact methods aren't 100% effective against pregnancy." She signed her comments, "A pregnant teen who was on birth control." Few young people would disagree: 92% maintain that "birth control information should be available to teens who want it." More possibilities, incidentally, are on the way. As you might be aware, a new monthly injectable contraceptive known as Lunelle, the first new birth control method since 1992, was introduced in the U.S. in late 2000. It is an alternative to Depo-Provera, an injectable drug that is given every three months. Both are administered by physicians.[26]

• About one in two teenagers (54%) approve of *homosexual* relations, with females (66%) considerably more likely than males (41%) to express approval. But 75%, led by females, maintain that homosexuals are entitled to the same rights as other Canadians. Among males expressing consternation is this 15-year-old male from Regina who says, "Gays should not have a special week or the right to adopt children." A grade 11 male from a small Alberta town comments, "One

Table 3.4. **Sexual Attitudes**

% "Strongly Approve" or "Approve"

	Nationally	**Males**	**Females**
Sexual Tolerance Limits			
Consenting adults doing whatever they want sexually	61%	67	56
Consenting teens 15 to 17 doing whatever they want sexually	56	66	46
Sexual Behaviour and Rights			
Sex before marriage when people LOVE each other	82	85	80
Sex before marriage when people LIKE each other	58	68	48
Sexual relations between two people of the same sex	54	41	66
Homosexuals are entitled to the same rights as other Canadians	75	62	87
A married person having sex with someone other than marriage partner	9	13	4
Cohabitation			
A couple who are not married living together	86	89	83
A couple having children without being married	63	61	64
Abortion			
It being possible to obtain a legal abortion when a female has been raped	84	85	83
It being possible to obtain a legal abortion for any reason	55	58	52

thing I would like to stress is that homosexuality is wrong. If they really want to be gay, they should do it in secret and not adopt kids."

- Merely 9% of young people condone *extramarital* sexual relations. It seems quite obvious that such behaviour has not been adding much to lives, however heralded it might have been by some at the time of the sexual revolution.

- *Cohabitation* receives the approval of almost nine in ten teenagers, while having *children without being married* is regarded as all right by about six in ten. Stigma in the latter case seemingly is higher for teenage single parents than couples. A 16-year-old in the Atlantic region says that, despite the fact that her boyfriend has stood with her in raising her child, "I get a lot of discrimination against my parenting skills."

- The availability of *legal abortion* when a female has been *raped* is approved of by some 80%, abortion *on demand* by just over 50%. One twelfth grader from Vancouver says he "applauds the availability of birth control in British Columbia" and adds that "abortion should never be withheld under any circumstances." The introduction of the RU-486 pill as an alternative to surgical abortion may or may not alter such attitudes. The pill, which can terminate a pregnancy up to about seven weeks after conception, was approved and made available to some U.S. doctors in late 2000[27] and is being tested in Canada. It has been met with strong opposition from pro-life groups. RU-486 has been available in France since 1989 and is also sold in Britain, Sweden, and China.[28]

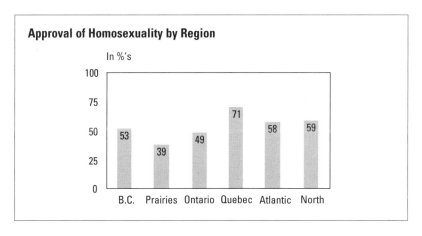

Approval of Homosexuality by Region

In %'s

B.C.	53
Prairies	39
Ontario	49
Quebec	71
Atlantic	58
North	59

In short, while one in two Canadian teenagers indicate that, in theory, consenting individuals technically and legally have "the right" to do what they want, teens nonetheless have some strong personal feelings as to what is sexually appropriate and what is not.

Sexual Attitudes and Service Attendance

Differences in sexual attitudes are readily apparent between teens who attend religious services weekly versus those who attend less often.

% Approving

	Weekly	Less than weekly
Consenting adults doing what they want sexually	36%	68
Consenting teens 15 to 17 doing what they want sexually	28	63
Sex before marriage when people LOVE each other	49	91
Sexual relations between two people of the same sex	25	62
Sex with someone other than one's marriage partner	4	10
Homosexuals entitled to same rights as other Canadians	59	79
A couple who are not married living together	57	94
A couple having children without being married	29	72
It being possible to obtain a legal abortion for any reason	24	64

We asked teens pointedly how often they engage in sex. About 25%, including 27% of males and 22% of females, claim they have sex at least once a week. Around another 10% indicate they have sex two to three times a month, a further 15% say less often. Approximately 50% of teenagers say they never engage in sex, with this category including some 45% of males and 55% of females. Among them is a 16-year-old male from southern Alberta who comments, "None of my friends or anyone I know have had sex. My friends and I feel that you should not have sex unless you are married." As for the one in two who do engage in sex, a *Globe and Mail* editorial has put it this way: "There is a principal reason why people engage in consensual sex: They enjoy it. Liking sex has little to do with age. Thinking about sex in terms of preventing unwanted consequences rather than preventing the sex act itself simply recognizes the fact that teenage sex is, well, common."[29] In responding to the question of how often she engages in sex, a 16-year-old female from suburban Montreal may speak for much of the nation in admitting, "When the chance comes up." In her case, she says, it's "hardly ever."

A cautionary note: "engage" in sex undoubtedly means "sexual intercourse" for most teens, but not all. One 15-year-old female from Williams Lake, British Columbia, reminds us that "some people engage in sexual activity which does not include actual sex," and that "there is a lot more sexual activity between 'neck and pet' and 'sex.'"

Table 3.5. **Teenage Sexual Activity**

"About how often do you engage in sex?"

	Nationally	Males	Females
Daily	6%	9	3
Several times a week	10	10	10
About once a week	8	8	9
2 to 3 times a month	7	8	6
About once a month	5	7	3
Hardly ever	13	14	12
Never	51	44	57
Totals	100	100	100

In sum, around 50% of teens are currently sexually involved, and 50% are not. A national survey of teenagers carried out in the mid-1990s by Statistics Canada reports similar levels of activity and adds some further details. First, 44% of males and 43% of females had had at least one sex partner in the year that the survey covered. Second, 21% of teen males had sex with at least two partners, compared to 13% of females. Third, close to three in four males (71%) but only one in two females (49%) claimed that condoms were used.[30]

Yet our current survey findings on sexual activity underestimate the lifetime sexual experiences of teenagers, because the item is asking specifically about *current* sexual behaviour. Fifty percent of teens are not virgins. An additional survey item reveals that 15% — 16% of males, 14% of females — are not sexually involved *currently*, but just 41% of teens (33% of males, 48% of females) say they have *never* been sexually involved. The "currently involved" and "previously involved" total consequently appears to be closer to 60%.

As for appropriate behaviour on dates, nine in ten teens think it is all right for two people to *hold hands* on the first date if they like each other and more than seven in ten approve of kissing on the first date. *Necking and petting*, however, is seen by six in ten teenagers as something that should not take place until after a few dates. Here, males and females differ significantly. Young women are much more inclined to indicate a few dates should have taken place, and about 15% don't think necking and petting should occur at all. In case you are wondering, no, we weren't all that excited about using the terms "necking and petting," but we wanted to use terms consistent with our previous surveys and, frankly, "making out" is too general. A 17-year-old from Nunavut was among those who wanted to make a distinction. Drawing an arrow to "necking," she said, "Yes, we did that after two months of going out. Me and my boyfriend neck, but I don't know what you mean by pet. If you mean 'feel up,' then no, never!" That's

Table 3.6. **Appropriate Behaviour on Dates**

"If two people on a date like each other, do you think it is all right for them to . . ."

	Yes, on the first date	Yes, after a few dates	No
Hold hands	89%	10	1
Males	92	8	<1
Females	87	12	1
Kiss	73	26	1
Males	78	21	1
Females	68	30	2
Neck and pet	32	57	11
Males	43	50	7
Females	22	63	15
Have sex	11	40	49
Males	18	50	32
Females	4	32	64

what we meant, and I think that's what most teens thought we meant.

Males and females differ sharply in their sense of when and if *sexual relations* are appropriate. Almost seven in ten males say sex is all right within a few dates, but fewer than four in ten females share their opinion.

Two common assertions of people observing the teenage sex scene is that the threat of AIDS has been (1) contributing to a reduction in sexual activity and/or (2) resulting in more protected sex. While the first assertion is seriously in doubt, about 60% of teens who say they are sexually involved acknowledge that AIDS has influenced their sexual habits. The remaining 40% apparently have been relatively unfazed by the existence of the fatal disease. One 16-year-old, who lives in a small city in northeastern Quebec, seems to express the sentiments of many teens in this latter category when she says, "Since I have been sexually active, AIDS has existed. For me, nothing has changed."

The Limited Impact of AIDS
"Has the existence of AIDS influenced your own personal sexual habits?"

	Yes	No
Males	56%	44
Females	62	38

Drugs

Since at least the 1960s, considerable publicity has been given to the problem of drug use among young people. It remains an area of major concern for adults. For example, we saw earlier that some 25% of males and 15% of females note that they frequently have conflict with their parents over the issue of drugs. Parents' and adults' fears are not neutralized by what they sense is the ready availability of drugs. If anything, those fears may be heightened when they learn of the current survey's finding that no less than 44% of teenage males and 49% of females acknowledge they have a close friend with "a severe alcohol or drug problem."

There is little doubt that Canadian teens have ample access to illegal drugs. No less than 77% say that if they wanted to use drugs, it is "not very difficult" (26%) or "not difficult at all" (51%) to obtain them; 6% think it is difficult and the remaining 17% say they "don't know." What's particularly striking is that access is not limited by whether or not someone is female or male, lives in one region of the country or another, or resides in a large city, small city, or a rural area. Illegal drugs appear to be just about everywhere. A 16-year-old in one Western Canadian city decries the availability of drugs where he lives:

> *I think the drug problem is very bad here. I mean, I try to stop doing drugs, but they are so readily available that it is very hard. There are so many drug traffickers in my school and I go to the best Catholic high school in the city. Kids need to be stopped from turning to drugs, but not by another one of the government's corny programs. Also, more stores should call for identification when people buy alcohol because I can buy it easily and I don't look a day over 16.*

A grade 12 student from New Westminster says "drugs are available on today's streets" and that "it is easier to buy drugs than alcohol." A 17-year-old in Hamilton notes, "Drugs are everywhere. I can get marijuana any time I want, day or night." A 16-year-old in a small city north of Edmonton concurs: "Pot is so easy to get, and cheap." Another Albertan, a 16-year-old male from a small town south of Calgary, takes the position that drugs are so readily available that laws should be relaxed: "I believe it shouldn't matter how old you are to buy liquor or cigarettes or pot because they are very easy to get if you are underage."

Availability, of course, doesn't equal use. A 15-year-old from Moose Jaw, Saskatchewan, observes, "There are a lot of drugs around here, but not all people use them." Yet the concern about drug abuse is shared by significant numbers of teenagers. As we saw earlier, almost one in two teens say that drug use is a "very serious" problem in Canada. One male, 16, who lives just outside Ottawa comments, "I really do feel that the use of drugs among teenagers is a big problem. I have many friends who engage in drugs weekly, daily, or monthly. I see this becoming more of a problem because I don't have a friend who hasn't at least tried drugs once or twice." A Grande Prairie, Alberta, teen expresses his alarm this way: "I strongly feel that heroin and crack cocaine are being strongly abused by teens and parents.

This is breaking up families and lives. I am very worried about it and scared for the future of our society." A 16-year-old female from a small Ontario town acknowledges that the problem exists and offers an explanation as to why: "I think that in our town a lot of our drug and alcohol problems are because we have nothing to do — no movie theatre, no bowling alley, no mall, nothing."

Table 3.7. **Access to Drugs**

% "Not Very Difficult" or "Not Difficult at All"

Nationally	77%
Males	80
Females	74
B.C.	81
Prairies	76
Ontario	75
Quebec	78
Atlantic	80
North	81
>400,000	77
399,999–100,000	79
99,999–930,000	76
Cities/towns <30,000	80
Rural non-farm	75
Farm	76

Given the prevalent consternation and access, what actually is happening?

Some 28% of teenagers say they smoke *cigarettes* monthly or more often, 9% rarely, and 63% never. Female smoking levels are marginally above those of males. These figures are consistent with Statistics Canada data for early 1999 that found 28% of teens, 15 to 19, to be smokers.[31]

Around 20% of teens say they drink *beer, wine, or other forms of alcohol* at least once a week, with the level for those under 18 only slightly lower than that of 15- to 19-year-olds as a whole. The weekly level for males is almost twice that of females; yet 75% of females drink at least on occasion, compared to 80% of males. One 15-year-old female from Edmonton helps to clarify the nature of alcohol use for some young people: "My parents often let me have wine or a cooler but I feel because of this I have grown a respect for alcohol. Because it's always available at home, I don't go out and get drunk with friends."

Approximately 15% of teenagers say they *smoke marijuana or hashish* weekly or more, with male use about twice that of females. However, about four in ten males and three in ten females admit to being occasional marijuana users.

Table 3.8. **Drug Use among Teenagers**

"How often do you yourself . . ."

	Weekly or more	Once or twice a month	Less than once a month	Never
Smoke Cigarettes	23%	5	9	63
Males	22	5	9	64
Females	24	6	9	61
Drink Beer, Wine, Other Alcohol	22	30	26	22
Males	29	29	22	20
Females	16	31	28	25
Under 18 total	18	29	26	27
Males	26	31	22	21
Females	14	31	29	26
Smoke Marijuana or Hashish	14	10	13	63
Males	19	11	13	57
Females	9	8	14	69
Use Other Illegal Drugs	3	4	7	86
Males	4	4	8	84
Females	2	4	7	87

Just 3% of young people acknowledge that they are using *other illegal drugs* on a regular weekly basis, including 4% of males and 2% of females. But again, occasional use is not insignificant — another 12% for males and 11% for females.

A 17-year-old from Montreal sums up the place of drugs in her life in a fairly matter-of-fact manner: "Every weekend I consume alcohol when I go to a pub or go out to eat at a restaurant. When I go to a rave I take illegal drugs, but I only go about once a month."

A grade 11 student who lives in a small community in New Brunswick explains her use of marijuana:

When you asked the question, "Do you smoke pot," I replied yes. This doesn't make me a drug addict. I'm getting an 80% average in school and doing well at work. I enjoy having a toke but I am very responsible. I never come to school or work high. I hope this shows that every teen who smokes pot is not a delinquent.

It's important not to lose sight of the fact that sizable numbers of young people maintain that they are *not* using drugs of any kind, including — in close to one in four cases — alcohol. Among them is another Montrealer, a 16-year-old female, who says, "Drugs do not interest me at all. I find cigarettes distasteful and I don't want to know anything about illegal drugs."

Top Five Most Popular Drugs

1. Marijuana	87%
2. Ecstasy	3
3. Hashish	2
4. Mushrooms	<1
5. Cocaine	<1

Two areas of controversy. One drug that has become increasingly controversial is **marijuana.** Use is extensive and the public seemingly divided as to whether or not it should continue to be treated as illegal. Interest groups have been arguing that its effects, short-term and long-term, pale compared to legal drugs such as alcohol and nicotine. Those opposed argue that its affects are highly detrimental, contributing to short-term dysfunctions and long-term disabilities.

In late July of 2000, the Ontario Court of Appeal ruled that Canada's marijuana law prohibiting the possession of marijuana is unconstitutional and gave Ottawa a year to amend it. People who require marijuana for medicinal purposes can apply for an exemption; the Ontario court asked that the exemption be written into law. At the same time, the court upheld a lower-court decision prohibiting the possession of marijuana for recreational purposes.[32] On the heels of the decision, Ontario NDP leader Howard Hampton called for the decriminalization of marijuana, saying that too many people are being turned into criminals for "smoking a little pot," and that such a move would free up police to fight real crime.[33] Indications that marijuana use may be on the increase means the debate can be expected to intensify.

Young people are not lost for views on the topic. One in two favour the legalization of the use of marijuana, with males (58%) more likely to be in favour than females (42%). A 15-year-old male from Hamilton protests, "No matter what anyone says, marijuana is addictive," while a 16-year-old Calgary-area female offers these thoughts:

> *I feel that the use of marijuana should not be illegal because it helps people relax; also, everyone does it nowadays so there is no way the law can keep it under control. If marijuana is illegal, then alcohol should be illegal, because it does the same things to your body and is just as dangerous or even more dangerous.*

We saw earlier that 18% of teens say they attend **raves** monthly or more, with the figure for males (21%) higher than that for females (15%). The media have given extensive attention to raves; *Maclean's*, for example, carried a cover story entitled "Rave Fever" in its April 24, 2000, issue. Writer Susan Oh noted that many see Toronto as the rave capital of North America, and that ravers can "dance until dawn most weekends" in other cities such as Vancouver, Calgary, Edmonton, Montreal, and Halifax, as well as some other smaller locales.[34] Critics say that these all-night parties are replete with drugs, notably ecstasy, which was given emphasis in the *Maclean's* story. In Ontario, a 13-day inquest was held in May 2000 following the death of Allan Ho, 21, who died at a Toronto rave after taking ecstasy. The inquest resulted in 27 recommendations to ensure the all-night parties are safe.[35] Concern about ecstasy was heightened in late August 2000 with news that Canada Customs officials in Montreal had seized a record-breaking shipment of ecstasy that was on its way to Toronto.[36]

Raves, according to Toronto police chief Julian Fantino, are "threatening the very fabric of Canadian life." Others, however, say they represent a new cultural party expression and are no more problematic than party gatherings of the past — and typically less turbulent than gatherings in bars. Edward Adlaf, a research scientist at the Toronto's Centre for Addiction and Mental Health, has said, "In many ways, the concerns raised over the rave scene are not that much different than for rock concerts in the 1970s." He points out that, in Ontario, about 60% of students who attended raves in the past year used cannabis but no other illegal substance. Just over 4% of all students surveyed had taken ecstasy in the past year.[37] A June 2000 article in *Time* magazine argued, "First we had the Beat Generation; now we have the Beats-per-Minute Generation. And it's not just about ecstasy." Rave culture, said writer Christopher John Farley, has started to exert a potent influence on pop music, advertising, films, and even computer games. According to some observers, rave culture has become youth culture. Drugs may or may not be part of "the rave scene."[38]

One of our survey participants, a 17-year-old male from Kelowna, B.C., has the following to say:

> *I know lots of kids who go to them and I went to them extensively myself. The thing is drugs! So many hard drugs are taken by kids ages 14 to 25 it's amazing. I've done ecstasy about 10 times and it was really fun, although I won't do it again, and I was able to stop unassisted. I know of kids who go to every rave that's put on (about 1 to 2 times a week) and do ecstasy, crystal, mushrooms, smoke dope, use acid, drink, huff nitric oxide, snort coke. People don't really know about this underground rave culture and parents would freak if they found out their 15-year-old daughter went to raves, got f...d out of her mind, and hooked up with some older guy. I can see how kids get addicted to raves but the drugs are the scary thing and it makes me laugh that parents have no clue!*

Despite such alarming reports, journalists such as Kevin Grace maintain that a consensus is forming in cities, including Toronto, that attempts to ban raves only drives them underground. He cites one suburban-Vancouver councillor who says, "They're not something I would ever go to, but my parents' generation had the same opinion of the dances we went to when I was young."[39] *Calgary Sun* columnist Bill Kaufmann writes, "The hysteria that swept city hall in the wake of an isolated stabbing incident following a rave was amusing to behold. It's as if raves have just arrived in Calgary in the past few weeks. In

A portrait of a rave

VANCOUVER, December 10, 1999 — *The music begins with a steady thump, thump, thump. It's a beat and a sound that goes on with unrelenting monotony for eight hours straight at the Plaza of Nations.*

Welcome to The Rave.

The room is filled with about 3,000 jostling kids of varying ages and costumes. Kids sucking soothers, kids wearing candy necklaces and silver sparkles on their cheeks, kids wearing cute little tops. On the dance floor, glow sticks whirr like insects in the night.

In a room tucked away from the dance floor, a girl sits next to a first-aid attendant, spaced out on drugs. Now what was it this time? Ecstasy, GHB, DXM, ephedrine, Quaalude? Police say a mind-boggling menu of chemical cocktails is turning up at these all-night, high-decibel dance fests.

Rave promoters like David Primack admit the drugs are there and that they are dangerous, but they point out that drugs are everywhere. "It's a societal problem, not a rave problem," he said, adding it would be absurd to ban raves because of them. Instead, he thinks there should be a massive drug-prevention campaign.

Having grown out of Britain in the early 1980s, raves start around midnight and go to 8 a.m. and they feature non-stop dancing to the music of disc jockeys rather than live bands. They're food-free and alcohol is largely eschewed, but bottled water is sold at inflated prices. On the sidelines at a rave is a new breed of young free enterprisers offering everything from massages to body painting. Now held in big, established venues, they've come a long way from what began as impromptu gatherings held in warehouses.

Ravegoers feel they have been misunderstood. The only problem, according to [police], is that so many of these nouveau hippies are on drugs. Police have given up trying to charge kids with drug-related offences at these events. "It's not cost effective. Far better to go after the clandestine [drug-producing] labs," they say.[40]

fact, they've been filling halls, party rooms and underground venues for years with little fallout." Predicts Kaufmann, "This current manifestation of youth culture — like so many others before it — will play itself out."[40]

So what do the data actually say?

To begin with, 6% of teens tell us that they go to raves once a week or more, 5% say they go two to three times a month, and another 7% about once a month. A further 18% say they "hardly ever" attend raves, and 64% say they never do. Almost 50% of monthly-plus ravers come from cities of 100,000 or more, but these consist of only about 15% of the teens in those same cities. Surprisingly, 40% of those who say they attend raves at least once a month come from communities of fewer than 10,000, suggesting that the term "rave" has come to have a fairly broad interpretation. Keeping things in perspective, approximately 20% of the young people living in those smaller communities go to raves that often.

An examination of general drug use among young people who attend raves and those who don't shows that rave-attendees are more inclined than non-attendees to use marijuana and other illegal drugs. It is not clear where exactly such use is taking place. However, what is

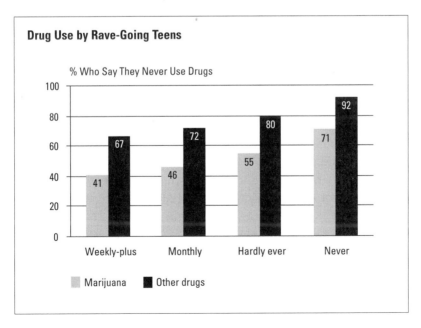

Drug Use by Rave-Going Teens

clear is that about 40% of teens who attend raves at least once a week say that they *never* use marijuana, and almost 70% claim they *never* use any other illegal drugs, including ecstasy. In short, lots of teens who attend raves claim they are partying without drugs.

Tracy Ford, a social worker with the Ministry of the Attorney General in Toronto and described as "a former enthusiast of the rave scene," is a member of the Party People's Project (PPP), a community-based group formed to protect the rights of ravers. Writing in a publication of the Alberta Alcohol and Drug Abuse Commission in late 2000, she maintains that false stereotypes of violence and rampant drug use have been used to discredit raves. What is required, she suggests, is not the outlawing of raves, but rather a combination of support, trained supervision, and education that can reduce rave-related harms. "The harm reduction model," she says, "accepts the choices of young people, and supports them, rather than criminalizing them." Ford writes:

> *The rave community is a place where young people can find a creative and open network of individuals that love to dance and love music. Young people have basic civil rights to associate, express themselves and enjoy the same freedoms accorded all Canadians in their leisure time. Whatever our concerns about the safety of young people, we must find options that will foster their development, and support their ability to make informed choices.*[42]

There is little reason to disagree.

Canada and Canadian Culture

As Canadians we have not made a lot of nationalism, especially in the post-Trudeau years. We continue to struggle with the perennial problem of who, in fact, we are. Moreover, it is not clear that we even have a sense of where we have been. Mark Starowicz, the executive producer of CBC's Canadian History Project that made its debut in late 2000, has lamented that Canada has few highways that link our particularities of region, language, age, belief, or taste. Unlike most European countries and the U.S., we do not locate the present in the past; we have "severed the arteries that connect us to the past."[43]

Nonetheless, Canadian culture increasingly has come to be

defined in terms of some distinguishable emphases and policies such as bilingualism and multiculturalism. In the words of the commissioner of official languages, Dyane Adam, bilingualism "is a critical element for the success of Canadian federalism."[44] And as the popular "Joe Canadian" rant and "Radically Canadian" CFL commercials remind us, we are not totally like Americans. We consequently have expectations that our young people will grow up with an appreciation for things Canadian, while, as typical Canadians, we want them to have global awareness and appreciation as well. Few may show the emotion for the country of a Simon Whitfield, the Olympic gold winner from Kingston who said after winning the triathlon in Sydney, "I've dreamed of this my entire life. I've dreamed about winning a gold medal. It happened today and I can't tell you how proud I am to be Canadian."[45] But we do want people to care about the country.

How are things looking? Well, actually, not bad at all. To begin with, some seven in ten teenagers say that being a Canadian is either "very important" (45%) or "somewhat important" (26%) to them. A few, like one Saskatoon male in grade 12, simply say, "Canada Rocks!" A grade 11 student from London, Ontario, comments, "I'm very, very proud to be pure Canadian. I love it here." A 15-year-old male from the Northwest Territories tells us, "I am a Canadian who loves Canada," while a 16-year-old female from a community west of Edmonton writes, "If I had a choice to be anything, it would be Canadian. It's one of the most important things to me, besides family and friends." A 15-year-old from Vancouver says, "Canada is the best country in the world and so are the people in it!" On the other hand, a 17-year-old Calgary female complains that "many Canadians have little pride in their country," a reality verbalized by a Toronto grade 10 student who says, "I'm not patriotic at all. We're all humans."

There is, however, a significant difference in the valuing of being Canadian between teens in Quebec (40%) and those in the rest of the country (80%). Quebec francophones (35%) are particularly disinclined to say that being a Canadian is important to them. Among them is this 18-year-old Montreal male who comments, "Canada oppresses us. We will never make progress with this country." A 16-year-old says that being a Canadian is not important to him at all and, when asked who he considers the greatest Canadian of all time, facetiously responds, "the Montreal Canadiens." Another 16-year-old, a female from Montreal, tells us that she places very low value on being a Canadian and says she sees herself as "Québécois(e)." Yet she sees the threat of separation as a serious problem: "Most young people today, above all, want to see the liberation of Quebec. Me, I detest such things." In contrast, a 16-year-old from a small community in the province sums up his sentiments succinctly: "Je suis Québécois! Vive le Québec Libre!"

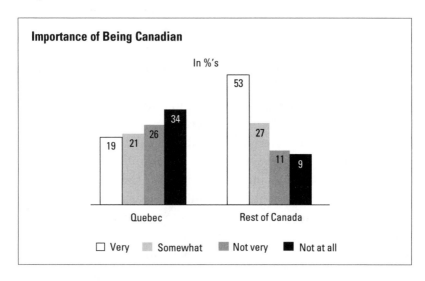

Importance of Being Canadian

In %'s

Quebec: Very 19, Somewhat 21, Not very 26, Not at all 34

Rest of Canada: Very 53, Somewhat 27, Not very 11, Not at all 9

□ Very   ▨ Somewhat   ▩ Not very   ■ Not at all

Seven in ten teens, led by those from Quebec, endorse the idea of Canada having two official languages. Close to the same proportion of young people indicate that they are opposed to Canada being a cultural "melting pot." One bilingual 17-year-old from Sherbrooke of English descent says of immigrants, "They should come, but not have to give up their culture." Yet, despite such apparent widespread approval of multiculturalism — and the enshrinement of the importance of one's national heritage — only 20% of teenagers say that their own cultural heritages are "very important" to them. Even in Quebec, heritage as such is not widely valued. Perhaps, in that provincial and linguistic instance, it is partly because being a Québécois in the present is more significant than whatever one's ancestors were. It is clear that some First Nations teens place high importance on their cultural heritage. One 16-year-old who lives on a reserve proudly says that his heritage is "Blood Indian from the Blackfoot Confederacy," adding, "I'm an Indian, not a Canadian." He tells us that the one thing he would like to accomplish in his lifetime is to "unite the people of the Blackfoot Nations."

Table 3.9. **Nationalism and Views of Policies**

	Nationally	Quebec franco	Quebec anglo	Rest of Canada
Highly value being Canadian	45%	15	37	53
Endorse bilingualism	73	80	83	70
Opposed to "melting pot"	66	59	70	68
Highly value cultural heritage	20	20	24	19

Canadians celebrate from coast to coast

OTTAWA (CP), July 1, 2000 — *Trailing plumes of Maple Leaf red-smoke, the Skyhawks sky-diving team floated over Parliament Hill as thousands of Canada Day revellers clapped, cheered and tried to get a glimpse of the prime minister wandering through the crowd Saturday. "The first of July is a fantastic day to be prime minister," Jean _____ said as he walked to the main stage with his wife Aline and shook hands with the pressing crowd.*

The hot day in the nation's capital drew about 100,000 people, including Joe Canadian, star of Molson's popular I AM Canadian ad, who gave his rant on the street across from the hill a few hours before the ceremonies began.

In Montreal, thousands converged on Dominion Square. Behind a backdrop of dancers, marching bands and about 4,000 participants in Montreal's largest-ever Canada Day parade, Finance Minister Paul Martin . . . helped cut a red and white cake, a 1,000-pound behemoth large enough to serve 2,000 people. "Quebecers are looking forward to building, not destroying, this great country," Martin told The Canadian Press. The turnout for the subsequent party was pegged by organizers at 100,000.

Fewer than one in four teens view core, ongoing Canadian social issues such as American influence, Native-White and French-English relations, and the lack of unity as "very serious" problems. Quebec francophones are slightly less inclined to view Canadian unity as a problem — not surprising, given that a good number are in favour of separation. A poll of just over 1,000 16- to 18-year-olds carried out in January 2000 for *Reader's Digest* found that 61% of Quebec teens favour independence. Nationally, male-female differences on these four issues are very minor.

Table 3.10. **Specific Canadian Concerns**

% Viewing as "Very Serious"

	Nationally	Quebec franco	Quebec anglo	Rest of Canada	Males	Females
American influence	25%	23	25	25	27	22
Lack of Canadian unity	22	13	33	23	22	21
Native-White relations	21	18	20	22	20	21
French-English relations	20	26	45	17	20	20

Much is being made of globalization, whereby our culture and other national cultures are interacting with one another as never before. Unprecedented global contact via the Internet, television, and travel have seemingly brought into being the global village of which forecasters such as Marshall McLuhan wrote. While globalization's impact on Canadian life culturally and economically may be self-evident, some observers have suggested that, in the Canadian instance, a cultural phenomenon that continues to be equally if not far more profound is Americanization.[47] In reality, what is packaged elsewhere, as well as "globalization," is often "Americanization," given that some 80% of the world's multinational companies are based in the United States.[48]

One way of exploring the impact of other cultures on ours is to look at the culture of young people. Teens were asked about "their favourites" in ten areas of interest: kind of music, TV program, movie, singer or group, athlete, web site topic, author, world leader, politician, and TV newsperson. A cursory glance at the results shows that a majority lack favourites in six of the ten areas, from athlete through TV newsperson. The dominant "favourites" that they do cite are typically

American; a few are Canadian; virtually none have origins outside North America.

- Programs, films, and names such as *The Simpsons*, *Friends*, *The Matrix*, *American Pie*, the Backstreet Boys, DMX, Michael Jordan, Stephen King, Bill Clinton, and Barbara Walters are far more numerous than Céline Dion, Wayne Gretzky, Jean Chrétien, and Pamela Wallin.
- The NBA Raptors' Vince Carter is a favourite, but obviously is an American based in Canada — sort of ours, sort of not, just a trade or free agency away. That's not to say he isn't having an impact on Canadian youth well outside Toronto. A 17-year-old male with six brothers and sisters, who follows the National Basketball Association "very closely" and cites Carter as his favourite athlete, says his life dream is to "make it to the NBA." He lives in Nunavut.

Table 3.11. **Top Three Favourites**

%'s Computed on Total Number Cited for Each Category

	#1	#2	#3	None cited
Kind of music	Rap/Hip-Hop	Alternative	Pop	
	[18%]	[15]	[11]	9
TV program	The Simpsons	Friends	Dawson's Creek	
	[13]	[9]	[4]	17
Movie	The Matrix	American Pie	Sixth Sense	
	[5]	[2]	[2]	20
Singer/group	Backstreet Boys	Blink-182	DMX	
	[3]	[2]	[2]	28
Athlete	Vince Carter	Michael Jordan	Wayne Gretzky	
	[9]	[8]	[4]	55
Web site topic	Music	Sports	Chat groups	
	[8]	[7]	[4]	56
Author	Stephen King	J.R.R. Tolkien	John Grisham	
	[8]	[6]	[4]	56
TV newsperson	Peter Mansbridge	Lloyd Robertson	Barbara Walters	
	[1]	[1]	[1]	81
World leader	Bill Clinton	Nelson Mandela	Jean Chrétien	
	[5]	[2]	[1]	84
Politician	Jean Chrétien	Bill Clinton	Lucien Bouchard	
	[2]	[2]	[1]	84

A footnote here for the information of more than a few cynical readers. *The Simpsons* has been North America's longest-running sitcom. In its twelfth season in 2000–2001 the animated social satire is seen in more than 70 countries. The show has been described by *TV Guide*'s editor-in-chief Steven Redcliffe as "one of the greatest comedies ever"; University of Syracuse television expert Robert Thompson maintains it is "among the greatest American comedies in all the arts and letters," adding that "mentioning *The Simpsons* right up next to Mark Twain does not bother me at all."[49] Canadian teens obviously have embraced this animated television commentary on Americana.

It is interesting to note that Quebec francophones are more likely than anglophones to cite favourites that are Canadian — beginning

---

Rap music

The term "rap music" was first coined around 1976 as black disc jockeys in New York dance clubs began to play extended dance tracks by using two turntables and a sound mixer. By switching from one record to another without stopping the music, they would get the crowd whipped into a frenzy while using a microphone to insert their own spoken personal commentary.

Rap music began to grow as a distinctively black urban alternative to white music. It has served a dual role in culture. First, it is an outlet for expressing the reality of trying to survive in the oppression of the ghetto. And second, rap fulfills a prophetic role by communicating messages that show how those stuck in the rut can cope, fight and survive.

What began in the ghetto is now mainstream. While the majority of popular rap artists are black — a prominent exception being Eminem — the majority of rap albums sold are purchased by white males and, increasingly, young white females.

Source: Drawn from Walt Mueller, "Eminem — Meet the real Slim Shady," *youthculture@2000. Newsletter of The Center for Parent/Youth Understanding* (Fall 2000): #3.

with *4 et Demi* as their favourite TV program, although *The Simpsons* is a very close second. Those anglophones, by the way, include anglophones in Quebec. Ironically, a Quebec that has been worried about losing its culture continues to know cultural distinctiveness. Upon the death of Maurice "the Rocket" Richard in May of 2000, a friend of the former hockey great commented, "He will never be forgotten. After the Pope, it's Maurice Richard."[50] The rest of the country has known or claimed few such icons in the past or present.

As I have previously suggested, in the course of analyzing Canadian social trends in general, our national effort to establish a rich Canadian culture through championing a multicultural country has contributed to a cultural blank in most of English-speaking Canada. Outside Quebec, people have a questionable sense of where they have come from, few heroes, and a passive acceptance of being inferior to the U.S. In lieu of having our own Canadian culture, the tendency has been to fill the void with American culture, contributing to the Americanization of Canadian life.[51] It's not a new phenomenon, but it has been intensified with the expansion of media ties between the U.S. and Canada, notably television and, increasingly, the Internet.

Table 3.12. **Favourites**

% Citing Canadian

	Nationally	**Quebec**	**Rest of Canada**	**Quebec franco**	**Quebec anglo**
TV newsperson	76%	80	74	90	40
Politician	61	81	55	88	52
Athlete	30	36	28	39	25
Singer/group	12	16	11	18	10
Author	8	15	6	17	7

In recent years, there have been attempts to draw attention to Canadian stars and heroes. For example, Toronto now has "Canada's Walk of Fame." Stylized maple leaves with the names of inductees appears on a downtown King Street West sidewalk and, to date, include the likes of William Shatner, Gordie Howe, Martin Short, Maureen Forrester, Neil Young, Donald Sutherland, and Luba Goy.

It's not yet apparent how successful such efforts are in elevating Canadians to genuine "star" status in the minds of young people. Asked who they regard as "the greatest Canadian of all time," some 60% either indicated that "no one comes to mind" or left the item blank. The top three Canadians? Wayne Gretzky, Terry Fox, and Pierre Trudeau. Females placed Fox, whose Marathon of Hope run ended in Thunder Bay in 1980, ahead of Gretzky. The number-one choice of Quebec teens by a considerable margin was "Rocket" Richard. Teens also were asked who they see as "the greatest American of all time." Interestingly, they showed no greater inclination to cite Americans than Canadians; here around 65% drew a blank. The top three Americans cited? Martin Luther King, Abraham Lincoln, and John F. Kennedy. It is clear that some young people simply don't like the idea of cultural heroes, period. A 16-year-old female from B.C. says she "is not one of those people who idolizes TV stars. I have to say the greatest people are the ones that brought me into this world — my mother and father."

Year after year, the United Nations has maintained that Canada is one of the best countries in the world in which to live. A World Health Organization report released in June of 2000 asserted that Canadians can be expected to live an average of 72 years — females 74 and males 70 — before health begins to seriously deteriorate. Averages in other countries range from 74.5 in Japan to below 30 in a number of African countries plagued by AIDS. The U.S. average is slightly below Canada at 70.[52] A Statistics Canada report released in mid-2000 compared incomes in Canada and the U.S. for 1974 through 1997. It found that average real incomes are higher and have been growing faster in the United States. However, inequality of disposable incomes has increased in the U.S., with the very rich in the United States pulling up the income average more than in Canada, leaving other people with less purchasing power than those here. Some 50% of Canadians are better off in terms of disposable income living here compared to the U.S. The tax advantage of a move to the south isn't obvious until a person earns more than $60,000.[53] In reflecting on this report and services that contribute to quality of life, David Suzuki commented, "Canadians live longer, healthier lives than do Americans, at least in part because of the more equal distribution of wealth in our country."[54]

Our current survey findings suggest that Canada's high standard of living and overall quality of life have not been lost on young people.

Teens were also asked what country they would live in if they could live anywhere in the world. Just over half maintain they would live in Canada, about 15% in the U.S., and the remainder would live elsewhere. An Edmonton female, 15, offers the view that "Canada is the best country in the world and so are the people in it!" A 17-year-old from Toronto is a bit more restrained but positive: "I believe a lot should change in Canada, such as violence and government. Overall, though, I love living in Canada." Those who would like to head for the States include an 18-year-old female from Vancouver who says, "I hope to become a doctor. When I do, I am going to work in the USA because of better wages and job opportunities." A Calgary 16-year-old expresses ambivalence, but is leaning southward: "The USA is nice but it has too much violence. Still, for my career, it would be a better place to live."

Slightly less than half of Quebec teenagers say they would choose to stay in Canada — including Quebec specifically, but to a larger extent than young people in the rest of the country they show an interest in living in a wide variety of countries around the world, not only the U.S.

Table 3.13. **If I Could Live in Any Country . . .**

	Canada	U.S.	Elsewhere
Nationally	52%	15	33
North	68	11	21
Atlantic	62	8	30
Prairies	62	12	26
British Columbia	55	15	30
Ontario	53	15	32
Quebec	44*	19	37

* Includes 6% who cite Quebec specifically.

Some of these teens aren't kidding about leaving. By way of an informative footnote, it's valuable to know what all this departing could mean. During the 1990s, Canada suffered a net loss of skilled workers to the United States. The people who left tended to have higher education and income levels than the population as a whole, and also were individuals of prime working age. Do you recall the Molson's Canadian commercial that ran in 2000, the one where the polite Canadian finally had enough of the wisecracks about Canada and pulled "the obnoxious American's" jacket over his head? Well, between laughs, remember what country he had chosen to work in.

But although movement to the U.S. accelerated during the '90s, so did the influx of highly skilled workers into Canada from other countries. As a result, we gained four university grads from abroad for every one we lost to the Americans. In fact, the average number of immigrants who entered Canada with a master's degree or doctorate totalled more than 10,000 people — higher than the total of Canadian university graduates at all levels who left for the U.S. (4,500, for example, in 1995).[55] Recent immigrants were twice as likely as people born in Canada to be working as computer scientists and engineers, as well as employed in the natural sciences.

We do not want to lose our young people to the United States. Yet, in recent years, thanks to international immigration, the "brain gain" appears to be exceeding the "brain drain."[56]

Religion and Spirituality

Religion historically has been a major part of Canadian life and many Canadian lives. While religion is officially separated from the day-to-day operations of most of our institutions, it only takes a high profile funeral of a Pierre Trudeau to remind us that religion remains a part of our culture; it is summoned even by government to share centre stage, complete with massive media exposure, during times when the limits of life are experienced. On an individual level, religion continues to know remarkable resilience in Canada. No organization in the country has more people, short of citizenship, who identify with it. One in four people claim to attend services close to every week; what organization, including professional sports teams, can even begin to think of having such followings? Much is made of the demise of organized religion. The demise is relative; organizationally, religion continues to be a significant force with a significant following in Canada.[57]

The lifeblood of religious groups is youth. Social scientists who have sought to understand who becomes involved in such organizations have come to a basic conclusion: religious groups grow primarily by recruiting their own children, retaining them, and adding a few outsiders along the way through relational ties — notably friendship and marriage.[58] Consequently, a good number of Canadians in this and every decade express concern about young people not being as interested in religion and spirituality as past generations. Given that more than 80% of adults identify with a religious tradition, such potentially concerned people represent a significant portion of the national population.

In other instances, adults are troubled by the possibility that young people, in lieu of being interested in traditional religion, will be lured into cults or fall prey to exploitive religious entrepreneurs. In the '70s, many felt anxiety over the proliferation of new religious movements, such as the Children of God, Hare Krishna, and the Moonies, especially in light of much-hyped stories from the U.S. about kidnappings, brainwashings, mass marriages, mass suicides, and the like. In the '80s and '90s, attention switched to a wide range of New Age–type organizations and entrepreneurs, complete with a plethora of diverse themes that included channelling, synchronicity, god within, psychic power, the spirit world, the unity of creation, pyramids, reincarnation, auras, healing, and, of course, love.

Then, too, there are some observers who, whether they are sympathetic with conventional religion or not, are concerned that contemporary emphases on materialism and consumption, technology and information, personal pursuits and personal gratification may be accompanied by a minimizing of the spiritual dimension of being human. The concern is that such impoverishment is increasingly evident in teenage lives. Yet no one knows for sure.

Part of the problem is that we have had considerable difficulty getting a good handle on the religious and spiritual leanings of their Baby Boomer parents, not to mention the younger adult Generation Xers. The pre-Boomers seemed fairly easy to profile; they were, for the most part, pretty traditional in their religious expressions. But the Boomers and the Xers have been something else. Harvey Cox, the well-known theologian from Harvard, sums up the religious complexity of Gen Xers this way:

[T]heir religious proclivities have remained a mystery almost as inscrutable as that of the Holy Trinity. Here is a generation that stays away from most churches in droves but loves songs about God and Jesus, a generation that would score very low on any standard piety scale but at times seems almost obsessed with saints, visions, and icons in all shapes and sizes. These are the young people who, styrofoam cups of cappuccino in hand, crowd around the shelves of New Age spirituality titles in the local book market and post thousands of religious and quasi-religious notes on the bulletin boards in cyberspace.[59]

In a provocative book entitled *Virtual Faith*, Tom Beaudoin argues that Xers are "strikingly religious" if, by many people's standards, "irreverently" so. He maintains that an examination of their culture points to four themes: suspicion of organized religion, the importance of personal experience, identification with suffering, and ambiguity as a central feature of faith.[60] Cox comments that Beaudoin may be right and he may be wrong. "God may be eternal," says Cox, "but Generation X is a moving target."[61] The same, of course, is true of the Millennials (people born since 1985) we are looking at.

Conscious of such complexities, our survey attempted to gain insight into the religion and spirituality of today's teenagers.

Organized Religion

About one in five teenagers today are highly involved in organized religion. Approximately the same proportion say that they are receiving a high level of enjoyment from their involvement. Among them is a 17-year-old from just outside Toronto who comments, "You can see from what I have been saying that my faith and the church are very important to me." A 16-year-old male who lives near Calgary and attends services every week tells us, "It's a shame that so many people in Canada and the world have lost touch with God and are looking to drugs and alcohol to fill the void only God can fill in their lives."

The fact that sizable numbers of teens are attending services is no accident. In the past, groups typically relied primarily on intergenerational recruitment to reach young people, whereby adults brought their children and teens to church whether the kids wanted to show up or not. These days, many groups — led by Conservative Protestant, "evangelical" groups such as Baptists, Pentecostals, Mennonites, and Nazarenes — have developed youth ministries that aggressively target young people. Many congregations have full-time or part-time ministers, and/or participate in cooperative ventures aimed at ministering to regional and local youth. Major features of such ministries and ventures include contemporary music, bands, and informal dress, with an emphasis on interaction and experience. In Hamilton, for example, a youth minister by the name of Dave Overholt, who was pretty young himself, felt that teenagers in the early '90s were in need of a worship service that could resonate with their unique spiritual interests and needs. He established such a service. Overholt's initial handful of young worshippers now numbers some 750 high school and university students. His group has evolved into what is known as the "Church on the Rock," which now is working to encourage youth ministry right across Canada.[62]

Apart from actual involvement, it's highly significant that some 75% of young people identify with a religious group, stating a preference such as Catholicism, Protestantism, Judaism, Islam, or something else. This means that, in a psychological and emotional sense, they still "think" they are "religious somethings," even if they are not actively participating. They are not lost to religious groups; on the contrary, they represent an important pool of affiliates.[63] Prominent American Catholic sociologist and novelist Andrew Greeley recently had this to say about Roman Catholic teenagers: "Young people are still strongly attached to Catholicism, if in their own way. Despite all we have done to them, we have not been able to drive them away."[64] Among this large group who identify but are not active is a 16-year-old female from a mountain community in B.C. who comments, "I do have a church but I never go. I'm not a religious person. I don't practice religion in my free time, and I don't talk about it."

Yet large numbers of such young people are not shutting the door on more extensive participation in the future. About 45%, double the number who attend weekly, say, "I'd be open to more involvement with religious groups if I found it to be worthwhile." One Alberta 18-year-old expresses things this way: "I am religious in my own way. I don't attend church, not because I don't want to but I really never get the opportunity. I believe in God, I pray often, and I try to live a good honest life. I would like to become more involved in my religion."

Table 3.14. **Organized Religion**

	Nationally	Males	Females
Attend weekly or more often	22%	21	23
Receive high level of enjoyment from	21	19	23
Identify with a religious group	76	73	78
Open to greater involvement	43	42	44

One specific area in which young people are anticipating future ties with religious groups is rites of passage. No fewer than nine in ten teenagers say that they anticipate turning to groups for future ceremonies relating to marriages and funerals, seven in ten in the case of births. Their choices will not be random; that religious identification I spoke of a moment ago, which often is sort of latent, will come to the surface during times when couples are thinking where and how they want to get married, what should "be done" now that the baby has arrived, where they should have a relative's funeral. And it's not necessarily a case of just bowing to family pressures. Ministers frequently encounter people who, frankly, have little understanding of theology, yet have a sometimes poorly articulated sense that "God needs to be brought in on the event." What's interesting to keep in mind is that such a desire for rites of passage means that religious groups will not have to go out and find those young people; they will be taking the initiative in contacting groups. It's an enviable position for any organization to be in.

Table 3.15. **Desire for Rites of Passage**

"In the future, do you anticipate having any of the following carried out for you by a minister, priest, rabbi, or some other religious figure?"

% "Yes"

	Nationally	Males	Females
A wedding ceremony	89%	87	90
A funeral	86	84	88
A birth-related ceremony	70	67	73

Young Roman Catholics in the millions

ROME (CP), August 19, 2000 — *Pope John Paul urged more than two million young people from around the world on Saturday to go against the tide and not be "swallowed up by mediocrity."*

The biggest crowd in living memory in Rome had gathered in blazing sunshine to await the Pope's arrival at twilight on a sprawling university campus as part of a youth festival.

Some of the young people, who came to Rome from 160 countries, waited for nearly 24 hours to get a good view of the Pope. "We are well over two million," Rome's Mayor Francesco Rutelli told reporters as the Pope arrived by helicopter on the eve of the Catholic Church's World Day of Youth, which commentators have called a Catholic Woodstock.

A number of the young people interviewed in the crowd acknowledged it was difficult for them to adhere to all the church's teachings, particularly those on sexual morality and contraception. "I believe in God and I love this Pope, but I don't agree with everything the church says," said Karin Dussaut, 20, from Montreal.

Searching and Spirituality

Apart from their involvement and interest in organized religion, today's teens indicate that they fairly frequently raise the so-called ultimate questions about life's origins and purpose, suffering, and life after death. Levels of questioning tend to be somewhat higher for females, yet are high for males as well. A 15-year-old Montrealer who describes his religious preference as "none" has this to say: "Once in a while you've got to stop and look at what is going on in your own personal life. Sometimes we as humans get too caught up in the fast-paced schedules that we have and don't stop to think about the meaning of what we are doing."

Table 3.16. **Extent to Which Ultimate Questions Are Being Raised**

% "Often" or "Sometimes"

	Nationally	Males	Females
What happens after death?	78%	74	81
How can I experience happiness?	73	70	75
What is the purpose of life?	72	69	75
Why is there suffering in the world?	72	60	83
How did the world come into being?	63	63	62
Is there a God or Supreme Being?	56	55	57

There's more. **In addition to asking questions about meaning, today's emerging generation gives evidence of being interested in and receptive to interpretations of life and existence that transcend "the human plane."** Approximately eight in ten maintain that life has meaning beyond what we ourselves give to it and are intrigued by synchronistic events, while some seven in ten assert believe in ultimate personal accountability and ultimate justice.

Such responses suggest this is not a generation of young people who think life is nothing more than what we decide it is, or that what is fair and what is just are solely in our hands. On the contrary, teens are exhibiting a high level of openness to the historical claims of religions — that there's a reality beyond ourselves, that existence has meaning and history has purpose, that people are accountable for how they live, that ultimately wrongs will be made right.

Table 3.17. **Views on Select Topics**

% "Strongly Agree" or "Agree"

	Nationally	Males	Females
Life has meaning beyond what we ourselves give to it.	86%	83	88
Some things seem more than just coincidence.	80	75	84
Somehow, someday injustices will be made right.	70	67	72
How we live will influence what happens to us after we die.	66	62	69

Today's Millennials are also expressing explicit spiritual interests and needs. Some 40% of females and 35% of males report that their friends are interested in spirituality. Further, 55% of females and 40% of males say that they personally have spiritual needs. Asked what they have in mind when they think of "a spiritual person," their thoughts are extremely varied, taking conventional as well as less conventional directions. Illustrative of the former is the observation of a 17-year-old Pentecostal from Montreal that such a person "attends church and follows the Ten Commandments"; the latter can be seen in the thoughts of another 17-year-old, a Roman Catholic who lives in rural Saskatchewan, who suggests a spiritual person "helps others by being around them and being their friend. It has nothing to do with church."

Such interest in spirituality has been both fuelled and legitimized by the extensive attention that media in Canada and especially the U.S. have given to spiritual quest since around the early 1990s. Major magazines including *Maclean's, Time,* and *Newsweek* have been proclaiming the new interest in spirituality, while a string of best-selling books, including Thomas Moore's *Care of the Soul*[65] and James Redfield's *The Celestine Prophecy,*[66] have served to both respond to and stimulate the quest for spirituality. Widely read social forecaster

---

"In my mind, a spiritual person is someone who . . ."

. . . believes that when the person dies the spirit lives . . . has a close relationship with God . . . respects whatever put us here . . . puts all their faith in a higher being . . . loves you . . . believes in God . . . is in touch with themselves and cares about others . . . has inner peace with one's self and others . . . cares deeply about others . . . believes . . . follows their beliefs . . . is inspired to be a good person because of a belief in a spirit . . . wastes their life but at least doesn't harm anyone . . . is looking for or has found God . . . is open-minded . . . believes in things they can't see . . . is in touch with themselves on more than one level . . . can't handle reality with their narrow mind . . . has a special power and can help a person find his way sometimes . . . loves God with all their heart and obeys Him . . . is in touch with themselves on a spiritual level . . . believes in an afterlife . . . there is no such thing . . . has some guidelines for their life . . . has a belief in something . . . questions life and their place in it . . . believes in something other than themselves . . . is open-minded but scientifically sound . . . believes in something rather than nothing . . .

John Naisbitt was among those who predicted heightened interest in spirituality well into the new millennium.[67] In Canada, highly regarded journalist Ron Graham spent two years travelling the country looking for "the soul of the dominion" and concluded that increasing attention is being given to spiritual issues.[68] I myself, in books such as *Unknown Gods*, have maintained, on the basis of our Project Canada national surveys, that there is widespread receptiveness to spirituality in Canada; findings like Graham's and mine have been enthusiastically co-opted by a media anxious to document their spirituality claims.

In the mid-1990s, one popular magazine, *Entertainment Weekly*, summed up the saturation of spiritual themes in the media this way:

> *In a year when the TV airwaves are aflutter with winged spirits, the best-seller lists are clogged with divine manuscripts and visions of the afterlife, and gangsta rappers are elbowed aside on the pop charts for the hushed prayers of Benedictine monks, you don't have to look hard to find that pop culture is going gaga for spirituality. . . . These days the Supreme Being seems to have His magic fingers in **everything.**[69]*

Little wonder that those born in the early 1980s and since have been exposed to all this talk of spirituality, are comfortable with talking and thinking about it themselves.

In addition to spirituality, **the media also have been giving enormous play to the supernatural.** Films such as *Ghost, Dogma,* and *The*

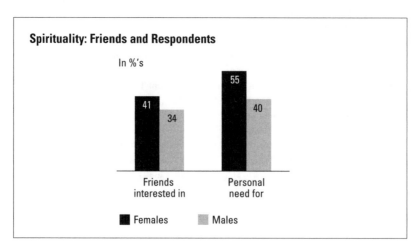

Spirituality: Friends and Respondents

In %'s

	Friends interested in	Personal need for
Females	41	55
Males	34	40

■ Females ▨ Males

Sixth Sense readily come to mind, along with television shows including *The X-Files* and *Touched by an Angel*. It's hard to know the extent to which such attention functions as the cause or effect of what goes on in the minds of teenagers. Regardless, what is unquestionably clear is that Canada's young people endorse a wide range of conventional and less conventional **ideas**. They readily express beliefs concerning God, angels, and hell; but they also readily hold beliefs relating to areas such as near-death experiences, astrology, and psychic powers. Belief levels in both the conventional and less conventional instances are consistently higher for females than for males. Yet the levels for males are still relatively high, with the rankings of specific beliefs very similar for both sexes.

Table 3.18. **Beliefs**

% "Yes, Definitely" or "Yes, I Think So"

"I believe . . ."	Nationally	Males	Females
Conventional			
In life after death	78%	73	82
In heaven	75	69	80
God exists	73	69	77
In angels	72	62	82
God or a higher power cares about me	68	63	73
Jesus was the Divine Son of God	65	61	69
In hell	60	58	61
Have felt presence of God / a higher power	36	36	37
Less Conventional			
In near-death experiences	76	71	82
Miraculous healing sometimes occurs	63	59	68
Have personally experienced an event before it happened (precognition)	63	59	67
In ESP (extrasensory perception)	59	55	62
In astrology	57	48	65
Some people have psychic powers	55	47	62
We can have contact with the spirit world	43	38	47

Besides holding a wide variety of beliefs concerning the supernatural, Canadian young people — again led by females — also engage in a number of related private practices. For example, in a given week, one in three say they pray privately. Among them is a 19-year-old from Nunavut who says he "hardly ever" attends services, but he reads the Bible and prays privately every day. He tells us that when he faces a serious problem, "I turn to my bed and Bible." Further, one in five teens claim they say table grace at least once a week. Two Toronto teens, both 16-year-old females, are among those who remind us that additional variations on prayer are being practised. One notes, "Although I do not pray to any god, I do often meditate, which I consider a spiritual act"; the second adds, "I don't pray but I do use native medicines to smudge and give thanks to the creator." About one in three teenagers read their horoscopes at least once a week, considerably more than the one in eight who indicate they are reading the Bible or some other form of Scriptures that often.

Table 3.19. **Private Practices**

"How often do you . . ."
% Weekly or More Often

	Nationally	Males	Females
Pray privately	33%	27	39
Say table grace	19	19	19
Read your horoscope	33	18	46
Read the Bible/other Scriptures	13	11	15

Teens are divided on the role that religion should play in life generally and in their lives specifically. A grade 11 Protestant female from Kamloops says, "I think we need God and prayer and religion back in our schools. There is too much hate in the world, shootings, and other things." But a 17-year-old Jewish male from Toronto disagrees: "Maybe it's my personal opinion only, but religion has no place in public life and should be confined to only those who desire it." At the individual level, one 18-year-old Roman Catholic from Saskatchewan finishes his questionnaire by saying, "My faith is important to me." In contrast, a Calgary 17-year-old Protestant, who says she hardly ever attends services, maintains "teens don't really make their decisions based on religion," adding, "Even though we don't want to admit it, we teens see a similar situation to ours on a favourite TV program and copy that."

Religion and Morality

It's generally assumed that, historically, religion has been a major source of values and morality in Canada. The dominant Christian tradition, for example, has stressed the importance of interpersonal considerations in the course of making moral decisions, attempting to transmit such ideas through Sunday schools and day schools.[70] **In light of current levels of involvement in and commitment to organized religion, it is therefore important to get a sense of what constitutes the basis for moral decision-making among teenagers.**

We put the question to young people, asking them, *"Generally speaking, on what do you base your views of what is right and wrong?"*

- Almost five in ten teenagers have an "internal focus" when they think of the basis for their moral views, citing personal judgment and, to a lesser extent, personal morality and how they feel at the time, along with beliefs, personal consequences, conscience, and values. One student from Toronto expressed things this way: "I base what I do on what I feel is right or wrong. I work on spur-of-the-moment thinking, and whatever my body wants to do I do. Impulse is what I go by." A 15-year-old from a small city in Manitoba states the situation succinctly: "Truth, right, and wrong are in the eye of the beholder."

- For just over four in ten, the moral basis is "external" and includes criteria relating to family, how they were raised, religion — with spirituality and God specifically mentioned occasionally — along with impact on others, and laws. Very few maintain that their friends provide the basis for their views of what is right and wrong.

- The remainder either cite other factors or admit they don't really know. Among those mentioning other criteria is this 18-year-old male from Sherbrooke: "The question assumes I believe in ultimate good and bad. However, I feel that this is an amoral universe and that good and bad are human inventions, as is morality." Another student, a 17-year-old from B.C., similarly writes, "Morality is a human invention to perpetuate human survival. Therefore, right and wrong are relative to the eye of the beholder."

Females are slightly more likely than males to indicate their moral criteria are external rather than internal in nature.

Table 3.20. **Bases for Moral Views**

"Generally speaking, on what do you base your views of what is right and wrong?"

	Nationally	Males	Females
Internal Focus	47%	51	44
Personal judgment	18	21	16
Personal morality	9	10	8
How I feel at the time	6	6	6
Consequences for me	5	6	4
Personal beliefs	3	2	4
Conscience	3	3	3
Personal values	3	3	3
External Focus	43	39	45
Religion, incl. spirituality and God	11	10	12
Family considerations	9	8	11
How I was raised	7	5	9
Impact on others	7	7	7
Laws	4	5	3
Friends	1	1	1
Other	4	3	2
Other	2	2	3
Varies	4	3	5
Don't Know	4	5	3
Totals	100	100	100

There are, however, some interesting variations in the religious identification of teenagers. Conservative Protestants are considerably more likely than others to cite religious sources for moral decisions. Teens with other religious ties tend to base their decisions about right and wrong on (1) personal factors and (2) external factors other than those of a religious nature. Other criteria, most frequently cited by Quebec youth, include the fairly individualistic response that "it depends" on the situation involved. These findings about moral criteria are fairly consistent with the widespread belief that morality is a matter of personal opinion — a view especially pronounced among Quebec

Roman Catholics, those who adhere to other faiths, and teens with no religious identification.

Table 3.21. **Bases for Moral Views by Religious Identification**

	Internal focus	External: religious	External: other	Other	Don't know	Totals
Nationally	47%	14	28	7	4	100
Protestant	31	38	27	3	1	100
Mainline	40	16	39	4	1	100
Conservative	21	58	17	3	1	100
Roman Catholic	45	10	30	9	6	100
Outside Quebec	53	10	29	4	4	100
Quebec	34	9	31	16	10	100
Other Faiths	50	15	23	7	5	100
No Religion	59	3	26	8	4	100

Overall, these findings point to a paradox: many young people who are not involved in organized religion are nonetheless seemingly interested in many things that organized religion "is about." In trying to make sense of the situation, highly regarded religion writer Douglas Todd of the *Vancouver Sun* writes, "Most young people probably would appreciate a safe, accepting — even fun — place where they can ask hard religious questions, and where 'doubt' is not a dirty word." He

---

"I base my views of what is right and wrong on . . ."

. . . what I feel . . . God's words and my parents as well . . . respect . . . my mom . . . what I've been brought up on . . . instinct . . . what I think . . . no one being hurt . . . my own opinions . . . the consequences . . . religion . . . what my brain tells me to do . . . my parents . . . how I affect others . . . conscience . . . treating others like I want to be treated . . . peers . . . the situation at hand . . . my moral and spiritual life . . . what I believe . . . God and parents . . . my opinion . . . not hurting and upsetting others . . . I just know . . . family morals and beliefs . . . common sense . . . my gut feeling . . . my morals . . . the law . . . my friends . . . what people say about it . . . what kind of mood I am in . . . law, my judgment . . . parents . . . personal values . . . Christian morals . . . my well-being . . . experience and morals . . . what I was taught at home . . . how I will feel afterward . . . information gathered over the years . . . my own judgment . . . how guilty I think I will feel . . . how it affects me and the people I care about . . . whatever we both want . . .

adds, "Either the clergy's genuine welcome is not getting out to teenagers, mass culture is just too hostile to faith institutions, or the spiritual message isn't one that clicks with most young people. Or all of the above."[71]

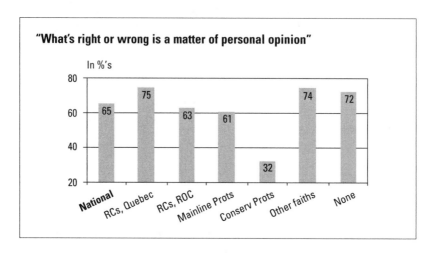

"What's right or wrong is a matter of personal opinion"

In %'s

Assessment
This has been a fairly long section on some of the primary concerns that Canadian adults have about teenagers. So, for the sake of helping us not to get lost in all the specifics, let me sum up what we have learned.

Violence, especially violence at school, has become a major area of concern in recent years. Considerably more females than males see violence and youth gangs as constituting very serious problems. Yet, more males than females report that they have close friends who have either been physically attacked at school or victims of gang violence. Variations in both perception and reported behaviour tend to be fairly small across the country, even though some communities, notably Toronto, have been particularly proactive in responding to school violence. Statistics Canada data call into serious question common beliefs about violence and youth. Young people under the age of 20 are more likely than people in other age groups to commit violent crimes and property crimes, but they are also more likely to be victims of violence. Rather than increasing, crime rates generally and violent crime rates specifically have been decreasing in recent years, and there is evidence that young offenders who are sentenced are actually treated more harshly than adults.

Teenagers, particularly males, exhibit considerable openness about sex. In theory they endorse the idea of people, including themselves, being free to do whatever they want sexually. However, when pushed on specifics, they have mixed opinions about when sex before marriage is appropriate, homosexuality, unmarried couples having children, and abortion being available on demand. They show far more agreement in condoning premarital sex when love is involved, homosexuals having the same rights as other Canadians, couples who are not married living together, and the availability of legal abortion in cases of rape. They also are nearly unanimous in disapproving of extramarital sex. Approximately 60% have been sexually involved and 25% engage in sex at least once a week, another 35% at least once a month. About 60% who are sexually experienced indicate AIDS has had an influence on their sexual habits.

Young people have ready access to illegal **drugs,** regardless of where they live in Canada. A minority of close to four in ten are smokers, and almost eight in ten use alcohol. Marijuana is reported to be the most popular drug virtually everywhere in the country, and is used at least on occasion by around four in ten teens. Some 50% would like to see the use of marijuana legalized. Other illegal drugs, in total, are being used by fewer than two in ten young people. Smoking is marginally higher among females than males, alcohol and marijuana use higher among males. Consistent with stereotypes, drug use tends to be somewhat higher among teens who regularly attend raves than those who do not. However, contrary to stereotypes, most regular ravers never use either marijuana or other illegal drugs.

With respect to **Canadian culture,** most teens say they value being Canadian, but the number who do so is much lower in Quebec than elsewhere. Bilingualism and multiculturalism are endorsed by a majority of young people, but relatively few place high importance on their cultural heritages. Issues that dominated the 1980s and 1990s, such as American influence, Native-White and French-English relations, and lack of national unity are seen as significant problems by only a minority of today's Millennial generation. An examination of their cultural favourites shows that, outside Quebec, the favourites are predominantly American. Quebec francophones are much more inclined to cite favourites who are Canadian and, more specifically, French Canadian. This is not a generation of teens that readily extends adulation toward so-called great people. Only about one in three cite someone when asked who they see as "the greatest Canadian of all time" and, despite being inundated with would-be American legends by the U.S. media, are no more inclined to cite someone when asked whom they view as "the greatest American of all time." Asked which country they would live in if they could live anywhere in the world, just over half choose Canada. Quebec teens show a particular interest in living in a wide variety of countries around the world, besides the U.S.

Contrary to widespread perception, a solid majority of young people exhibit receptiveness to **religion**. A noteworthy proportion of teens — about one in five — are actively involved in religious groups. In addition, the vast majority continue to identify with a religious tradition and anticipate that groups will be providing them with future rites of passage. Close to half are open to greater involvement. They are raising questions of meaning and purpose and assume that there is more to life than life itself. About one in two readily acknowledge that they have spiritual needs. Teens generously embrace both conventional and less conventional supernatural beliefs, and as many as one in three pray privately at least once a week. Most perceive the basis for moral decisions as lying with themselves, rather than with an external authority, including religion; those with Conservative Protestant ties are an exception, acknowledging faith's authoritative place. In virtually all of these instances, the pro-religious and pro-spiritual levels for females are consistently somewhat higher than those for males.

Five areas of concern, **five** very brief points.

First, concern about **youth violence** is warranted. The "hard data" point to crime being more prevalent in this age cohort than any other. Older teens are commonly both culprits and victims. Given this milieu of violence, it shouldn't shock anyone that the violence spills over into the physical confines of schools — especially when so many diverse teens are gathered together in one place. Yet any attempts to deal with "violence in schools" has to address violence in our society more generally. Otherwise it is like complaining that we've got a draft in our tent when a hurricane is going on outside.

Second, teenagers are very open about **sex**. But that is not to say they no longer have sexual standards. Females, in particular, tend to expect sex to be accompanied by caring. Both males and females have reservations, for better or worse, about homosexuality, children without marriage, and abortion on demand. Very few approve of extramarital affairs. Just as adults have sexual standards, so do teens.

Third, illegal **drugs** are all over the place. For whatever reasons, only a minority of teens bother to use them. Maybe that's the *real* drug story. The big things they are into are alcohol and cigarettes. Marijuana use is substantial, but part of "the problem" is that many young people see "pot" as a recreational drug that needs to be legalized. It's not clear that, when it comes to drugs, teens differ all that much from their anxious parents in what *they* were doing at the same age.

Fourth, we actually might be starting to convince young people that there is something to the notion of **Canadian culture**. Pro-Canadian sentiments seem reasonably high and, even in Quebec, there is at least an appreciation for Québécois culture over something outside the province and the country. Nationally, acceptance of cultural diversity is extensive, but interest in the preservation of national heritages is limited. Perhaps it's time to re-focus the mandate of multiculturalism, so that rather than merely celebrating our differences, we pursue ways of tapping those differences so that they have life-enriching net effects for all of us.[72] Such a focus would facilitate interpersonal and national harmony, in sharp contrast to the tired and debilitating method of biennially declaring we have a unity crisis and seeking unity for unity's sake. To tell people to coexist is to present them with an uninspiring national goal that in the end may very well fail. To emphasize and tap the collective benefits of diversity is to produce a culture and a country where the quality of life will speak for itself.

Fifth, today's teens do not warrant any labels that depict them as not interested in organized **religion**, or in any sense unreceptive to things supernatural and spiritual. This is a generation of young people whose current involvement in religion is appreciable. Further, their terms for greater involvement in groups are reasonable; if they can find their participation "worthwhile," they are open to it. In light of their widespread interest in meaning and mystery, the supernatural and the spiritual, religious groups who have something to bring need to bring it — and, to put it bluntly, stop complaining about the apathy of youth.

As we look at these five areas of concern, all of us need a general reminder that we are not Americans. Too often, the ways American media and American researchers portray life are assumed to apply to Canada. Sometimes they do, but often they don't. This reminder applies to the assumptions and data on how young people live life. Following American views of reality can be not only misleading; such a procedure can lead to irrelevant, ineffective, and wasteful responses to life in Canada.

These five areas of anxiety are important cases in point. Violence levels in the U.S. are considerably higher than they are in Canada, including a higher level of violence in schools.[73] The massive American media portrayals of sexuality are hardly accurate depictions of the sexual attitudes and behaviour of our young people — or theirs. Drug use in the U.S. is far more rampant than it is in this country. American media are virtually oblivious to Canadian culture, leading us to assume that young people see our culture, institutions, and even our heroes as inferior to theirs. The religious market in the U.S. has different dominant groups, higher levels of participation, and is far more volatile; American devotion is not Canadian devotion.

In short, in making sense of Canadian youth, we need a good set of Canadian eyes.

And, oh yes, in almost all five areas, our young women keep differing from our young men.

Chapter Four

Their Hopes...
and Expectations

CANADA'S TEENS ARE DREAMING AND DREAMING BIG. THIS IS NOT A generation of young people that shows signs of disillusionment with what they can accomplish. If doomsayers are correct in their predictions that the newest emerging generation is going to have to settle for less than their parents, the message has not got through. Young people in this teen cohort not only expect to emulate whatever success their parents have known; most expect to do better. The Millennial generation plans to accomplish much.

The General Picture
A grade 10 student from rural Nova Scotia complimented us on "a very good survey," saying, "This is a good way to get inside the mind of a teenager, to try to see what we really think about, plan for, and hope for." She playfully added, " What we want is . . . sex, sex, sex (just joking!!) . . . a happy future, lots of love, and to be secure and safe." She has summed up the general goals of most Canadian young people — happiness, good relationships, material and physical security. And, of course, life-giving humour.

For many teenagers, it all starts with the dream of a university education. As they look to the future, more than six in ten expect to graduate from *university* and another one in ten anticipate at least attending university. Another two in ten say they expect to complete a *vocational* or commercial program, while fewer than one in ten indicate their formal education will end with *high school*. For all the pressure many feel in high school, fewer than one in a hundred students do *not* expect to graduate. About 4%, incidentally, acknowledge they dropped out of high school at some point.

How realistic are such expectations? As of the last census in 1996, 13% of Canadians over the age of 15 had university degrees, up from 6% in 1976. The 1996 figure was similar for males and females.[1] Obviously the level of grads will not come close to 70% in the next decade. What's important here is that most teenagers undoubtedly would agree that 70% is an unrealistic figure. Nonetheless, most think that they personally can be part of the degree pool, regardless of how large it actually is going to be. Individually, they have high hopes.

Table 4.1. **Education Aspirations**

"How much education, in total, do you expect you will eventually get?"

	Nationally	Males	Females
Graduate from university	62%	58	65
Some university	7	8	7
Complete vocational*	18	18	17
Some vocational	6	6	5
High school	7	10	5
I don't expect to finish high school	<1	<1	<1

* Includes commercial college/CEGEP (Quebec)

Beyond education, expectations of Canada's teenagers are extremely high. A Toronto 17-year-old illustrates the range of expectations youth have when she says, "Being part of this survey has helped me to see what is important to me. I realize my future family life and future career and future residence are the most important things to me if I am going to know a good and happy future."

- Almost everyone plans to pursue a *career*, and close to nine in ten expect not only to be able to find work but to get *the job they want* when they graduate. Undoubtedly such high hopes are fuelled in part by a jobless rate that in mid-2000 was the lowest since the mid-1970s, and was expected to drop even lower.[2] Some 60% maintain they will stay with the *same career* for life. That isn't to say that teens are clear on what exactly that career is going to be. One New Westminster student in her last year of high school admits, "I have many aspirations but I don't know what to go into — no real career goal. I fear for my future." Those 60%, if they fulfill their dreams of having one career, will be an exception to the rule: career movement is becoming increasingly common, with most people now expected to have at least three careers during their employment lifetimes.

- Nine in ten teens expect to *marry*, with the same proportion further anticipating staying with the *same partner* for life — this in the midst of daily reports that marriage is on the way out and as many as one in three marriages end in divorce.
- Close to half of young females report they eventually expect to *stay home* and raise their children; what is surprising is that a slightly higher proportion of males also claim to have the same expectation. Hmmm. We'll come back to this.
- Virtually all teenagers say they anticipate eventually *owning their homes*, despite the dramatic escalation of the price of homes in many parts of the country, notably Toronto, Vancouver, and Calgary.
- A solid eight in ten expect to be *more financially comfortable* than their parents. In the process, they are taking on experts who have made the widely publicized claim that the generations following affluent Baby Boomers would be the first in history to have to settle for less than their parents. Mind you, the same thing was said of Boomers.[3] In the case of Generation Xers, a recent Royal Mutual Funds study claims they actually might do better than their parents. Time will tell, but they expect to be better off and — according to Simon Lewis, the president of Royal Mutual Funds — "if we end up having another decade of sustained growth, they are going to be in terrific shape."[4] The current generation of teenagers expects to follow suit in exceeding the financial accomplishments of their parents.
- Less than half, however, think they will have to *work overtime* to do it. Some are in for a bit of a surprise. Not only will a good number of unfortunate souls put in extra hours; they'll be doing it gratis. Statistics Canada reports that, in 1997, about 10% of employed Canadians worked overtime and were not reimbursed either with extra pay or time off. Perhaps a mild shocker, given the high-status expectations of almost everybody, unpaid overtime was most common among white-collar workers, especially teachers and managers.

Status-maligned blue-collar workers were generally more likely to be paid for the overtime they put in.[5] I guess the moral of the story is that, when it comes to overtime, job prestige carries a price.

- Additionally, about three in four expect to *travel* extensively outside Canada; just under the same proportion say they anticipate being *involved in their communities*. Only about one-half say they expect the *national debt* will be paid off in their lifetimes. One 16-year-old francophone from Montreal succinctly sums up the sentiments of many on the debt's elimination: "It'll never happen."

Table 4.2. **Expectations of Teenagers**

"Do you expect to . . ."

% Indicating "Yes"

	Nationally	Males	Females
Pursue a career	95%	93	96
Get the job you want when you graduate	86	86	86
Stay with the same career for life	62	61	62
Get married	88	87	89
Stay with the same partner for life	88	87	89
Eventually stay home and raise your children	45	47	43
Own your own home	96	97	96
Be more financially comfortable than your parents	79	81	77
Have to work overtime in order to get ahead	44	48	41
Travel extensively outside Canada	72	68	77
Be involved in your community	65	62	68
See the national debt paid off in your lifetime	49	51	47

The survey findings suggest that "the Canadian dream" is alive, well, and pervasive. No less than 71% of teenagers agree with the statement "Anyone who works hard will rise to the top." In the words of one 16-year-old from a small town in Alberta, "I believe we live in a country where anyone can succeed and where most things that hold a person back are self-made." The expectation figure is exactly the same for females and males. Gender discrimination may be out there,

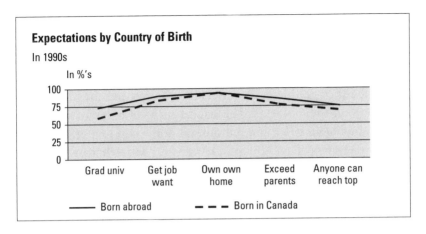

Expectations by Country of Birth

In 1990s

In %'s

| | Grad univ | Get job want | Own own home | Exceed parents | Anyone can reach top |

——— Born abroad   – – – Born in Canada

but young females don't see much of anything as a barrier to their experiencing success. The same is true of young immigrants. Teens who were born outside Canada, if anything, are more likely to have high expectations than young people who were born here. It appears that Canada, as seen from other parts of the world, is the proverbial "land of opportunity."

Expectations are also very high regardless of young people's socio-economic backgrounds, as measured by the education of their parents. Although teens who come from homes where either parent

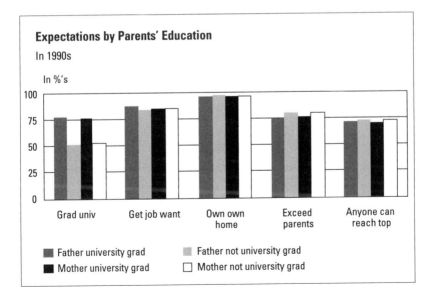

Expectations by Parents' Education

In 1990s

In %'s

| | Grad univ | Get job want | Own own home | Exceed parents | Anyone can reach top |

■ Father university grad   ▨ Father not university grad
■ Mother university grad   ☐ Mother not university grad

is a university graduate are more likely than others to expect to graduate from university themselves, the education of parents has no bearing on other expectations. Simply put, teenagers from diverse socio-economic backgrounds are equally likely to expect to get good jobs when they graduate, own their own homes, and be more comfortable than their parents. The education level of parents and the accompanying lifestyles and outlooks at home also matter little with respect to teens believing that "anyone who works hard will rise to the top."

Those who plan to get a university degree themselves are only a bit more likely than others to think their education will enable them to know material success. A solid majority of those with less-ambitious education goals also are expecting to know "the good life." In part this seems to reflect the fact that Canadian youth have considerable faith in the principle that hard work will lead to success. But let's not get overly idealistic or naive: in many instances it probably simply reflects the fact that some teens think they can take an education shortcut en route to success.

Table 4.3. **Success Expectations**

Anticipated Education

"I expect to . . ."	Nationally	University degree	<University degree
Own my own home	96%	97	95
Be more comfortable than parents	79	81	76
Travel extensively outside Canada	72	77	65

Careers

A quick peek at the relation between the education goals and career expectations of young people shows that those who expect to graduate from university are only slightly more likely than others to say they will pursue careers or get the jobs they want when they graduate. Those who don't expect to obtain a university degree are just as likely as others to think they will stay with the same career for life; they also are no more likely to believe they will have to work overtime to get ahead. According to the data we just looked at, ironically, in this rare overtime instance those with less education just might be right — or at least have the satisfaction of getting paid for the extra effort.

In short, a majority of the country's teens feel they are university-bound. But even those who don't intend to graduate from university are inclined to have very high career expectations. And young females tend to have hopes just as high as young males.

Table 4.4. **Career Expectations and Education Goals**

Anticipated Education

"I expect to . . ."	Nationally	University degree	< University degree
Pursue a career	95%	98	90
Get the job want when graduate	86	88	82
Stay with same career for life	62	61	63
Have to work overtime	44	44	45

A Reality Check on Career Expectations

It is worth taking a closer look at those kinds of expectations. Statistics Canada reports that the employment rate in 1997 for the majority of young adults of post-education age — 25 to 34 — was about 91% (90% for males and 92% for females), the same as the national level. So employment prospects in general are good for most of today's teenagers. Regional variations, however, are important to keep in mind: overall unemployment rates the same year ranged from around 15% in Atlantic Canada through 11% in Quebec, 9% in Ontario and B.C. to 6% in the Prairies.

But beyond sheer employment, education makes a big difference with respect to both the kind of employment one can experience, as well as income potential. StatsCan notes in one release, "For generations, parents have urged their kids to stay in school. Today, young people ignore this advice at their peril." The report says that, during the '90s, close to 20% of jobs requiring high school skills or less disappeared, while the number of jobs for people with at least a high school education grew by nearly 30%. Further, Canadians who hold a post-secondary degree or diploma earn 40% to 45% more than those who don't complete post-secondary studies.

School for the rest of your life

NEW YORK (AP), John Cunniff, July 16, 2000 — *Before the great Internet revolution changed society, a high school diploma or a post-secondary degree was seen as preparing a person for a long and perhaps permanent career in one company.*

Today, an "education for life" has evolved into "a lifetime of education," meaning you are never through with the educational process. It goes on and on — should it cease, workers might find their skills outmoded. There's no end to the need for education, self or formal.

Information technology has provided jobs and good wages and profits. But in the midst of plenty, it has also created job insecurity. The quest for greater productivity has put a premium on newer skills. Blue-collar job requirements, unchanged for decades, now may require workers to have a knowledge of computers and information systems. Millions of workers worry about the changes. Perhaps as many welcome the new opportunities.

It appears that young Canadians in the 1990s were getting that message, staying in school or going back to school in unprecedented numbers. Over the course of the decade, the percentage of 15- to 24-year-olds in the labour force declined from about 70% to 60%, while those in school either full-time or part-time rose to a record of more than 60%.[6] In addition, while close to one in five teens had dropped out of high school in the early '90s, about 25% of these same teens returned to school and eventually graduated.[7]

Education is consequently almost essential to the prosperity that so many of today's teens hope to know. Those who forgo post-secondary work will seriously jeopardize their material dreams. That said, to repeat an old philosophical cliché, education may be a necessary cause of career attainment and success, but it is not a sufficient cause. In plain English, education may be needed for success, but it doesn't provide a guarantee. Despite the fact that Canadians have become more educated in the past two decades, Statistics Canada found that more than 20% of Canada's well-educated workers in the mid-'90s felt they were overqualified for the jobs they were doing. Almost half of these workers were younger than 35.[8]

A Warning to Women

In the midst of all this optimism, some gender realities mustn't be overlooked. As of the late '90s, women were still earning an average of 80 cents for every $1 earned by men. Almost 20% of this wage gap reflected the fact that women tend to have less work experience than their male counterparts, and less often have supervisory and administrative responsibilities. Another 10% of this difference can be accounted for by differences in job tenure and the fact that more men than women graduate from programs such as engineering that lead to higher-paying jobs. Still, government analysts acknowledge that "much of the wage gap still remains a puzzle." Encouraging is the news that single women who had never been married were earning 96 cents for every $1 earned by men. What remains to be seen is whether this is indicative of a closing of the gender gap or points to temporary equity that decreases with life-cycle changes, notably marriage, children, and aging.[9]

Apart from pay disparity, it's readily apparent that women are still having difficulty securing top management positions. A Conference Board of Canada study released in mid-2000 found that the median percentage of women executives in the private sector is only 20%, versus 40% among public sector organizations. Half the women surveyed felt that women managers are perceived as less professional and not as committed to a corporation as males; only 25% of male CEOs felt that view is accurate. The author of the report, Barbara Orser, pointed out in an interview, "If chief executives do not see that a problem exists, they're not likely to do anything about it."[10] Mobility and equality still appear to be problems for women, even at the top executive levels of companies and other organizations. Many young females underestimate the ongoing societal barriers to the realization of their career dreams.

What a Good Job Looks Like

What qualities are young people of high school age looking for in that "good job" they expect to get when they graduate? Well, the number-one quality, valued by some 85% of males and females, is that the work be *interesting.* Next, females give high priority to the job giving them a *feeling of accomplishment,* a trait that males rate on an equal level with the job *paying well* and providing a chance for *advancement.* Females are also somewhat more likely than males to place importance on the desire that co-workers and colleagues be *friendly and helpful,* and that a job add to *other people's lives.* Job *security* is important to about 60% of both males and females.

Table 4.5. **Characteristics of "a Good Job"**

% Indicating "Very Important"

	Nationally	Males	Females
The work is interesting.	86%	84	87
It gives me a feeling of accomplishment.	76	70	81
There is a chance for advancement.	68	70	66
It pays well.	66	72	60
Other people are friendly and helpful.	63	59	67
It adds something to other people's lives.	59	53	64
There is little chance of being laid off.	57	60	55
It allows me to make most of the decisions myself.	49	53	45

Teens, especially females, give relatively low priority to the job being one in which they are allowed to *make most of the decisions themselves.* It seems that almost one in two would prefer to leave the decisions to others, putting much more importance on interesting and gratifying work, complete with a good salary.

A Statistics Canada national study of what college and university graduates in the mid-1990s were looking for in a job suggests these priorities might change slightly when some high school grads are introduced to that — "oh my gosh!" — reality of student loans. The study found that by the time people had finished their post-secondary education, they were ranking pay first and liking the work second. Next, pretty much tied for third, were chances for advancement, the people, job security, and feelings of accomplishment.[11] Obviously we want different things from our jobs at different points in our lives. With the onset of bills to pay, making good money tends to shoot to the top of people's charts. Logically, the next hurdle is hanging on to that well-paying job. If we like the work and get gratification from it, great. If we have the chance to advance, that's terrific. And if we can enjoy the people, well, let's just say that's a pretty unique bonus.

In the midst of dramatic social change grounded in the Internet and its impact on culture and the economy, these kinds of ideals about work, including spending an entire lifetime in one cherished career, are extremely precarious dreams for the vast majority of Canadian young people.

But they've all got to start somewhere, and — what the heck — who knows where their dreams will take them? In a recent interview, Canadian rock superstar Bryan Adams, who had just recorded a duet with Elton John for the latter's new live record at Madison Square Garden, was asked what he considered his greatest achievement. His response? "Being able to pay my rent and get out of Burnaby."[12] Someday, some dreams will be realized.

Family

Most teens are expecting to have traditional families. We saw earlier that they exhibit considerable tolerance toward people cohabiting, and a slight majority say they approve of a couple having children without being married. But as for their own personal preferences, nine in ten say they expect to marry and the same proportion anticipate having children.

Marriage

Such findings fly in the face of popular portrayals of marriage as a dying institution. In August of 2000, for example, *Time* magazine, in both its Canadian and U.S. editions, ran a front-cover story showing the four female stars of *Sex and the City* with the heading, "Who Needs a Husband?" and a subheading, "More women are saying no to marriage and embracing the single life."[13] A Rutgers University study of young men and women in their 20s, which was released in the fall of 2000, concluded that romance and marriage are out and casual sex and low-commitment relationships are in. The study's report, co-authored by sociologists David Popenoe and Barbara Dafoe Whitehead, carried the less-than-subtle title, *Sex Without Strings, Relationships Without Rings*. It did concede, however, that most young adults do expect to meet and marry someone someday who fulfills their emotional and spiritual needs. But the authors express concern that the current mercenary mating habits of young people do not easily lead to the fulfillment of that goal.[14]

In Canada, as in most highly developed nations, the past 50 years has seen a decline in the marriage rate, and increases in both divorce and cohabitation. Approximately one in three marriages are projected to end in divorce and one in seven couples are living in common law unions. This latter pattern is particularly pronounced in Quebec. But disenchantment with marriage as such is not evident. Offsetting trends are also readily evident both in the form of remarriage and cohabitation frequently being transitional rather than permanent.[15]

Ironically, around the same time that *Time* ran its cover story, famous feminist Gloria Steinem, who once said "a woman needs a man like a fish needs a bicycle," married for the first time at age 66. Steinem commented, "I'm happy, surprised and one day will write about it. Though I've worked many years to make marriage more equal," she said, "I never expected to take advantage of it myself. I hope this proves what feminists have always said — that feminism is about the ability to choose what's right at each time of our lives." Reflecting on Steinem and marriage more generally, *Toronto Sun* columnist Linda Williamson wrote, "Low marriage rates or not, marriage is still alive and well and sought after by happy, loving, equal couples who realize there's more to a relationship than cohabitating. Marriage remains special."[16]

In light of the prevalence of divorce, it is particularly noteworthy that no less than 88% of teenagers say they expect — not *hope* — to stay with the same partner for life. The fact that many come from homes where their biological parents are no longer together does not

Table 4.6. Family Expectations and Family Background

	Nationally	Parents together	Parents not together
"I expect to ..."			
Marry	88%	89	86
Have children	92	91	92
Stay with same partner for life	88	91	83
"I want to have ..."			
A home like the one I grew up in	70	75	60

in any sense dull the inclination of these sons and daughters to marry and have children. In addition, young people whose parents are not together are only slightly less likely than others to say that they expect to stay with the same partner for life.

An aberration or a peek at the future?
I love you, now sign this

LOS ANGELES, *Globe and Mail,* Doug Saunders, July 8, 2000 — *If celebrities are the barometers of our age, the windsocks of fashion's shifting breezes, then Michael Douglas and Catherine Zeta-Jones' peculiar celebration ought to be held aloft as a banner of our era's late-capitalist zest.*

Over chateaubriands and tiny vegetables, they were toasting the fact that their lawyers had finally worked out the terms of their eventual divorce. Their wedding was still months away, they were in the bloom of love, their child was quietly gestating, and they were both in bliss, for their impending marriage and their future divorce were both settled, inscribed, and notarized.

It had been an angry and fractious divorce battle between Catherine and Michael, and their lawyers had worked feverishly to get its ugly skirmishes out of the way in time for their wedding. Michael, whose fortune is estimated at $225-million (U.S.), had wanted to pay off Catherine with $1.5 million a year and the use of a house that would remain part of his estate, should they ever divorce. She had reportedly wanted a house of her own plus $4.5 million for each year they were wed. Eventually, it appears that their lawyers met somewhere in the middle. The prenuptial agreement was settled to both parties' satisfaction. A blissfully married life could now be theirs.

More and more, people seem to be examining their relation-ships and coming back with what might become the marital vow of the 21st century: "I love you, but I love my money even more, and while it would be unfortunate were I to lose you it would be even worse if I were to lose half my money as well." Till tort do us part. Sign here, and kiss the bride.

As one Statistics Canada writer put it in summing up national data on marriage and remarriage patterns, "It seems the underlying commitment of Canadians is to family life of one sort or another: once having tried and failed, one simply tries again."[17] Our teen survey findings suggest that what is true of adults is true of their teenage offspring: they don't give up on marriage; rather they hope for better things for themselves. One 16-year-old from the Yukon is among them. She comes from a home where her parents are divorced, but expects to stay with the same partner for life. Asked what one thing she would like to accomplish in her lifetime, her succinct response was this: "A lasting marriage."

In chapter 2 we noted that some 75% of teens whose parents are together say they want a home like the one they grew up in; that percentage comes in at about 60% in step-parent and lone-parent homes, and slips to around 50% in homes where a biological parent is living with a partner. Given that most teenagers want to marry and plan to marry, it would seem fairly obvious that what has been valued — and sometimes not so valued — in many home instances is the atmosphere that has been cultivated, versus the sheer presence of two parents rather than one.

Children

Most teens want to have children of their own. Some 96% of those who plan to marry want children, as do 62% of those who do not plan to marry. As for numbers, about 50% would like to have two kids, and 30% would like three or more. The remaining 20% are almost equally divided between those who expect to have just one child, and those who do not anticipate having any. Forget the talk about childless relationships; marriages and kids are both on the way.

Earlier in this chapter we saw that a surprising number of males, as well as females — around 45% in both instances — say they expect to eventually stay home and raise their children. Then again, this generation is being told that our information-based economy frequently can be served by links to a computer. People can know increasing autonomy and flexibility, including working out of their homes and being self-employed.

The desire to stay home and possibly carry out one's career from there may also reflect a sense, on the part of some, that children would benefit from the "full-time presence" of at least one partner. Maybe that provocative philosopher, Allan Bloom, was right when he argued in the late 1980s that the .5 + .5 child-rearing contributions of two employed parents doesn't equal 1 when that "1" is one of the parents staying home and taking on a child in a focused, full-time way.[18] For what it's worth, a U.S. survey of parents of children under the age of six, conducted in mid-2000, found that 70% of parents felt the best child-care arrangement for children in their early years is to have one parent at home. Another 14% felt the best arrangement would be parents working different shifts. Close relatives and quality daycare each were the preference of 6%; the remaining 4% were divided between favouring another mother in the neighbourhood and having a babysitter come into their homes. The study concluded that not staying at home sometimes involves "necessary compromises," usually related to finances.[19]

"Compromises," however, seems to be the key to what in fact takes place. Apart from being able to have a permanent "stay at home" situation, many couples find that even for a mother to remain at home for any length of time when a child is born is sometimes difficult. On the plus side, today's teens have been growing up at a time when not only women but men are able to experience paid parental-leave benefits.

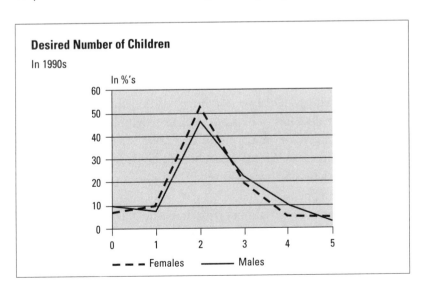

Desired Number of Children

In 1990s

As of January 2001, those benefits, which are available to either a mother or father, were increased by the federal government to one year. Basic benefits are 55% of average earnings, to a maximum of just over $400 a week. But to date, stay-at-home dads, either short-term or long-term, are relatively few. They have made up only about 3% to 4% of Canadian parents on leave since the early 1990s,[20] and perhaps about 1% of U.S. households with children under six during that time.[21]

The problem is that the ideal of staying home for any length of time is compromised by financial need, not only for dads but also for moms. Some important Canadian national-trend research carried out by StatsCan, charting the same people over time during the '90s, shows that two in ten women who gave birth had returned to work within *one month* of the birth. A further six in ten had returned within six months, and eight in ten within eight months. The primary factor dictating their return time was lost income, an issue felt particularly acutely by self-employed women.[22]

For millions of Canadians, staying at home is great in theory, but nearly impossible in practice because of financial needs, whether they be pressing or perceived. Such a reality is something many stay-at-home-minded teens will eventually have to confront.

Outlook

The majority of Canadian teenagers claim to be happy with life and buoyant about the future.

Asked to generalize about personal happiness, three in ten teens — led by males — say that they are "very happy," while another six in ten claim they are "pretty happy." About one in ten indicate that they are "not too happy," and two in a hundred that they are not happy at all. While males tend to be a bit more overtly upbeat than females, gender differences for unhappiness are quite small (females 13%, males 7%). There also are only marginal differences in reported levels of happiness between those whose natural parents are still together and other young people.

Such a lack of variations with happiness is to be expected. Happiness, as we saw earlier in looking at sources of enjoyment, is not something that depends on one magic variable — such as family background, gender, income, region, religion, or whatever. Any number of factors contribute to people's joy. In the case of teenagers, the key sources are friends, music, other significant people, and a varied range of activities. Family is one source, and unquestionably an important source. But the overall high level of happiness reported suggests there are many pathways to the happiness mountaintop, and most young people have found ones that get them there.

Table 4.7. **Emotional Outlook of Teenagers**

"All in all, would you say you are . . ."

	Nationally	Males	Females
Very happy	28%	32	25
Pretty happy	61	61	62
Not too happy	9	6	11
Not happy at all	2	1	2

The relatively low number of unhappy and perhaps "troubled youth" does not, of course, minimize the importance of being responsive to them. Their voices can be heard in a 17-year-old female from Brampton, Ontario, who says, "If some of my answers seem confusing, it's because I suffer from depression and don't think highly of myself" — or the terse words of a 15-year-old male from Scarborough who writes, "Life is Hell; there is no need for death." Life is good for most teens, but not all. Research suggests such young people are

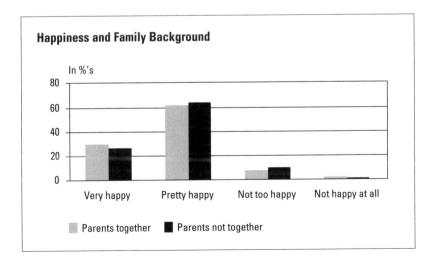

more susceptible than others to a variety of problems. A recent national study in the U.S. has found that girls who join gangs, for example, are characterized by particularly high levels of social isolation and particularly low levels of self-esteem.[23]

Yet many experts remain optimistic that, with adequate support, even teens who are experiencing severe problems can live healthy lives. Among such observers is psychiatrist Dr. Jalal Shamsie, who has worked with troubled young people since the 1960s and has founded the Institute for the Study of Anti-Social Youth at Toronto's Centre for

---

Kids remarkably resilient

LETHBRIDGE, February 26, 2000 — *Chris Windle is no longer surprised by the resilience she sees in children and adolescents with whom she works. Windle, an adolescent addictions counsellor with the Alberta and Alcohol Drug Abuse Commission (AADAC), conducted a session called Resources for Resilience at the 101st Annual South Western Alberta Teachers' Convention.*

AADAC has become actively involved in resiliency projects. The seven different kinds of resilience they see in the children of alcoholics and drug-addicted adults include independence, insight, relationships, initiative, creativity, humour, and morality.

In a study of 700 "at risk" children, Windle says two-thirds demonstrated the survival instincts that helped them on the road to a successful life. Windle encouraged teachers to support those children who are considered high risk. "Behaviour does not necessarily equal the child's capacity."

She used the example of Anita, a child who is defined by her lack of academic progress and inability to get to school on time. Behind the scenes, however, Anita is caring for a younger brother while her drug-addicted mother struggles with her own demons. Sometimes you just have to look a little deeper to see the child's strengths and support those strengths, she said. For many children, school is their only safe place. A teacher can sometimes be their only friend.[24]

Addiction and Mental Health. "In the past, people thought nothing works with anti-social youth," says Shamsie, "but there are approaches that work," including those that stress good relationships with parents and positive social environments.[25]

Another person who is not giving up on so-called troubled youth is Carol Johnson, who runs a Calgary business called Chaos Consulting and Training. She works with teachers and others who are relating directly to young people with behavioural problems. Johnson asserts that 85% of school children do really well, 15% need support, and 5% of those draw about 95% of teachers' resources. She urges teachers to look at their own behaviour and attitudes first when coping with challenging students. "They don't come to school hungry and tired because they want to irritate you," Johnson told teachers recently. "They come to school hungry and tired because they are." She estimates that in a class of 20 students, two will be from a home where they're victimized by sexual or physical abuse while another two students are witnessing abuse in their homes. "If you knew that child was being sexually abused or knew that child was hiding in a closet while his mom and dad abuse one another, you wouldn't want to further punish the victim." Sometimes, she says, teachers just have to cut a student slack. Johnson says she focuses her attention on "helping one more kid not get kicked out of one more place."[26]

The Future and Canada

Significant numbers of young people say that uncertainty about the future of Canada has made their plans for the future problematic. Is anyone surprised? When many of them were in elementary school, they heard some alarmists proclaim that if the "Yes" side didn't win some kind of an obscure nationwide referendum, Canada as we knew it would die. When many were in junior high, Quebec was holding a photo-finish referendum on what seemed to be separation, or sovereignty, or something along those lines. Now that they are in high school, the unity file has been stored somewhere on the national hard drive. But they know it hasn't exactly been deleted.

So it is the survey has found that 58% of teens feel "Canada's uncertain future makes it difficult to plan for the future." Apprehension levels are fairly consistent across the country. Concern about the

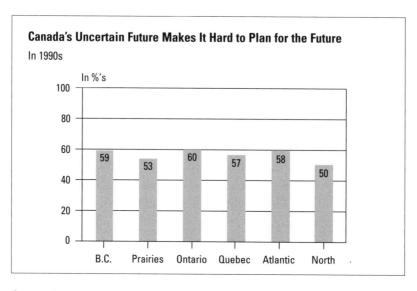

Canada's Uncertain Future Makes It Hard to Plan for the Future

In 1990s

In %'s

B.C.	Prairies	Ontario	Quebec	Atlantic	North
59	53	60	57	58	50

future, however, is *no higher in Quebec,* leading one to conclude that young people there have been coping with the unity issue as well as their counterparts in the rest of the country. Among those who are not letting Canada's future get in the way of their personal plans is a 16-year-old francophone from a community in the northeast part of the province, who says, "I have confidence in the future. We are young, full of ambition and believe in our goals. With all the possibilities that are being offered, scholastic programs, etc., practically nothing is closed off or impossible!" His optimism seemingly does not depend on Quebec's staying or leaving. Either way, he is convinced he can fly.

Despite apprehensive and, in some instances, negative feelings about Canada, we saw earlier that 52% of teenagers say that, if they could live anywhere, they would still choose Canada. They do, however, show a definite preference for some parts of Canada, particularly — after their own province — beautiful British Columbia along with Alberta. Ontario is the second choice of many young people who live in the Atlantic region. Teens in almost every province choose their own province first, and then somewhere else. Alas, such is not the case with young people who live in either Saskatchewan or Manitoba: in both instances more teens would prefer to live B.C. than in their home provinces. The same situation appears to hold for the North, although we may have erred in asking about provincial choices and not mentioning the territories specifically. Overall the main mobility message? British Columbia, brace yourself for an onslaught of young adults from the Prairies and the North, as well as more than a few from just about everywhere else!

Table 4.8. **Provincial Residence Choices**

"If I could live in any province, I would live in . . ."

	BC	AB	SK	MB	ON	PQ	NB	NS	PE	NF	North
Nationally	29%	13	1	1	31	17	1	2	2	2	1
British Columbia	77	9	<1	1	8	2	<1	1	1	<1	<1
Alberta	32	57	1	<1	7	<1	<1	1	1	<1	<1
Saskatchewan	34	26	29	1	6	1	<1	3	<1	<1	<1
Manitoba	31	23	<1	27	13	2	<1	2	<1	2	<1
Ontario	21	4	<1	<1	65	3	<1	2	2	1	1
Quebec	16	2	<1	<1	15	64	1	1	1	<1	<1
New Brunswick	23	8	<1	<1	13	4	34	8	3	4	3
Nova Scotia	17	15	<1	<1	21	<1	<1	38	4	2	2
Prince Edward Island	7	5	<1	<1	19	<1	2	9	56	2	<1
Newfoundland	12	10	<1	<1	19	2	<1	2	<1	55	<1
North	32	32	1	1	10	4	3	3	1	<1	13

A finding we brushed over rather quickly is one that could have some important implications for the quality of life in Canada, if young people follow through with their intentions. **A fairly high 65% of teens say that they expect to be involved in their communities in the future.** Variations in such expectations are small by both region and community size, meaning that their geographical mobility should not affect their potential contributions to the communities in which they eventually come to live.

This finding is consistent with how a number of American observers are seeing counterpart Millennials in the United States. William Strauss, whom you may remember for his "They're not bowling alone" idea cited back in chapter 2, and colleague Neil Howe, have recently written that the newest generation of U.S. teenagers are "cooperative team players." According to Howe and Strauss, teens' gravitating toward group activities can be seen in such areas as team learning, community service, and even school uniforms. These two generational trend-watchers believe that Millennials are going to be "community shapers" and institution builders."[27] In light of what Canadian teens are saying about their community involvement intentions, this alleged pattern among young people in the U.S. bears watching in Canada.

And finally . . . asked to use *one word* to describe their feelings about the future in general, teenagers are far less positive than they are about their personal futures more specifically. Some 47% offered terms that are positive, 40% negative, and 13% words that express ambivalence. Alberta and B.C. teens — those people who are living where many of the geographically-mobile want to be — are slightly more likely than others to be positive about the future, while teens from Ontario are slightly more inclined to express negative feelings about what lies ahead.

Table 4.9. One Word Describing Teens' Feelings about the Future

	Positive	Negative	Ambivalent
Nationally	47%	40	13
Males	51	38	11
Females	48	36	16
Prairies	52	33	15
B.C.	51	36	13
Atlantic	49	39	12
North	47	40	13
Quebec	46	41	13
Ontario	44	44	12

"What one word would you use to describe your feelings about the future?"

edgy . . . optimistic . . . wow . . . hectic . . . intense . . . happiness . . . unique . . . chaos . . . new . . . hazy . . . excited . . . crazy . . . foggy . . . blur . . . scary . . . hopeful . . . dark . . . unpredictable . . . cool . . . scared . . . uncertain . . . exciting . . . downhill . . . confused . . . unlimited . . . shaky . . . curious . . . unclear . . . bright . . . troubled . . . groovy . . . successful . . . lost . . . confident . . . open . . . morbid . . . promising . . . excellent . . . peaceful . . . nervous . . . unknown . . . great . . .

Assessment

Teenagers have **high expectations**. A solid majority expect to graduate from university, pursue careers, and get the jobs they want, with more than half anticipating staying with the same career for life. Whether or not they graduate from university, young people are almost unanimous in anticipating that they will own their own homes and be more financially comfortable than their parents. Less than half think they will have to work overtime in the process.

Financial and career expectations are high for both those who plan to pursue a university education and those who don't, despite well-documented differences in income by education. Females tend to have career and financial aspirations similar to those of males, even though there frequently continue to be gender differences in occupational mobility and income. For the majority, the primary characteristics of that "good job" they *expect* to get are that it is interesting, provides a sense of accomplishment, pays well, and leads to advancement.

Teens have high hopes when it comes to **family life**. Most plan to marry and stay with their partners for life. Almost all plan to have children, and close to half want to eventually stay home and raise them. Marrying and having children are obviously the easy parts; staying together and staying home will be the unpredictable parts of the story.

Generally speaking, today's teenagers are **upbeat and optimistic** about the future. So-called problem youth need to be taken very seriously. But based on these and earlier findings relating to personal concerns, they constitute a fairly small minority of young people. Teens say the uncertain future of Canada has made planning for the future somewhat difficult. Yet most see themselves continuing to live in this country, preferably in B.C., Alberta, and Ontario, with a majority indicating they are interested in community involvement in the future. Young people tend to be more positive about their personal futures than they are about the future more generally.[28]

Two fast observations . . .

First, this is a generation that believes in **the Canadian Dream**. They believe that their interpersonal and material goals can be realized. In our examination of values, we saw that the vast majority of teens want good relationships and want to be loved. Here we see that they are looking to establish their own homes, complete with marriage and children. It doesn't matter what kind of family structures they have come out of; most still believe they can have lasting and fulfilling marriages. They also tell us they place high value on success and a comfortable life. They believe they can experience both through finding good jobs, and in turn owning their own houses and being more financially comfortable than their parents. It matters little whether they are female or male, were born in Canada or have arrived as immigrants, have parents of high socio-economic standing or not. If they work hard, teens maintain, they can share in the good things that Canadian life has to offer. Affluent times, if anything, make the dream seem all the more attainable.

Second, **their personal resilience** in not abandoning these relational and success components of the Canadian dream is, in many instances, quite remarkable. Despite the experiences that many have had at home, they continue to embrace the idea of family and children and are determined to have permanent relationships of their own. Despite in many instances having disadvantaged backgrounds, most believe they can transcend those backgrounds — along with national instability, if need be — en route to education, occupational, and financial success. That kind of resilience and determination is something else.

Will their expectations be realized? Or are they really not so much what young people are expecting as much as what they are hoping for, what they are dreaming about?

Here, as in the past, I would simply say what is fairly obvious. In many instances, those expectations probably will not be realized. But, as a country and as adults who have helped to instill and nurture those dreams, we need to do everything we can to enable as many of these young people as possible to see their dreams come true.

Part II

Teens Yesterday

Chapter Five

What Teens Were Like in the Early '80s and '90s

I DON'T KNOW ABOUT YOU, BUT I HAD A RECURRING THOUGHT AS we were going through all that material: Are things really very different today from what they were in the past?

Sure, we all know there has been a massive information explosion. It's been estimated that the sum total of human knowledge doubled between 1750 and 1900, and in the period 1960 to 1965 began doubling every five years. Today it is said to be doubling every two years and, by 2020, will double every 73 days! I'm not quite sure how anyone could know all that, but there's no question that we have been experiencing a geometric jump in the volume of information available to us. And with more information has come dramatic technological innovations, typically computer-related. Even there, change seems relentless. Someone, for example, has said that today's average consumers wear more computing power on their wrists than existed in the entire world before 1961.[1] Such technological production, combined with unprecedented multinational corporate marketing, has created a sense that the world is becoming new every day. Moreover, we are expected to indulge in this emerging newness or face the prospect of becoming dinosaurs. There also is a widespread assumption that technology is not just helping us but changing us — how we think, how we live, what we want.

But beyond all the hype about change, when we get right down to what people value and want out of life, are teens and the rest of us really all that different from people in the past? Or are we just sharing in the latest and, according to the hype, "the greatest advances in technology the world has ever seen"?

There are probably people in every era of history who have proclaimed that their technological offerings and even their eras were "new and unprecedented." Who wouldn't have felt such an inclination to have said such things during the arrival of writing, fire, the steam engine, electricity, the telephone, the automobile, radio, television, and remote car-starters specially created for cold Canadian winters? But there is nothing particularly significant about such aggrandizing, "histocentric" claims.[2] Advances in technology and new eras are both, by definition, "unprecedented." Both also inevitably come and go, replaced by "newer," "unprecedented" eras and technological offerings.

The important social question in all this is, what is the impact of changing technologies on people — on what they value, want, and enjoy, their attitudes, concerns, beliefs, and hopes? Technocrats, such as Don Tapscott in his book *Growing Up Digital,* seem to assume that there is something inherent in the Internet, for example, that is making its impact both dramatic and positive.[3] It's as if it has a life of its own, an autonomous power to influence. A minor digression: by way of a possibly helpful parallel, I'd remind everyone that we have done the same thing with television. Over time we have come to see television not as an innocent item sitting over there in the corner, but as something that takes on a life of its own, complete with motives and any number of other qualities. For example, we talk about liking "it" or having no use for "it," how "it" allows us to laugh or how "it" isn't good for our kids. We somehow don't get as personal when we talk to people about our pop-up toaster, or even our radio or VCR. William Stahl of Regina's Luther College cringes at talk about the presumed impact of computers and the Internet, warning in his book *God and the Chip* against what he calls "technological mysticism." He emphasizes that computer technology is just that, neither good nor bad. The onus is on us, he argues, to decide how *we* want to use it, thereby making the best use of it.[4]

Apart from the important question of whether technology drives us or we drive it, a very old voice from yesteryear reminds us not to get overly presumptuous about its net novel effect on who we are as humans. From an era of some 5,000 years ago — a time that people undoubtedly thought was unprecedented — comes this radical hypothesis from the writer of the book of Ecclesiastes: "There is nothing new under the sun."[5] We need to be careful not to equate technological change with social and personal change. The correlates of technological developments need to be critically examined, not rhetorically assumed.

The way to explore the question of the influence of technology is to take a careful look at people at different points in time. If it were possible, it would be great, for example, to be able to look at change over the last century by using some kind of "back to the future" time machine to bring teens today together with their teen counterparts from the '40s, '60s, and '80s, and have them compare their eras.

We are going to try to do something fairly close to that.

Two Sets of Glasses

But before we do, we want to set the stage for looking at differences between generations by taking a few pages to bring some additional thinkers into our conversation. **Observers of today's young people include many who are inclined to believe that this generation is very different from past generations.** In part, such an assumption is based on the current prominence of two approaches to understanding culture and youth — postmodernism and generational analysis. Some see the two approaches as highly complementary. As we prepare to look at what has been happening to teens over time, it's important that we have a sense of what the experts are saying about the changes that have been occurring. Some of you are already very familiar with their thinking. In making our reflections on the pending findings more meaningful for everyone, it's helpful for the rest of us as well to have some understanding of these two prevailing frameworks.

Postmodernism

The term "postmodernism" was first used in the 1950s and 1960s to refer to a movement in architecture that was a reaction to the rigidity of modern styles. It was soon broadened to include developments in areas such as literature and art, and subsequently moved into philosophy, sociology, history, and theology. Generally speaking, postmodernism arose out of the disillusionment of European intellectuals with many modern ideals following World War II.[6] It started as largely a French perspective on cultural and historical analysis, and made significant academic inroads with the French publication of Jean-François Lyotard's *The Postmodern Condition* in 1979,[7] as well as the work of Michel Foucault,[8] and Jean Baudrillard.[9] Today the term is much in vogue in academic circles and is being used by consultants who attempt to interpret the times to a wide range of people, including those who deal with youth.

In capsule form, *postmodernity* is seen as a new historical period that started to emerge in approximately the 1960s, characterized by important new cultural emphases that people have dubbed "postmodernism." Among those heralding the arrival of a new era was Aleksandr Solzhenitsyn, who had this to say in his 1978 commencement address at Harvard: "The world has reached a major watershed in its history, equal in importance to the turn from the Middle Ages to the Renaissance."[10] Postmodernism is viewed as succeeding the modern period, which dates back to approximately 1600, which in turn follows the premodern period, with origins in the beginning of human history; obviously those periods can be subdivided in any number of ways by observers, and frequently are. Religion and reason respectively are seen as key sources of the dominant worldviews of the first two periods, while postmodernism is seen as emerging largely in reaction to the shortcomings of modernity.

If it is relatively simple to speak of "postmodernity" in chronological terms as a period following modernity, confusion abounds when people speak of "postmodern" in cultural terms. In a recent review of postmodernism, sociologists Kenneth Allan and Jonathan Turner note that the term encompasses vast, complex, and contradictory fields. "Still," the authors continue, "one organizing feature of postmodernism is clearly discernible: postmodernism is always understood in contrast to modernism."[11] The problem, suggests theologian Daniel J. Adams, is that "the postmodern is a way of recognizing that the world is in a period of transition. . . . At the present time, however, no one knows for certain what will arise to take modernism's place. The postmodern is the name given to this space between what was and what is yet to be."[12]

Adams maintains that the postmodern era can best be understood in terms of four main characteristics: (1) the decline of Western world emphases on reason, science, and the belief in human progress; (2) the decline of authoritative "meta-narratives" such as belief in unlimited development, the Judeo-Christian sexual ethic or Marxism[13] — for Lyotard there are only small stories from the position of different perspectives; (3) the decline in the control of power, be it power of information or power over people; and (4) "deconstruction," unveiling the contextual nature of all ideas, including scientific research, by examining materials from different perspectives, and uncovering the implicit values and interests beneath the surface.[14]

Together, says Adams, "these four characteristics result in a world of almost unlimited pluralism." Objective truth gives way to social subjectivity. The downside of all this, he suggests, is that we are left with "no way of evaluating this plurality of ideas, values, and products."[15] Social theorist Ben Agger writes that "social science," for example, "becomes an accounting of social experience from these multiple perspectives, rather than a larger cumulative enterprise committed to the inference of general principles."[16] What's real is only what individuals and groups perceive to be real and is frequently simulated by the media and other cultural sources. In the process, people lose the ability to distinguish between simulations and reality. But postmodernists such as Baudrillard go further: there is no "true reality" against which social constructions of reality can be measured. Such a vision of reality, says Canadian sociologist Sylvia Hale, "is both liberating and frightening. It also is paralyzing."[17]

Not everyone has been excited about postmodernism. Allan and Turner write that "many sociologists," for example, "have rejected postmodernism as too arcane and obscure"; their article is, in fact, an attempt to make some of the key ideas of postmodern thinking "more readily accessible to sociologists and perhaps other social scientists as well."[18] Sylvia Hale suggests "it is far too soon to attempt to assess the possible impact of postmodernist thought on the future of sociology." She also cautions us, "In some respects, the ideas are not so avant garde. The notion that ideas are real and the world of the senses mere appearance is as old as Plato. The notion of multiple subject positions is also not new." She concludes, "The challenge is to draw on the critical strengths of postmodernism while redressing its limitations."[19]

Yet, interestingly, postmodernism has been embraced enthusiastically by many people who attempt to "interpret the times," including large numbers of specialists and practitioners who work specifically with young people. In May of 1999 I attended a conference at McMaster University in Hamilton aimed at leaders who are extensively involved with youth, including those engaged in varied forms of youth ministry. I came not as a speaker but as the proverbial fly on the wall, wanting to listen lots and get a sense of the dominant interests, concerns, and thought-forms of such leaders. What was almost immediately apparent was the pervasiveness of the term "postmodernism" in presentations and discussions, with the adjective of "postmodern" applied matter-of-factly to today's young people. Those who are seen as youth culture experts, particularly Americans, such as Walt Mueller, a Pennsylvania-based consultant on youth who frequently speaks in Canada, are telling their audiences that "postmodernism is something you have to grasp if you are going to understand today's kids." In Mueller's words, "Postmodernism is a world-view — a system our kids are growing up with whether they know it or not."[20]

"Experts" on youth culture commonly extract a number of themes from postmodernist thought, including the inclination of people today to: (1) reject reason, (2) emphasize the subjectivity of truth, (3) place primary importance on experience, and (4) question authority. Many

---

How the Postmodern Mind Views Truth

Recently I heard a story about a group of umpires who got together and compared notes on how they decided to call a strike or a ball. The first umpire said, "I call them as they are." The second umpire disagreed and said, "I call them as I see them." The third umpire told the other two, "You are both wrong; they ain't nothing until I call them."

The first umpire represents the naive realist, to whom it is obvious that things are exactly as they appear on the surface. The second umpire admits that his view of the strike zone will vary from day to day. He is a twentieth-century relativist. The third umpire lives in what we would call virtual reality. There is no truth or falsehood, only choices. The third umpire represents the coming postmodern generation.

Source: Jimmy Long, *Generating Hope.* Downers Grove, IL: IV Press, 1997, pp. 56–57.

such popularizers present postmodern characteristics as polar opposites of those found in the modern era — for example, preference versus truth, community versus the autonomous self, virtual reality versus scientific discovery, and human misery versus human progress.[21]

Generational Frameworks

Postmodernist thinking in turn has become fused with generational analysis. The media have led the way in popularizing terms such as "Boomers" and "Xers," "Busters" and "Echo," "Generation Y" and "Millennials." The terms have emerged from a relatively recent strategy whereby observers, led by marketing people, attempt to make sense of national populations by segmenting or stratifying them by age. They then have conceptualized those age categories as "generations," and asserted that they have characteristics that set them apart from other age cohorts.

Only a few years ago, when most of us were using the term "generation," we had a fairly straightforward meaning in mind that was summarized well by Webster's — "persons born about the same time."[22] That was all that co-author Don Posterski and I meant, for example, when we entitled our first youth book in 1985, *The Emerging Generation*. However, what started out as a fairly simple procedure of age segmentation has been evolving into a belief that generations are "real," complete with fairly fixed age boundaries. Influential American proponents of generational analysis, William Strauss and Neil Howe, have gone as far as to maintain that, to date, the United States has had seven generations since the Civil War: the Missionary Generation (1860–1882), the Lost Generation (1883–1900), the G.I. Generation (1901–1924), the Silent Generation (1925–1942), the Boom Generation (1943–1960), Generation X (1961–1981), and the Millennial Generation (1982 through the present). They proceed to describe the dominant features and personalities of each of these eras, thereby seemingly providing a succinct guide to American cultural history.[23]

In the midst of such efforts to delineate generations, it is interesting to note that, according to historians, the word "teenager" didn't even exist prior to the 1950s. People in the United States and the rest of the Western world who were born after 1945 appear to have been the first young people to be designated "teenagers." They also gave rise to the use of generational frameworks. Because of the relatively large size of this postwar cohort in the United States, a resurgent economy, and the potential economic impact of their numbers, these teens were additionally dubbed "Baby Boomers" by marketers. Boomers, of course, became the object of extensive studies by social scientists, who proceeded to refer to them as "a generation" and to define their birth dates as approximately 1945 to 1964.

This was a cohort that, in the U.S., proceeded to experience the prosperity and family stability of the '50s as well as the tumultuous days of the '60s. They lived at a time when traditional views on sex and the family were turned upside down by the "sexual revolution," when conventional lifestyles were jolted by the emergence of the hippies, drugs, and plain "dropping out." In a relatively short time, they grew up and entered the workforce, and were transformed into young urban professionals, better known as "Yuppies." In Canada, many of the features of U.S. Boomers were emulated, including the term, some social dissent, family and sexual changes, and a measure of drug use and dropping out. At one point in the 1960s, hippy-like hitchhiking across Canada was so common in the summers that the federal government actually provided buses to help young people get from place to place. Here, as in the United States, by the '70s nomadic young people were drifting into careers and family life.

The preoccupation with Baby Boomers began to dissipate in the early 1990s as marketing people gave increasing attention to the fact that the offspring of Boomers — born between approximately 1965 and 1984 — were coming of age as teens and young adults. With the help of Canadian author Douglas Coupland's best-selling novel, this new cohort was given the name "Generation X." Many onlookers saw this generation as paying a price for Boomers' preoccupation with careers and consumption, dual incomes and divorce. Xers were commonly viewed as discouraged in view of the difficulty of emulating the career and financial success of their parents, but also as lacking clear goals and a solid work ethic. They pejoratively were labeled "slackers"; if Boomers were viewed as living to work, Xers were seen as working to live.[24]

Attention now is being given increasingly as well to young people born since around 1985, a generation widely referred to as *"Millennials."*[25] This cohort is seen as living during a time of unprecedented peace and prosperity. They have been exposed to dramatic technological innovations relating to sight, sound, and, of course, the Internet. All this change, according to youth and culture expert Dawson McAllister is something with which they are comfortable: "For Boomers, change was a mandate. They were out to change the world. Change was threatening to Xers, who felt unsafe and unstable in the world the Boomers created for them. Millennials, however, thrive on change. It is the air they breathe, and the more of it, the better."[26]

And so it is that generational thinking has become widespread in Canada and the United States as people try to make sense of the age variations they see in how life is being experienced. Beyond speculation, considerable generational research is taking place, not only in the U.S. but in Canada as well. Recent books disseminating findings have included David Foot and Daniel Stoffman's best-seller *Boom, Bust & Echo*,[27] pollster Michael Adams's *Sex in the Snow*,[28] which looks at Elders, Boomers, and Xers (just in case you weren't sure), and the recently released *Chips & Pop*, in which authors Robert Barnard, Dave Cosgrave, and Jennifer Welsh examine Xers, or what they refer to as "the nexus generation."[29]

The Postmodern-Generational Link

In view of the fact that many proponents of postmodernism maintain its effects began to be felt in cultures such as ours in approximately the 1960s, some observers have maintained that Generation X, comprising young people born between 1965 and 1984, is "the first postmodern generation."[30] In making such a connection, the tendency is to ascribe alleged postmodern traits to Generation X and Millennials, assuming that if they are living in a postmodern world, they must be exhibiting postmodern traits, whatever they are. I have been at gatherings where leaders have drawn charts with the headings "Modern" and "Postmodern," based on a year of birth such as 1975, under each of which is a list of characteristics. The two lists are the previously mentioned polar opposites. Everything is seemingly reduced to modern and postmodernist outlooks, based solely on date of birth. My response to that kind of speculative procedure is simple: "Show me the data."

Having looked at what the postmodernist and generational experts are saying about the changes that allegedly have been taking

place in the lives of younger people and older people, we now are ready to take a look for ourselves.

The Teens of the Early '80s and '90s

I think I have a particularly good feel for what older teens were like in the '80s, and not just because of my national surveys. I have three sons, all older Gen Xers, who were born in the late '60s. Their teenage years spanned the decade. Reggie hit 15 in 1981, Dave in 1983, and Russ in 1984; the guys consequently celebrated their nineteenth birthdays in 1985, 1987, and 1988, respectively.

As a parent I experienced firsthand what every parent experiences — the multidimensional emergence of our children into young adults, complete with their physical and social maturation, their friends, music, parties, and girlfriends, the concerns about school, alcohol, drugs, sex, safety, and their staying out of trouble. It was a good decade for us.

It also was a good decade for much of the country. The economy was reasonably good. There were no major wars. It probably could have been a pretty good decade for those Generation X teenagers. But never content with excessive normality or tranquility, in lieu of having a war, the media succeeded in convincing people that we *might* have one of unprecedented proportions. Our Project Canada national survey in 1985 found that 47% of Canadians believed a nuclear war would "definitely" or "probably occur"; a mere 6% were convinced it would "undoubtedly never occur." What's more, in the event that such a war took place, 38% felt it would "mark the end of human life on earth," while another 57% maintained there would be "destruction beyond anything in the past," even though life would go on. The illusory nuclear war cloud hung over us for a good part of the '80s. Fortunately the threat of nuclear war turned out to be only that.

The teens of the '90s, the younger Gen Xers, well, they were a bit different. Unlike their counterparts of the '80s, they were living in a time when Canada's politicians, media, teachers, and just about every other opinion leader was telling them that the most urgent problem facing the country was unity; without constitutional change, the country had no future. Yet, with or without constitutional change, there were no guarantees that Quebec would bother to stick around.

Children are scared of nuclear war threat

HAMILTON (CP), November 23, 1984 — *Children know much more about nuclear war than most adults believe, but the issue is still governed by a code of silence, says a member of the Peace Education Network. Helene Fallen said children "know about the arms race and the effects that nuclear war would have on a global scale and they're scared." There is a "real need for more open communication between parents and children."*

A survey by Dr. Ross Parker, chairman of Physicians for Social Responsibility, indicated 55 per cent of the children asked said the war-peace issue was second only to the death of a parent among their greatest fears. "We as parents, doctors and educators have a duty to help our children deal with this issue," Parker said following a presentation this week of the award-winning film Under the Nuclear Shadow. *"We have to find ways in which we can help our children prepare for the world they're going to inherit. We have to be able to leave them with some hope.*

What's more, the economy was not in good shape. The '90s, especially the early '90s, were unsettling years for young people, who wondered about their futures in a country that itself had a questionable lifespan. It was a time of national means-end inversion; it was difficult to look ahead when the focus of the political, media, and education elites — and, in turn, the economic elite — was on the country's precarious existence. Our 1990 Project Canada national survey indicated that such leaders were badly out of touch with average Canadians. The alleged "unity crisis" was seen by only 37% of Canadians as representing a "very serious" problem; just 27% had a similar sense of seriousness about the need for constitutional agreement. In contrast, 57% felt that the economy was a "very serious" problem. Perception in Quebec was similar to perception elsewhere in the country. Understandably, given the difference in preoccupations, 49% of Canadians maintained that lack of leadership was a severe problem, with a mere 13% indicating that they had "a great deal" or "quite a bit" of confidence in the federal government. Prime Minister Brian Mulroney was seen as "doing a pretty good job" by a paltry 19% of Canadians; by way of comparison, Pierre Trudeau had been given that rating by 57% of Canadians in 1975 and by 44% during fairly tumultuous times in 1980. No, the early '90s were not days that made for happy and enthusiastic living. In a time when their leaders were saying the sky was falling, most people weren't looking heavenward.

Very few of these young people in 1984 or 1992 would have anticipated that cultural analysts would be viewing them as "Generation X." Even fewer would have had any sense that they had arrived during the postmodern era and could therefore be expected to exhibit some of the features of an increasingly postmodern world. Regardless of whether young people knew it or not, say observers, the emerging influence of postmodernism was beginning to show. What's more, those characteristics associated with postmodernism that were appearing in Xers logically should be even more visible in the Millennial generation — today's teenagers.

So much for the theoretical and historical backdrop. Without getting into excessive repetition, we want to turn to the teens of the early

'80s and early '90s, and see how they were putting the world together and living out life compared to teens today.

What Mattered

In 1984 the top five *valued goals* of Canada's teenagers were friendship, freedom, being loved, success, and a comfortable life. There were only minor differences in the ranking of these top values by males and females. An Ottawa 15-year-old back then summed things up this way: "A person will go to almost any lengths to feel or be loved. Believe me, I know." A 16-year-old Quebec male reminded us, "Freedom is something every human being wants," while a CEGEP female added, "You can take care of us by creating more jobs for us. But we can take care of ourselves."

Over the past two decades, these five values have remained the most important goals for the country's young people. Their ranking by males and females has changed slightly, but the five top values have remained the same as they were in 1984.

Table 5.1. **Top Five Valued Goals, 1984–2000**
Ranked . . .

| | MALES | | | FEMALES | | |
	1984	1992	2000	1984	1992	2000
Friendship	1	2	2	1	1	1
Freedom	2	1	1	3	3	3
Being loved	3	4	5	2	2	2
Success in what you do	4	3	4	4	4	5
A comfortable life	5	5	3	5	5	4

What is different now from the early 1980s is the decreasing importance that teenagers are placing on a number of *interpersonal values.* In 1984, larger proportions of females and far larger proportions of males viewed traits such as honesty, forgiveness, and politeness as "very important" than is the case today. Most of the decreases appear to have taken place by 1992; since then, the levels have either remained essentially the same or risen slightly. In 1992, an 18-year-old from London wrote, "Morality is losing its importance. Our governments need to be giving more attention to morality and values." A Walkerton,

Ontario, 17-year-old was even more direct: "I think the world is a self-ish and cold-hearted place to be."

Table 5.2. **Interpersonal Values, 1984–2000**

% Indicating "Very Important"

	MALES			FEMALES		
	1984	1992	2000	1984	1992	2000
Honesty	80%	57	62	90	82	83
Concern for others	**	48	51	**	75	73
Forgiveness	62	45	47	72	71	67
Politeness	60	46	51	70	60	65
Generosity	**	32	37	**	47	47

*** Not asked in 1984.*

In 1984 the two top sources of enjoyment for teenagers were their friends and music. Moms and dating were also among the top five sources of enjoyment, as were sports for males and dads for females. The importance of friends and music, we suggested, could be summed up in the image of two teenagers we saw walking down a beach wearing headsets, linked together by a patch cord from a Walkman.

I myself found that the '80s were a time when friends were plenty and music seemed to be always in the background of any socializing and partying, and in the foreground when bands could be watched in person. Whether I liked it or not, I was introduced to groups and people like Kiss, Cheap Trick, Ozzy Osbourne, and Alice Cooper. And those were just some of the artists I could comprehend.

As I indicated earlier, "my guys" and I had a good life together during those teen years. And, thank goodness, a majority of teens in our survey were saying they were getting high levels of enjoyment from their mothers and fathers. The survey findings, however, also served to remind me of what I, and many readers, knew well — that this wasn't always the case. Our house was a refuge for a few kids who were having some tough times. I remember one teen who on a couple of occasions came over to the house just after 7 a.m.; years later, I was told his father had beaten him and he needed a place to go. I remember one Christmas Eve when I was almost a bit annoyed to find a group of friends filing through the back door, heading to the large

Jackson clears air on sexuality

Calgary Herald, September 6, 1984 — *In a virtually unprecedented move, singer Michael Jackson's personal manager called a news conference Wednesday in Hollywood at the superstar's request to deny "once and for all" that Jackson is gay. Jackson's manager Frank Dileo said Jackson would take legal action against any future remarks he considered libelous or slanderous.*

In the statement attributed to him, the 26-year-old Jackson said, among other things: "NO! I've never taken hormones to maintain my high voice. NO! I've never had my cheekbones altered in any way. NO! I've never had cosmetic surgery on my eyes. YES! One day in the future I plan to get married and have a family."

Meanwhile in Montreal, it was announced that the Jackson brothers' mammoth Victory Tour will touch down at the Olympic Stadium there on Sept. 16 and 17.

game and TV room in the basement where the guys frequently congregated with their friends. Reggie came up to the kitchen area at one point and — fortunately, before I had a chance to express my mild consternation — said softly, "I hope you don't mind these guys coming over here tonight. Things aren't so great for some of them at home, and they really didn't have anywhere to go." One grade 12 student who participated in the 1984 survey helped to keep parental enjoyment in perspective with the observation, "Mothers, fathers, and kids aren't as close as they should be."

I would be remiss if I didn't add another footnote on pets. In 1992 we found that 49% of all Canadian teens reported they were receiving a high level of enjoyment from their pets, with the level 68% for those who actually had pets. That latter level compared favourably with enjoyment of either mothers (69%) or fathers (65%). Two Montrealers in the '92 survey offered some insightful comments. One, 16, said he was receiving little or no enjoyment from either his mother or father, adding, "What I enjoy most is my dogs." An 18-year-old was a bit more generous toward her mom and dad, writing, "When something big goes wrong, I want to talk to my friends, my dog, and my parents."

Unlike a few of my colleagues and friends, I think I understand something of their sentiments; I know many readers do. We had a core of two small dogs and two cats during most of the '80s. Jojo, Nik, Tee, and Mitt added much to our home. They taught the three boys and me much about appreciation of life in its array of forms. I used to be taken by the warmth and sensitivity and affection that our pets could bring out in the guys, humoured and moved to come around a corner and hear a budding young rock star — with dyed black hair, an earring or two, and snakeskin pants — muttering baby talk to a pup. . . .

Over the past two decades, changes in major sources of gratification have been relatively small.[31] Friends and music have remained one-two and, for males, sports have continued to hold down third place. Mom and Dad have held their place in the top five for young women while, among males, Mom has returned to that elite group, after slipping out in 1992. She also has regained her number-three rating with females. Mom's movement may reflect her ongoing effort to juggle a career with home life. Often she wants a career. As Seinfeld and his friends would be quick to add, "Not that there's anything wrong with it." The point is that when such choices are made, everything does not always stay the same. Mothers as a whole show signs of having found an improved balance.

Table 5.3. **Top Five Sources of Enjoyment, 1984–2000**

	MALES			FEMALES		
	1984	**1992**	**2000**	**1984**	**1992**	**2000**
Friends	1	1	1	1	1	1
Music	2	2	2	2	2	2
Your mother	4	—	5	3	5	3
Sports	3	3	3	—	—	—
Dating	5	4	4	4	3	4
Your father	—	—	—	5	—	5
		↑			↑	
Your boyfriend/girlfriend		5			4	

Despite the high ranking that dating and relationships have enjoyed, there is some evidence that, in contrast to 1984, increasing numbers of teens are content to "hang out" with members of both sexes versus actually "dating" or seeing themselves as having a boyfriend or girlfriend. The interaction and the enjoyment are still there. It's just that the style of socializing is being redefined by many teens who have emotional and physical ties with people.

Conventional Relationships and Dating Losing Popularity?

Between 1984 and 2000, there has been a modest decline in the percentage of males and females who report high levels of enjoyment from relationships and dating.

	MALES			FEMALES		
	1984	1992	2000	1984	1992	2000
Boyfriend/girlfriend	70%	66	62	72	72	62
Dating	78	71	70	77	75	68

In 1984, 82% of males and 65% of females were reporting that they were getting a "great deal" or "quite a bit" of enjoyment from sports. More males than females were following sports, attending sporting events, and participating in team sports. Those figures were 80% and 55% respectively in 1992; the current levels are similar for both males (77%) and females (57%). The importance of sports to some teens could be seen in this 1992 comment of a 15-year-old who was living in a small community in Quebec: "I am worried about what will happen to me in the future, and what will happen to Quebec, to the environment, to the economy, and to the marvelous world of sports."

During the 1990s, there was a tremendous increase in the corporate sponsorship and media exposure given to professional sports, particularly leagues based in the United States. Many National Hockey League arenas, for example, took on corporate names — the Molson's Centre, Air Canada Centre, the Corel Centre, the Canadian Airlines Saddledome, the Skyreach Centre, General Motors Place. Corporate luxury boxes and corporate sales more generally became the mainstay of team revenues. Symbolic of the growing corporate influence were ads that first covered the boards and then the ice itself, as well as post-game press conferences against backgrounds carrying the logos of an array of corporate sponsors. The emergence of growing numbers of sports specialty channels, including TSN, Sportsnet, and Headline Sports, significantly supplemented the coverage already provided by national networks and local stations.

However, somewhat remarkably during the past decade there appears to have been a general decrease in the interest that teenagers have in major professional sports.

- While interest in the NHL has remained steady, there has been a significant drop in interest among both males and females in Major League Baseball, and more modest declines in the proportion of teens who are following both the NFL and CFL.

- In contrast, there has been a slight increase in interest in the NBA, reflecting in large part the arrival of new teams in Toronto and Vancouver in 1994, and the aggressive marketing of the league, including young stars such as Vince Carter and Shareef Abdur-Rahim.

The big drop-off in interest in Major League Baseball is corroborated by the drop-off in TV ratings in Canada. One October 2000 playoff game between Chicago and Seattle attracted a mere 138,000 viewers; more significantly, a mere 3,000 — 2% — were in the 18-to-34 age group. Looking at such figures, *Toronto Star* media columnist Chris Zelkovich commented, "If the folks at Major League Baseball aren't worried about the future of their sport, they should be."[32] The 2000 World Series between the Yankees and Mets averaged the lowest ratings in the series' history. Reflecting on the change in baseball's popularity, Steve Simmons of the *Toronto Sun* had this to say on the day after the first game of the 2000 Series: "When I was a kid, the World Series meant everything to me. Time stopped for baseball. You devoured every inning, ever at-bat, every piece of the drama. You left school early to watch or listen. There was something magical about the game." Simmons adds, "Last night, the World Series began and not a child I know seemed to notice or care. How and why this changed, I still don't understand. But somehow you yearn for an innocence lost and a sport that doesn't hold the same magic anymore."[33]

It is noteworthy that these major professional sports have had limited success during the '90s in expanding their markets among young females. Pro hockey, baseball, basketball, and football remain sports that primarily intrigue men. However, that is not to say women are not receptive to sports — just not necessarily the high-contact sports of men. For example, as we saw earlier, 18% of females do say they are closely following figure skating.

Table 5.4. **Interest in Professional Sports, 1992–2000**
% Indicating Follow "Very Closely" or "Fairly Closely"

	NATIONALLY		MALES		FEMALES	
	1992	2000	1992	2000	1992	2000
National Hockey League	45%	34	63	51	28	19
Major League Baseball	33	17	48	25	19	9
National Basketball Association	27	30	37	40	18	20
National Football League	26	21	44	34	10	8
Canadian Football League	22	16	37	26	9	6

Why the big drop-off in interest? Young people are trend-oriented when it comes to entertainment. In the early '90s through the present, the NBA has succeeded in linking itself to the entertainment world more generally, notably in the form of rap music. It also has strong links to U.S. urban African-American life, which itself moved in the '90s to the unexpected role of feeding pop culture more generally. So it was that, in 1992, before Canada had any NBA franchises, four in ten males and two in ten females said that they were closely following the

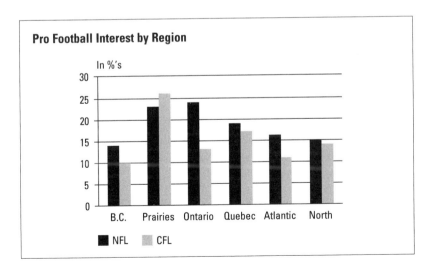

NBA and that Michael Jordan was their favourite athlete. Just as today's young people are abandoning the rockers of even a decade ago, so, when it comes to sports, yesterday's flavour has limited appeal if it is not perceived as "in." Baseball, in particular, is no longer "in," football has never been "in" with females, and the CFL — especially in Ontario — and the NFL are not as "in" with males as they were a decade ago.

Teens in the 1980s saw the way they were brought up, their own willpower, and their mothers as the three key sources of influence on their lives. Close behind were fathers and friends. Illustrating the roles of self and friends, one 16-year-old from Edmonton told us, "My friends often influence my actions, but if there is something I feel isn't right or shouldn't be done, *I don't do it.*" A grade 11 female from Ontario pointed out that one's own willpower is of central importance even in the selection of friends: "I don't take peer pressure as an excuse for doing anything. If a person is strong enough and mature enough to make her own decisions, she should be able to decide not to hang around people that force her into something."

Teens today continue to see the same factors — how they were raised, their own willpower, and their mother — as having the key influence in their lives, although they place a bit more emphasis on friends.

Young people in the '80s tended to place less emphasis than teens today on the impact of the characteristics they were born with, while more saw their lives influenced by teachers and what people in power decide. They also were somewhat less inclined to see God or luck as having a significant influence on their lives than their counterparts of the new millennium.

In short, teens today, like those of the '80s, see themselves as influenced by genetics and upbringing, family and friends. But they are somewhat more likely to think they can transcend social constraints, and more likely to believe there is a chance element to what happens in their lives, be it in the form of supernatural forces or luck. Cultural emphases on personal empowerment and equality of opportunity, along with getting breaks and even a little supernatural help, all seem to be having an impact on their perception of what influences their lives. In a "Just do it" world, the individual typically is seen as being able to overcome social constraints.

Table 5.5. **Perceived Sources of Influence**
% Seeing as Influencing Their Lives "A Great Deal" or "Quite a Bit"

	1984	2000
The way you were brought up	85%	91
Your own willpower	82	89
Your mother specifically	80*	81
Your father specifically	73*	70
Your friend(s)	73	78
The characteristics you were born with	60	71
Your teacher(s)	41	36
What people in power decide	39	25
God or some other supernatural force	36	40
Television	34**	34
Luck	21	31
The Internet	—	15

* Data from Project Teen Canada 87; see Methodology.
** In 1984, "media" was used.

Their Primary Concerns

In an interview a short time ago, well-known demographer David Foot of the University of Toronto noted that high school students are worried about getting good jobs. He commented, "I think if you polled the same 18-year-olds ten years ago, 20 years ago, you would have heard some of the same concerns."[34] He is right.

Teens of the early 1980s had one dominant personal concern: what they were going to do when they finished school. Two other primary concerns were the lack of both money and time. A grade 12 student in a small northern Alberta town summed up some of these problems this way:

My major problem is what to do after I graduate. If I can't get a summer job, I can't go to college, and my plans will be ruined. I need a job and there aren't many jobs to be found.

Over the past two decades those three major concerns have persisted, joined by two issues that were not explored in the first survey — pressure to do well at school and not being understood by parents.

- A comparison of various other personal concerns in 1984 and 2000 — such as boredom, the meaning of life, looks, loneliness, sex, inferiority feelings, and their parents' marriages — shows that levels have remained remarkably similar during this 16-year period.
- What is striking is that levels of concern for almost all these issues were higher in 1992 than in either 1984 or 2000.

Table 5.6. **Personal Concerns, 1984–2000**

% Indicating Concerned "A Great Deal" or "Quite a Bit"

	MALES			FEMALES		
	1984	1992	2000	1984	1992	2000
Pressure do well at school	**	73%	64	**	78	69
What do when finish school	67	70	63	71	74	70
Money	53	71	52	56	71	54
Not understood by parents	**	52	41	**	64	48
Never have enough time	47	69	52	51	78	61
Losing friends	**	49	39	**	64	53
Boredom	41	**	44	45	**	41
Meaning/purpose in life	41	**	38	49	**	46
No girlfriend/boyfriend	**	40	36	**	37	32
Looks	38	**	38	52	**	51
Loneliness	31	**	26	40	**	33
Height/weight	31			56		
Height	**	21	19	**	22	21
Weight	**	26	21	**	53	45
Sex	29	32	30	27	28	22
Inferiority feelings	23	**	27	35	**	43
Parents' marriage	17	**	24	24	**	29

** The item was not included in that year's survey.

With respect to social issues, similar patterns to those for personal issues are readily observable. There was a considerable jump in the levels of concern regarding almost everything in 1992, but levels of concern in 2000 have returned to 1984 levels. And over the years, more young females than males have expressed concern about social issues that are person-centred versus institution-centered.

- Obviously, some of the "big problems" have changed over time. I wasn't exaggerating about the widespread concern about the threat of nuclear war in the 1980s. One in two teens back then saw it as one of the dominant social concerns. A 15-year-old from the Interior of British Columbia told us, "Nuclear war is the worst problem in the world today. It should be the foremost object of concern!" In the 1990s, nuclear war and other front-running issues were replaced by concerns about AIDS and the environment. Today, violence is school is among the primary social concerns; the environment is not.

- Concern about many issues, at least rank-wise, has remained fairly consistent over time.

Table 5.7. **Social Concerns, 1984–2000**

% Viewing as "Very Serious"

	1984	1992	2000
AIDS	**	77%	55
Child abuse	50	64	56
Threat of nuclear war	48	**	24
Crime	48	**	40
Drugs	46	64	48
Violence against women	46[1]	58	42
Teenage suicide	41	59	49
The environment	37[2]	69	42
The economy	37	57	25
Poverty	33	**	41
Racial discrimination	22	58	47
Unequal treatment of women	15	40	32
Youth gangs	**	40	32
Native-White relations	**	39	21
Lack of Canadian unity	13	39	21
Violence in schools	**	36	50
French-English relations	13	31	20

[1] *"Sexual assault" was used.*
[2] *The word "pollution" was used.*

What's clear from these trend findings on personal and social concerns is that teens in 1992 were feeling a level of stress and strain far greater than what their counterparts of 1984 and today feel. As suggested earlier, it should surprise no one. Remember 1992? This was the year of the National Referendum, when an October national vote approving widespread constitutional changes allegedly would

Canadians literally sick of unity squabble

TORONTO (CP), October 12, 1992 — *The whole referendum debate is making people sick. Call it "referendum angst." Stress counselors say they're seeing the effects of a bitter debate over the country's future hard on the heels of an economic recession.*

"What is going on isn't healthy," says Warren Shepell, a Toronto psychologist whose company runs employee stress programs for a string of large corporations across the country. Shepell says more and more people are mentioning the referendum during counselling sessions for stress, a condition that can cause everything from sleeplessness and allergies to nervous breakdowns and heart disease.

"When they listen to the consequences being drawn up for them, they're not pleasant and the views are exaggerated," says Shepell. "The economy had depressed them and now they're hit with doom and gloom over the future of Canada."

And with anxiety already so high over the economy, the added stress of the referendum is going to tip the balance for some people.

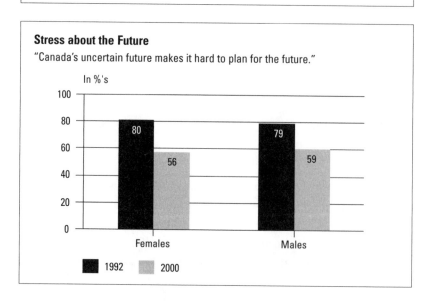

Stress about the Future

"Canada's uncertain future makes it hard to plan for the future."

In %'s

Females: 80 (1992), 56 (2000)
Males: 79 (1992), 59 (2000)

Legend: ■ 1992   ▨ 2000

determine the future of Canada. Media and politicians told us that Canada was at a critical crossroads. "The Day After" hysteria of 1984 that followed the television program on the effects of nuclear war was replaced with dire predictions of what would happen to Canada "the day after" the Referendum, if the motion put to the Canadian people by the government failed. The motion failed to receive national support.

The day after, life in the country continued pretty much as usual. The media and politicians turned to other things. But our findings suggest many Canadian young people had believed their personal and social skies were falling. They paid a considerable price for the fabricated crisis.

Sex and Drugs

Two areas that seem to have been a source of stress and strain for almost every parent over the past few decades are sex and drugs. In both cases, most parents have been wondering when and if their kids are "doing it." The sex possibility is often met with consternation, heightened by anxiety about the additional possibilities of pregnancy and disease. With drugs there is flat-out anguish, accompanied by extra concerns about health, safety, and problems with the law.

In the 1980s, some eight in ten teenagers approved of sex before marriage when people love each other, and just over five in ten were personally engaging in sex. A 15-year-old from Alberta playfully said, with some exaggeration, "This is 1984, wake up, Mom! Everyone has sex." More than nine in ten felt birth control information should be available to teenagers who want it. A grade 11 student from New-foundland suggested that such information should be made available in school, adding, "I think many of the unwanted pregnancies would not have happened if there was information on birth control available."

Just 26% approved of homosexual relations two decades ago, but seven in ten believed that homosexuals are entitled to the same rights as other Canadians. Males were more likely than females to disapprove of homosexual relations and to be opposed to according rights to gays and lesbians. Just over one in ten teenagers approved of extramarital sex. Almost nine in ten felt it should be possible for a woman to obtain a legal abortion when rape is involved, with the figure dropping to four in ten in situations when she does not want to have any more children.

Heterosexual attitudes and behaviour today are pretty much what

they were in the 1980s; what has changed is attitudes relating to homosexuality.

- Now, as then, young people are nearly unanimous in endorsing birth control information for teens who want it, with large majorities approving of sex before marriage when love is involved and disapproving of extramarital sex.

- The approval level for the availability of legal abortion when a female has been raped has remained about the same since 1984. Attitudes toward abortion on demand, cohabitation, and having children without being married have been charted since 1992 only. Approval of abortion for any reason has increased from about 40% to 55%. There has been a modest decrease in the approval of unmarried couples having children.

Table 5.8. **Sexual Attitudes, 1984–2000**

% "Strongly Approving" or "Approving"

	1984	1992	2000
Sexual Behaviour			
Birth control information available to teenagers who want it	93%	—	92
Sex before marriage when people LOVE each other	80	87	82
Sex before marriage when people LIKE each other	—	64	58
Sexual relations between two people of the same sex	26	38	54
A married person having sex with someone other than their marriage partner	12	8	9
Homosexuals entitled to the same rights as other Canadians	67	72	75
Abortion			
It being possible to obtain a legal abortion when a female has been raped	86	88	84
It being possible to obtain a legal abortion for any reason	—	41	55
Cohabitation			
A couple who are not married living together	—	88	86
A couple having children without being married	—	70	63

- The proportion of teenagers who approve of homosexual relations, however, has more than doubled since 1984, from 26% to 54%. Some 75% of teens now maintain that homosexuals are entitled to the same rights as other Canadians, compared to 67% in the '80s.

In 1984 more than 80% of teenagers thought that, if people liked each other, kissing was OK on the first date, with around 80% to 90% saying that necking and petting were appropriate within a few dates; some, led by males, didn't even think one needed to wait beyond the first date. Slightly over half of the 1984 teen cohort felt sexual relations were acceptable within a few dates. Differences between males (70%) and females (36%) were pronounced.

The sense of highly pervasive sexual activity had many parents troubled. One grade eleven female from Montreal wrote:

I believe that because of all the nasty things that my parents hear about teenagers outside the house, I am more and more forbidden to do anything at all now. I would like to know why my parents are so strict, and also do they have this right to treat us strictly because of what they hear?

Table 5.9. **Appropriate Behaviour on Dates, 1984–2000**

	KISS			NECK			PET			HAVE SEX		
	1st	Few	No	1st	Few	No	1st	Few	No	1st	Few	No
Nationally												
2000	73%	26	1		**		32	57	11	11	40	49
1992	82	17	1	52	44	4	33	53	14	12	44	44
1984	82	18	0	50	45	5	28	56	15	11	42	44
Males												
2000	78	21	1		**		43	50	7	18	50	32
1992	85	14	1	61	36	3	43	49	8	20	53	27
1984	84	16	0	59	38	3	42	50	8	19	51	29
Females												
2000	68	30	2		**		22	63	15	4	32	64
1992	78	21	1	44	51	5	23	57	20	5	35	60
1984	80	19	1	42	52	6	16	63	20	3	33	59

* Where totals are less than 100%, the balance is made up of other responses.
** Necking and petting combined as option in 2000.

A Quebec City female complained, "I have never been able to go out with a guy and I am 17 years old, because my parents don't want me to."

Attitudes toward appropriate behaviour on dates changed very little from 1984 to 1992. They also have remained fairly similar through 2000. Close to the same proportions of teens today as in 1984 approve or disapprove of necking/petting, and sex on first dates or within a few dates. Further, those male-female differences we were taking note of in that first 1984 survey are continuing into the new century. One minor difference — perhaps a blip, perhaps something more — is the slight decline in thinking kissing is appropriate on the first date, possibly reflecting the need to exhibit a bit of caution in light of the harassment issue. There is no such decline, however, in the proportion of people approving of necking/petting, and even sex on first dates.

Beyond just attitudes, the level of actual sexual activity of teenagers has remained almost the same as it was in the 1980s. Approximately six in ten males and five in ten females continue to acknowledge that they have been sexually involved. Incidentally, U.S. levels and patterns for high school students are similar, having been around 50% over at least the past decade. Speculation that there has been an increase "is flat-out wrong," says Victor Strasburger of the University of New Mexico.[35]

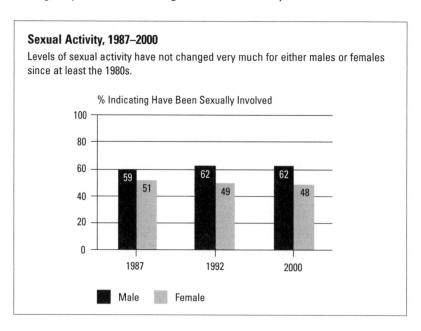

Sexual Activity, 1987–2000

Levels of sexual activity have not changed very much for either males or females since at least the 1980s.

% Indicating Have Been Sexually Involved

Male   Female

In short, apart from more positive attitudes toward homosexuals and homosexuality, sexual attitudes and behaviour among teenagers have changed little in at least the past twenty years. What we have been witnessing in the years after the sexual revolution of the 1960s is not an ongoing revolution of sexual mores and behaviour. After all, how much change is possible in the sexual arena? With respect to premarital sex specifically, the ensuing years have seen older and younger Baby Boomers who had shared in the revolution proceed to have Gen X and Millennial children who, in turn, have embraced similar open views of premarital sex. National levels of sexual permissiveness have risen with the passing of Boomers' grandparents and older parents, not because of ongoing changes from Boomers to Xers to Millennials.

As with sex, concern about drug abuse was fairly widespread among Canadians in the 1980s. A Project Canada national survey at the beginning of the decade found that the issue was ranked fifth in seriousness, behind only the economy, unemployment, crime, and violence.[36] Teens were routinely stereotyped as drug users. A 16-year-old female from a small community in British Columbia protested, "Our minds aren't warped, or whatever. All teenagers shouldn't be grouped together — not all of us go out and get drunk every weekend or get abortions. It's just adults who think that." Another respondent offered this insightful observation: "I've been a teenager for five years and this is the first time I've been asked what I thought about anything other than drugs." Still, almost one in two teens back then acknowledged that drugs were a very serious problem. One male from Saskatchewan commented:

> I feel that the older generation of Canadians don't understand the pressure that the younger generation faces concerning such areas as sex, drugs, and alcohol. Many parents grew up in a time when drug abuse wasn't a problem, and they don't understand the peer pressure involved.

The levels of reported drug use among teenagers in 1984 were fairly similar to what they are now, with one important exception — marijuana. Pot use has been on the rise.

- Cigarette smoking overall was 38% in 1984, and is 37% today, with the female level continuing to be somewhat higher than that of males.

- Alcohol use was twice as high as cigarette use, and the same situation as exists today.
- However, marijuana and hashish use has doubled from 1984 and 1992 levels, led by a sharp increase among males.
- The use of other illegal drugs, such as ecstasy, cocaine, and mushrooms, is up slightly from earlier levels, after having declined marginally between 1984 and 1992.

In light of their increased use of marijuana, teens today understandably are much more inclined to favour the legalization of its use. In 1984, 28% felt the use of marijuana should be legalized, as did an almost identical 27% in 1992. The pro-legalization figure has now jumped to a whopping 50% — comprised of 58% of males and 42% of females.

Table 5.10. **Drug Use among Teenagers**

% Indicating Regular or Occasional Use

	1984	1992	2000
Smoke Cigarettes	38%	34	37
Males	34	32	36
Females	42	37	39
Drink Beer, Wine, or Other Alcohol	76	75	78
Males	77	75	80
Females	76	76	75
Smoke Marijuana or Hashish	16	18	37
Males	18	19	43
Females	14	17	31
Use Other Illegal Drugs	11	8	14
Males	12	8	16
Females	9	8	13

Apart from actual drug use, it's very apparent that teenagers have even greater accessibility to drugs than they did two decades ago. In the light of such widespread availability, perhaps it is particularly noteworthy and newsworthy that, apart from marijuana, drug use has not increased markedly over the same time period. Greater access has not changed the drug headline that seldom is seen and needs to hit papers across the country: *Most teens not bothering with drugs.* In terms of public relations, it would be a gift to teens weary of an unfair stereotype.

Accessibility of Drugs

Dating back to the '80s, teens have been saying that they have ready access to drugs, if they want to use them, regardless of where they are living in Canada. Access has been increasing, say teens who claim to know.

	1987	1992	2000
Nationally	76%	87	93
B.C.	73	90	95
Prairies	83	86	94
Ontario	78	87	93
Quebec	69	84	92
Atlantic	81	92	93
North	—	90	96

The Culture and the Country

In 1984 teenagers were only a short distance removed from the passing of the *Official Languages Act* (1969) and the introduction of the Multiculturalism policy (1971). A majority of about 70% expressed support for **bilingualism**, while 80% indicated their opposition to Canada having a **"melting pot"** approach to cultural diversity.

Today support for bilingualism among young people remains virtually unchanged from 1984, as was also the case in 1992. What is noteworthy is that the endorsement of the "melting pot" idea has increased rather than decreased in the ensuing years since the unveiling and promotion of official multiculturalism. The 20% who approved of the idea of a melting pot in 1984 rose to 41% in 1992 and now stands at 34%. Economic and unity volatility in the early '90s may have spilled over into hostility toward cultural diversity.

In cultivating whatever they saw as "Canadian culture," almost eight in ten teens in the early '90s saw the CBC as "important to Canada." Today that support has slipped to seven in ten, but nonetheless is impressive in an ever-growing, multichannel television universe. Maybe Peter Mansbridge is resonating with more people than we thought with those commercials praising the unique role of his network and reminding us, "There's only one CBC."

In 1984 about two in three teenagers felt that average Canadians do not have any **influence on what the government does.** Many were vocal about their frustration with limited input. A 16-year-old male from a private school in B.C. told us, "We are willing to contribute responsibly to our society, but we have no avenue." A rural-Ontario grade 10 student said, "I think Canadian young people have more to offer this country than you give us credit for. Give us a chance!" Today approximately the same two in three proportion lament the inability to influence government, although that represents a slight decline from the level of those disenchanted teens in the unity-fixated days of 1992.

Table 5.11. **Attitudes toward Culture, Government, and Law, 1984–2000**
% Agreeing

	1984	1992	2000
Language and Culture			
Canada should have TWO official languages — English and French.	71%	66	73
Canada should be a "melting pot" where people coming here from other countries give up their cultural differences and become Canadians.	20	41	34
The CBC is important to Canada.	—	77	67
Government and Law			
The average Canadian does not have any influence in what the government does.	64	74	65
The death penalty should sometimes be used to punish criminals.	73	—	59
People who break the law are almost always caught.	36	—	27

Some other attitude highlights

- More than 70% of young people in the '80s maintained that **capital punishment** should sometimes be used. Today's young people are not as "hawkish"; the figure has dropped to about 60%. There has been growing cynicism about what happens to individuals who break the law. In 1984 one in three teens felt such people **almost always get caught**; now just one in four feel that way.
- Teens in the early '80s were nearly unanimous in asserting that people with insufficient incomes have a right to **medical care**; the same support holds today.
- Optimism about the ability of young people to **"rise to the top"** if

they work hard characterized seven in ten teenagers in 1984. One grade 12 female from a small southern Ontario town proclaimed, "At our age we can do anything and be whoever we want to be if we want it bad enough." That 70% level persisted through the '90s and remains virtually unchanged for the latest emerging generation. The current mood is summed up by a grade 10 male from a small Manitoba community: "Anything is possible for those who want it."

- In keeping with such perception of opportunity, about 60% of teens think **women** now encounter little discrimination, up slightly from the early '90s.
- In 1984 many teens expressed concern about **values changing for the worse**. One grade 10 student from Vancouver, for example, commented, "I feel that the morals of today are very low. I myself have little respect for many of the people I am in contact with because of their moral beliefs." She added, "This includes my parents." In 1992 we put the issue directly to teens, asking them to respond to the statement "In general, values in Canada have been changing for the worse." Some 68% agreed. Today, however, the figure has fallen to 52%.

Table 5.12. **Attitudes toward Equality and Interpersonal and Global Issues, 1984–2000**

% Agreeing

	1984	1992	2000
Equality and Interpersonal Issues			
People who cannot afford it have a right to medical care.	91%	—	92
Anyone who works hard will rise to the top.	74	75	72
In general, values in Canada have been changing for the worse.	—	68	52
Women in this country now encounter very little discrimination.	—	56	61
A stranger who shows a person attention is probably up to something.	—	39	37
Global Matters			
We need to worry about our own country and let the rest of the world take care of itself.	44*	—	38
War is justified when other ways of settling international disputes fail.	—	44	30

* *Data from Project Teen Canada 87.*

- If skepticism about the values of people is down a bit, suspicion is not: close to four in ten think **a stranger** "who shows a person attention is probably up to something," the same level as a decade ago. Stateside, incidentally, distrust seems to have been increasing. In 1975, 35% of high school seniors in the U.S. believed "most people can be trusted"; by the early '90s the figure had fallen to about 20%. During the same period, the proportion who felt "you can't be too careful in dealing with people" increased from 40% to 60%.[37]
- **Globalization** may be making young people more aware of the rest of the planet. But that's not to say it's making them appreciably more compassionate toward people elsewhere. In the 1980s, some 44% of teens maintained Canada should look after itself and let the **rest of the world** take care of itself; today's level is only a slightly lower 38%. As for the appropriateness of **war** when international disputes cannot be resolved otherwise, only 30% of teenagers agree with such an option, down from the 44% of young people who, on the heels of the Gulf War, felt war is sometimes justified.

Postmodernists, in particular, are inclined to think that confidence in institutions has been decreasing. In 1984 solid majorities of Gen X teens said they had a high level of confidence in people in charge of a variety of Canadian institutions. Today confidence in leadership among Millennials is still appreciable, but tends to be down from earlier levels.

The demolition of an orphanage

ST. JOHN'S, Nfld. (CP), April 2, 1992 — *The Mount Cashel orphanage will be demolished and the land sold to fund programs to help victims of sexual and physical abuse. The property, worth an estimated $8 million, will go to public tender as soon as the buildings are destroyed, Archbishop James MacDonald said today.*

The Roman Catholic Church owns the site, now notorious for abuse of young boys at the hands of orphanage staff belonging to the Christian Brothers, a Catholic lay order.

- In the 1980s large numbers expressed confidence in people responsible for law enforcement, the schools, the court system, and religious organizations.
- Close to half said they had confidence in the leadership being given the television and newspapers industries, while some 40% claimed to have confidence in provincial and federal government leaders.
- Today a solid majority of teens express confidence in the police, schools, and the newspaper, movie, and music industries. But, with the sole exception of newspapers, the numbers are consistently down from 1984 and, to a lesser extent, from 1992.
- A significant decline in confidence shown leaders of religious organizations took place between 1984 and 1992, undoubtedly related in large part to highly publicized charges of sexual abuse; confidence has not rebounded among teens over the past decade.
- Confidence in governments has risen following a sharp dip in the turbulent early '90s. Media leadership confidence is currently highest for newspapers and the movie industry, lower for the music and radio industries, and lowest for television. The largest increase in confidence of any institution since 1984 has been shown to newspapers. Teens enjoy television, but they clearly see newspapers as a more reliable medium.

Table 5.13. **Confidence in Leaders**

"How much confidence do you have in the people in charge of . . ."

% Indicating "A Great Deal" or "Quite a Bit"

	1984	1992	2000
Police	77%	69	62
Schools	69	67	63
Music industry	—	68	54
Court system	67	59	52
Radio	—	65	48
Religious organizations	62	39	40
Television	57	61	44
Newspapers	48	—	60
Movie industry	—	58	60
Provincial government	41	32	41
Federal government	40	27	41

Such findings lend some support to postmodernists' claims that today's young people are less likely than their counterparts of the past to have confidence in institutions. Yet confidence levels nonetheless remain fairly high in a number of instances. It's an overstatement to say, as one prominent American youth consultant does, that postmodern youth "have no faith in institutions and put little stock in a chain of command."[38] That might be the case one day. But that day has not yet come.

What They Believed

Teens of the 1980s were reflective about the meaning of life, suffering, and death. More than seven in ten said they "often" or "sometimes" raised these "ultimate questions" and another two in ten said they had reflected on such issues in the past. Although levels are down somewhat from 1984 in almost every instance, some 60% to 80% of young people today nonetheless say they are raising these kinds of questions.

Table 5.14. **Extent to Which Teens Raise Ultimate Questions**

	OFTEN OR SOMETIMES		NEVER HAVE	
	1984	2000	1984	2000
What happens after death?	84%	78	5	7
Why is there suffering in the world?	82	72	6	10
What is the purpose of life?	79	72	8	11
How can I experience happiness?	78	73	10	10
How did the world come into being?	72	63	6	13
Is there a God or Supreme Being?	69	56	13	19

The 1980s was not a time when teenagers had difficulty believing in supernatural phenomena. Conventional beliefs about God, the divinity of Jesus, and life after death were held by some eight in ten, while less conventional ideas concerning psychic phenomena, astrology, and contact with the spirit world were also endorsed by close to half or more of the country's young people. One particularly articulate Ontario respondent expressed things this way:

I really believe that humans have a sixth sense, or an extra dimension of perception, if that sounds plausible. The human mind is a far more complex piece of machinery and I don't think we've even begun to develop it to its fullest potential.

Today's youth mirror the belief levels of teens in the '80s with two important exceptions: there has been a significant decline in both belief in God and belief in the divinity of Jesus — primarily associated with teenagers who do not identify with any religious group or, in the case of Jesus, a faith other than Christianity. Belief in ESP has remained high, but cynicism is evident concerning people having psychic powers. What still is impressive overall is the ongoing pervasiveness of supernatural beliefs more generally, as described in detail in chapter 3, unquestionably fuelled by a media that have been both responding to and creating interest in the supernatural.

In addition to beliefs, spiritual needs were explicitly acknowledged by close to six in ten teens when the subject was first raised in 1992; that level stands at about five in ten today. Since 1992, some six in ten young people have also been indicating that spirituality is either "very important" or "somewhat important" to them. Here again, a media that have given spirituality considerable play through the '90s and into the present have undoubtedly played a key role in covering, popularizing, and legitimizing spiritual pursuit.

Table 5.15. **Beliefs and Spirituality**

"I believe . . ."	1984	2000
Conventional		
God exists	85%	73
Jesus was the Divine Son of God	85	65
In life after death	80	78
Have felt presence of God/a higher power	34	36
Less Conventional		
Some people have psychic powers	69	55
In ESP	54*	59
In astrology	53*	57
We can have contact with the spirit world	45*	43
	1992	2000
Spirituality		
Spirituality is important to me.	62	60
I have spiritual needs.	58	48

Project Teen Canada 87 data.

In the 1980s, about one in four young people were actively involved in religious groups. Close to 25% said that they attended religious services "very often," and about the same proportion indicated they were receiving a high level of enjoyment from their religious group involvement. A 16-year-old from Saskatoon seemed to speak for some teens who were "temporarily inactive" when he said, "Religion is important, but not too important for me right now. I suppose I will practise my faith more when I'm older." Then again, the one-shot look at involvement levels in 1984 offered no guarantees that anything close to a majority of teens would become more involved as they got older. A grade 11 male from a small Alberta town was among those who showed little indication of "returning" in the future, because he had never been involved in the past:

> I don't see where religion plays a part with us. I have never been to church in my life except for funerals and weddings. I am doing just as good or better than anyone else who has been going to church for years.

In the 1992 survey, a number of teens were explicit about their interest in spirituality but disinterest in organized religion. "I am a non-practising Catholic," said one 17-year-old male from St-Georges, Quebec, "but I am interested in spirituality." A grade 12 student from Toronto wrote, "I believe in God, but I don't think I have to go to church to prove it." A 17-year-old male from Bedford, Nova Scotia, commented, "I have no belief in religion, but I enjoy studying all the varieties because spirituality is interesting, if not realistic."

Table 5.16. **Religious Group Involvement, 1984–2000**

	1984	1992	2000
Identify with a group	85%	79	76
Committed to Chrisitanty or another faith	39	24	48
Attend weekly	23	18	22
Receive high level of enjoyment	24	15	21

Despite such skepticism and conjecture about young people's becoming less and less involved in organized religion, levels of participation in organized religious groups have returned to the level of the

'80s after slipping somewhat in the '90s. So have levels of enjoyment.

Further, identification with religious groups has dropped, but relative to attendance, it remains remarkably strong. In 1984, 85% of teenagers indicated that they had a religious preference, identifying with Roman Catholicism, Protestantism, Judaism, Buddhism, and so on. That figure now stands at 76%. Still further, the proportion of young people who claim to be committed to Christianity or another faith has rebounded, following a decline in 1992, to a new post-'80s high of almost 50%. Future religious rites of passage are also widely anticipated, particularly in the case of weddings and funerals.

These findings suggest that rumours of the departure of teenagers from organized religion in recent decades and in the future "have been greatly exaggerated."

What They Hoped For

Back in the '80s, teenagers did not have university aspirations to the extent they do today. In 1984 and again in 1987, our surveys found that some 50% of males and 60% of females expected to attend university; the corresponding figures now are about 65% for males and 75% for females. In the 1980s, more than 30% of teens expected to attend a vocational school; these days that figure has dropped to around 20% to 25%.

In 1984, almost all of those Generation X teens said they planned to pursue employment after they finished their education; only a very small number said they eventually would not work outside the home. More than 70% also anticipated that when they finished school, they would be able to find a good job. Only a minority shared the realism

Table 5.17. **Education Aspirations, 1987–2000**

"How much education do you expect you will eventually get?"

	1987		1992		2000	
	Male	**Female**	**Male**	**Female**	**Male**	**Female**
Graduate from university	48%	55	56	65	58	65
Some university	5	5	11	9	8	7
Complete vocational*	26	23	19	17	18	17
Some vocational*	7	8	6	5	6	5
High school	12	8	7	4	10	5
Less than high school	2	1	1	<1	<1	>1

* Includes commercial colleges and CEGEPs in Quebec.

expressed by a grade 11 female from Charlottetown: "I might have the job requirements but the jobs might not be there." Even fewer admitted to the pessimism of a Newfoundland grade 10 student who said, "There won't be any jobs around. If old people who are more qualified can't find jobs, how can I?"

Some 85% of teenagers in the '80s anticipated getting married and having children at some point. We noted that this was probably a minimum figure, since many of the remaining 15% would undoubtedly surprise themselves by getting married, after all. More than 50% planned to have two children, while another 35% thought they would

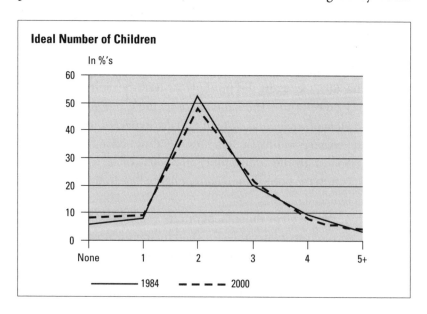

have three or more; the remainder either wanted one child (7%) or none at all (8%).

The 1992 and 2000 surveys have similarly found younger Gen Xers in the early '90s and the first group of Millennials today to be close to unanimous in wanting careers, marriage, and children. There has been little change in these three areas during the past two decades. Expectations that were high have continued to be high; if anything, they increased between the '80s and '90s and have remained extremely high ever since.

Teenagers have expected and continue to expect to get the jobs they want when they graduate, to have children — even the same numbers of children, and to stay with the same partners for life. Moreover, they anticipate owning their homes, with the vast majority expecting to be more financially comfortable than their parents. The optimism of today could be heard a decade ago in the words of a 16-year-old male from Richmond, B.C.: "In this country, I feel that anyone of any race, sex, or sexuality can achieve power if they can do the job." Some, like this 16-year-old from Winnipeg, were in a militant mood in the early '90s: "You tell Mulroney to get this country in order, 'cause I want a job when I get out of school." Today young people see the economy as essentially in pretty good order. For the most part, Prime Minister Jean Chrétien has been spared such admonitions. Teens in 2000 were giving him an approval rating of 60%, compared to a paltry 19% for former Prime Minister Brian Mulroney in 1992.

Table 5.18. **Expectations of Teenagers, 1992–2000**

"Do you expect to . . ."

% Indicating "Yes"

	1992	2000
Career		
Pursue a career	96%	95
Get the job you want when you graduate	83	86
Have to work overtime in order to get ahead	41	44
Family		
Get married	85	88
Stay with the same partner for life	86	88
Have children	84	92
Success		
Own your own home	96	96
Be more financially comfortable than your parents	77	79
Travel extensively outside Canada	73	72

It's interesting to note that the emergence of an information-based economy in the new century versus the legacy of an industrial economy in the last century, so far at least, has not significantly altered what young people are looking for when they think of "a good job."

- In the '80s teens primarily wanted interesting and gratifying work, with good colleagues.
- Today they still want interesting and gratifying work, but more are now also giving more attention to salary. Greater numbers are also

valuing being in a position to make most of the decisions, but decision-making still lags well behind other valued characteristics. Some one in three teens showed temerity about having to make decisions on the job in the '80s; the current figure is one in two.

Table 5.19. **Characteristics of a Good Job**

% Indicating "Very Important"

	1987	2000
The work is interesting.	81%	86
It gives me a feeling of accomplishment.	73	76
Other people are friendly and helpful.	71	63
There is a chance for advancement.	67	68
There is little chance of being laid off.	64	57
It pays well.	57	66
It allows me to make most of the decisions myself.	32	49

Assessment

In order to understand what's happening to today's young people, it's important to compare them with their counterparts of the past. While some observers assume that the emergence of digital technology, the Internet, and the dramatic escalation of information mean teens today are different from their predecessors, such an assumption needs to be tested.

Any effort on our part to locate today's teens in relation to both the past and the future should take into account two approaches that currently are being widely used — postmodernism and generational analysis. Both see present-day youth as highly unusual, but for different reasons.

Postmodernists emphasize the **historical context** in which young people find themselves, viewing them as living in an era that differs from the preceding modern era in its disenchantment with science and reason, rejection of systems of belief, decline in the control of power, and the contextualizing of ideas. Together these themes are seen as contributing to a new historical era characterized by pervasive pluralism, extending to the blurring of reality itself. Postmodernism has been widely embraced by people working in the youth industry. In their hands, commonly extracted themes include an emphasis on the rejection of reason, the subjectivity of truth, the importance of personal experience, and the questioning of authority.

A second prominent approach is **generational analysis.** This approach owes much of its origin and popularity to market research and "market segmentation," where the population is broken down into manageable categories — often initially by age — and prominent characteristics are identified, typically with the help of fairly broad historical generalizations. The tendency is to emphasize cohort distinctives rather than continuities. This popular approach has created "Baby Boomers," "Generation Xers," "Echoes," "Ys," "Millennials," and any other number of categories that analysts have chosen to bring into being.

A brief critique of the two sets of glasses. At the level of the individual, both the postmodern and generational approaches tend to be deductive, starting with a conclusion, then adding the facts. The postmodernist point of view is highly theoretical, rather than empirically derived. Its claims are important and warrant careful research. But at this point, it is largely what sociologist C. Wright Mills called "grand theory."[39] It's a big idea in need of lots of data. Generational frameworks have their origins in marketing research, and the excellent work of people like Canadian Michael Adams[40] or American Wade Clark Roof[41] provide good starts in isolating cohorts and their characteristics. But here again, what is needed is additional research that verifies and clarifies initial findings. In the case of Baby Boomers, considerable research has been done, particularly in the United States. But it has taken years to get a clear picture of that postwar cohort and its commonalities and peculiarities.

The problem is that, in the hands of the users, postmodern and generational approaches are taken to be truth, rather than treated as approaches that, at this point at least, can at best be used to suggest some possible people patterns. At their worst, practitioners use them dogmatically, literally stereotyping people based on their age, ironically doing so on the basis of appealing to scientific thought and research. Not only that (you can see I'm on a roll) but practitioners, including the media, frequently commit the mortal scientific sin of "reification" — equating their concepts and categories with the real thing. They don't just interact and write about people of certain ages; they now are interacting with and telling stories about people who are "Modern" and "Postmodern" "Boomers" and "Millennials." In Canada the satirical lead-in to Molson's "Obnoxious American" ad, "So, I hear you're from Canada, eh?" becomes, "So, you're a Boomer, eh?" or "So, you're Postmodern, eh?" and the imposing of any number of stereotypical and precarious characteristics, whether they apply or not. Sometimes these labels degenerate into terms used for purposes of name-calling, both bad and good; one writer dubbed postmodern by his critics commented, "I have the impression that [postmodern] is applied today to anything the users of the term happen to like."[42] Such labelers, like the obnoxious Greg in the commercial, are going to get some jackets pulled over their heads!

My approach has been to try to start with the data and see how well the two frameworks fit.

A comparison of today's Canadian teens, essentially young Millennials, with those of 1984 and 1992 — older and younger Gen Xers, respectively – shows considerable consistency in a large number of areas. They include valued goals, major sources of enjoyment, and dominant personal and social concerns, in that the specifics of the last have changed but still centre around the broader issues of "staying alive and living well." Personal and social concern levels jumped in 1992, but now have essentially returned to 1984 levels. Sexual attitudes and behaviour have remained fairly steady, with the exception of a growing acceptance of homosexuality. Drugs have become more readily available, but apart from an increase in the use of marijuana, drug use has not increased markedly.

Social attitudes toward issues such as bilingualism, input into government, hard work leading to success, the right to medical care, and the motives of strangers have remained at essentially the same levels as in previous years, but in many instances they represent a decrease in negativity expressed by teens in the early '90s. Today's religious involvement level is similar to that reported in 1984, following a slight drop in 1992; belief and spiritual interest levels have remained fairly constant since the '80s. Expectations about education, careers, family, and success have also varied little over time; they have been consistently high, even in the troubled times of the early '90s.

There has even been consistency where some observers may not expect or want to see it; for example, *gender differences* have persisted over the past two decades in pretty well all these areas. Females, collectively at least, consistently exhibit differences from males in their values, attitudes, beliefs, outlook, and behaviour, regardless of whether we are looking at teens in 1984, 1992, or 2000.

Some **differences** among the three cohorts of teenagers are readily observable. There has been a decrease, particularly, among males in the importance placed on some civility traits, including honesty, politeness, and forgiveness. A decline has taken place in interest in a number of major professional sports, especially baseball. Teens have a greater tendency today to think they can transcend social constraints in the course of pursuing their goals, yet show more openness to the possible role of supernatural factors and "luck." Social attitudes toward multiculturalism and lawbreakers being caught have become more negative, while attitudes toward some issues like capital punishment and war have softened. Confidence in institutions is considerable but generally down from earlier levels, although confidence in governments has rebounded to 1984 levels after dropping significantly in 1992.

So what do we make of it all? Three things jump out of these findings.

First, **similarities** are more common than dissimilarities. What young people want out of life and how they see themselves going about getting there have changed little over time. Of course technological resources have changed. But what teens want and what they value have tended to remain steady. A measure of disillusionment with institutions is apparent. Yet ongoing commitment to marriage and children means that old institutions are not necessarily being abandoned, while increases in confidence in governments suggest that disenchantment with institutional structures is not necessarily permanent. Revitalized and relevant institutions are sometimes re-embraced, rather than discarded.

Second, the **autonomy** theme persists. Rather than buying into a rigid deterministic model of behaviour, teens are convinced they can do battle with their social environments — starting with their family backgrounds and extending to "what people in power decide" — and still come out the winners. Interestingly, these days they acknowledge that "luck and the gods" may play a part, even a bigger part than people in power. They either don't know the odds or choose to ignore them.

Third, the finding that teens at the beginning of the '90s and teens today have almost **identical levels of expectations** about just about everything is really quite something, given the very different social milieus in which the two teen cohorts found themselves. As emphasized, the young people who participated in the 1992 survey were living in fairly turbulent times, when the economy was poor, divorce was on the rise, and the future of the country was up in the air. Yet somehow the majority of teenagers felt they could rise above the social world in which they found themselves and still get the jobs they wanted, have lifelong partners, and know financial success. And so it was that a 16-year-old from Wolfville, Nova Scotia, told us that "some people do not know what it feels like to go through a divorce, especially when you are only 10 years old . . . the pain, the anguish, the hurt, the hate, and the confusion." But she went on to tell us that she expects to stay with the same partner for life. In like manner, a 16-year-old from Chipman, New Brunswick, when asked to describe his feelings about the future in one word, responded, "Canada's — shaky; mine — confident." In the words of educator Arthur Levine, many such Gen Xers may have seen themselves as riding on a societal *Titanic*; but even if society sank, they themselves were going to go down in first class.[43]

The fact that today's teens know the reality of more buoyant times may contribute to their having similar high expectations. But the high hopes of teens in the '90s suggest that, good times or not, today's teens likewise would probably dig in and set their sights on "great expectations."

We also have now **put some interesting numbers** on postmodern Gen Xers and Millennials. For now, you be the judge of what kind of support the findings provide for postmodern thinking as you understand it, along with generational generalizations. No, I'm not dodging those questions. I'll continue to reflect on the merits of the frameworks as we look at additional findings.

Oh, and by all means — we have to talk some more about those ongoing **gender** differences.

Chapter Six

What Their Parents and Grandparents Were Like as Teenagers

COMPARING TEENS IN 1984, 1992, AND 2000 PROVIDES US WITH A **good look at short-term change.** But it doesn't tell us very much about broader intergenerational change, since we are looking only at Generation Xers and the youngest members of the next and newest generation, the Millennials. As such, the 1984, 1992, and 2000 comparisons shed only limited light on the extent to which young people born after 1960 exhibit, for example, the much-heralded postmodern cultural characteristics. We need to go further back.

That's what we now want to do. **We are going to extend the years of comparison by bringing the parents and grandparents of today's teens into our conversation, along with younger adults under the age of 35.** The latter typically include their older brothers and sisters, aunts and uncles, friends, and such people as younger teachers, co-workers, coaches, and youth leaders.

First, we want to look at how these three generations remember what life was like when they themselves were teenagers. Next, we want to briefly examine how they view teenagers and how teenagers view them. Third, we want to compare how these three adult generations are putting the world together, compared to today's teens.

Their World

The majority of parents of today's 15- to 19-year-olds are Baby Boomers, born between 1945 and 1964 and now approximately 36 to 55 years old. Teens' grandparents tend to be over 55, born approximately between 1925 and the end of the Second World War. Some observers have called them "The Silent Generation."[1] Through tapping memories, media, and the musings of historians, we can revisit the lives of these two generations, along of course, with younger adults, Generation Xers. In the words of James Garbarino, "While I cannot go to my children's future, they can at least view my past."[2]

A Profile of Three Adult Generations				
	Born	Current age	Years when a teenager	Generational label
Grandparents	c. 1925–44	56–75	1940s and '50s	Silent Generation
Parents	1945–64	36–55	1960s and '70s	Baby Boomers
Younger adults	1965–80	20–35	1980s and '90s	Generation X

The parents of today's teens were teenagers themselves in the 1960s and 1970s. A fair number were the children of immigrants who came increasingly from Western and Eastern Europe. As most readers are well aware, these were decades characterized by renewed emphases on freedom and equality. The American-based civil rights and women's movements were felt and supplemented in Canada with royal commissions on language and culture and the status of women. Ensuing legislation, policies, and programs were put in place across the country. In addition, the Quiet Revolution in Quebec in the late '60s and early '70s further placed the issue of unity squarely before the eyes of the nation.

These two decades were characterized by a strong emphasis on lifestyle freedom. The 1960s marked the sexual revolution, the American counterculture, and an increase in the use and profile of drugs. This was a decade when the most popular movies included *Lawrence of Arabia, The Sound of Music,* and *The Graduate,* when two of the top-rated programs were *Bonanza* and *The Beverly Hillbillies.* Teens were listening on 8-tracks to the likes of the Beatles, Simon and Garfunkel, the Rolling Stones, and Peter, Paul and Mary. Television comedies such as *Laugh-In* and *Wayne and Schuster* were now being seen in colour; *W-5* and *Man Alive* made their debut. The Maple Leafs and the Canadiens were taking turns winning the Stanley Cup, and Russ Jackson and the Ottawa

Rough Riders were winning more than their share of Grey Cups. The Montreal Expos became Canada's first Major League Baseball team two years after Expo. Near the end of the decade, one man landed on the moon and another received the world's first heart transplant.

The cable TV explosion of the '70s

by Phil Lind
Senior Vice-President and Director of Canadian Cablesystems and Rogers Telecommunications, 1979

Canadians had a love affair with cable television during the 1970s. In one decade, Canada became the most heavily cabled nation in the world, with nearly 60 percent of all households taking the service. The reason for the popularity was that cable provided more viewer choice, more distant stations (often U.S.) and better picture quality.

More than 75 percent of all viewing by Canadians is of U.S. programming — programs that appear for the most part on Canadian television stations. This lack of popularity of Canadian programming is a serious problem and it is imperative that ways be found to repatriate viewers to Canadian productions. For, as Pierre Juneau noted, if we don't have a national communications system, we don't have a nation.

The future for the cable industry looks promising indeed. [The] interface with the computer . . . will allow interactive, two-way television for home shopping, information-retrieval services and alarm systems. Pay television, allowing further audience specialization, will revolutionize the concept of programming choice, as cable systems deliver more than 100 channels. The '70s saw radical changes to the Canadian communications structure, changes that will continue into the '80s.[3]

The early '70s seemed like a time of relief from the heavy life of the freedom-movement '60s — functionally similar to the way the '50s followed the war-torn years of the '40s. The decade saw teenagers flocking to movie theatres to see *Jaws*, *Rocky*, *Star Wars*, and *Saturday*

Night Fever, and popping in their cassettes to hear the Eagles, Olivia Newton-John, David Bowie, and Elton John. Television offerings such as *All in the Family, Happy Days*, and *Charlie's Angels* were particularly popular, but perhaps the biggest news in TV viewing was the explosion in channel choices, thanks to the arrival of cable. The '70s saw the Flyers and Canadiens dominating the NHL and the Eskimos the CFL, with the Blue Jays making their debut in 1977. If the alleged "happy days" of the '50s had the Cold War as its political backdrop, the early '70s had the end of the Vietnam War and Watergate — "imported social problems" that nonetheless invaded Canadian media, households, classrooms, and teenage lives on a day-to-day basis. Imported social problems didn't stop there; the emergence of California cults and the Jonestown mass suicide also resulted in concern about cults in this country. The birth of OPEC led to an oil shortage crisis, dire predictions of a world that would soon be without fossil fuels, and the call for the public to implement a wide array of energy-saving practices, including average people turning down their thermostats. Environmental concerns became paramount, nuclear plant accidents and oil spills viewed with heightened anxiety.

The grandparents of today's teens tend to be approximately 56 to 75 years old, born between 1925 and 1944. Most were living out their teen years in the '40s and '50s. Large numbers were children of immigrants, mostly from Britain and other Western European countries. Their early years were frequently difficult years. The older members of this cohort were children during the depression of the 1930s, then, along with younger members of the cohort, found themselves in the midst of a world war that lasted through 1945. Wartime entertainment gave rise to new stars such as James Cagney, Elizabeth Taylor, and Debbie Reynolds, to crooners like Frank Sinatra and Eddie Fisher, to groups like the Ink Spots and movies that included *Casablanca, Going My Way*, and *The Best Years of Our Lives*. Radios carried such widely listened to programs as *Arthur Godfrey, Twenty Questions*, and *The Lux Radio Theater*.

The post-1945 years were a time marked by social instability and economic uncertainty as the country attempted to return to normal. The arrival of the H-bomb in 1952 brought with it a Cold War that kept nerves frayed. Consumers were introduced to Minute Rice, Tupperware, disposable diapers, the hula hoop, and *Playboy*. Young people were introduced to rock 'n' roll, complete with Elvis Presley, the Platters, Buddy Holly, and the Everly Brothers, whom they listened to on 78s, 45s, and 33 LPs. Television, in glorious black and white, began to take off in Canada in the '50s, providing such popular offerings as *Father Knows Best, I Love Lucy, The Ed Sullivan Show, Dragnet, The Plouffe Family*, and the CBC's national news and *Hockey Night in Canada* — minus the first period! This cohort has been described as coming of age too late to be war heroes and too early to be free spirits, whose surge to power coincided with fragmenting families, cultural diversity, and institutional complexity.[4] Prior to their emergence as adults, many knew a world close to that depicted in the popular film *Peggy Sue Got Married* and, more recently, *Pleasantville*. Seen through the eyes of today's youth, this era was formal but nice, structured but safe.[5]

Other adults in teens' lives today are a bit younger than most of their parents — essentially "Generation X" sisters and brothers, aunts and uncles, teachers and acquaintances who are now 20 to 35, born between 1965 and 1980. These people were teenagers in the '80s and

---

Life for People Born before 1945

You were born before television, before penicillin, before polio shots, frozen foods, Xerox, contact lenses, Frisbees, and the Pill. You were born before radar, credit cards, split atoms, laser beams, and ballpoint pens. You were born before panty hose, dishwashers, clothes dryers, electric blankets, air conditioners, drip-dry clothes, and before man walked on the moon. Fast food, pizza, Kentucky Fried Chicken, and instant coffee were unheard of. You were before househusbands, gay rights, computer dating, dual careers, nursing homes, FM radio, artificial hearts, and yogurt.

You got married first and then lived together. Closets were for clothes. Bunnies were small rabbits and rabbits were not Volkswagens. You were not before differences between the sexes was discovered, but you were before the sex change; you made do with what you had. And you were the last generation to think you needed a husband to have a baby.

Time-sharing meant togetherness, not jobs or condominiums; a "chip" meant a piece of wood; hardware meant hardware, and software wasn't even a word. You hit the scene when five and ten–cent stores sold things for five and ten cents. Cigarette smoking was fashionable, grass was mowed. Coke was a cold drink, pot was something you cooked in. Rock music was a grandma's lullaby and aides were helpers in the principal's office. But you survived. What more reason do you need to celebrate?[6]

'90s and consequently were part of our national surveys of teens in 1984 and 1992. Many were in at least junior high school when the Charter of Rights and Freedoms came into being in 1982, and a good number were high school students during the Meech Lake and national referendum unity crises of the early '90s. The younger Xers have been sharing increasingly in the so-called Information Society, with those under 30 particularly exposed to the high-tech revolution, complete with the Internet.

The Xers who were teens in the '80s were commonly using Walkmans and ghetto-blasters and tuning in to MuchMusic to listen to and watch Michael Jackson, ACDC, Madonna, and Bruce Springsteen. They sat with friends watching *Raging Bull, A Fish Called Wanda,* and any number of *Rocky* and *Friday the 13th* installments — frequently on video. Their television favourites included *Dallas, Cheers, Miami Vice,* and *Married with Children.* Younger adults who were teens a decade later in the '90s were often catching movies like *The Silence of the Lambs, Pulp Fiction,* and *Titanic,* and enjoying *Beverly Hills 90210, ER,* and *Friends* on television; in Quebec, *Chambre en Ville* was particularly popular. Their favourite CDs included music by Guns 'n' Roses, Bryan Adams, Sheryl Crow, and an array of rap and hip-hop artists such as L.L. Cool J, with video channels like MuchMusic now a normal part of their entertainment lives. They watched the Blue Jays win two world series in 1992 and 1993, saw Wayne Gretzky finish out his career, and were big Michael Jordan fans even before the Raptors and Grizzlies arrived on the Canadian sports scene in 1995. Increasingly they were being wooed by the heavily marketed NFL, while the CFL struggled with expansion to the U.S. and stabilizing its own future.

In the course of carrying out the new **Project Canada 2000** national survey, we asked Canadian adults a number of questions about life when they were teenagers, how they think they have changed since they were teens, and how they view today's teens. A 17-year-old male from Toronto commented at the end of his youth questionnaire, "I believe questions like these should be introduced not only to teens but to adults, to see what they think as well." We've done just that, asking the nation's adults many of the same questions about their attitudes, beliefs, and values that we put to teens in our **Project Teen Canada 2000** survey. Consequently we can compare the thoughts and behaviour of today's young people with those "teenagers from yesterday" — adults.

A quick methodological note to eliminate some possible confusion. In what follows, I am taking the liberty of describing the three adults' age cohorts of (1) 36 to 55, (2) 56 and over, and (3) 35 and under as "parents," "grandparents," and "younger adults," respectively; in generational language they correspond closely to the Boomer, Silent, and X generations. The matches are not perfect; obviously not everyone who is 40 to 55 is a parent and there are both "non-grandparents" and some great-grandparents among people over 55. And heaven knows the cutting points, for generational analyses, tend to slip and slide from writer to writer. But naming the three age cohorts, rather than listing ages or using only generational names, will give readers a clearer sense of whom we are talking about when we are comparing the thoughts of Canadian adults and teenagers. We'll intersperse age and generational lingo for variety's sake, but hope to keep things clear.

Now to the findings. We've learned a lot.

Intergroup Relations, School, and Violence

As all of us are well aware, consternation about teenagers is often accompanied by the claim that "life was different when I was a teenager." Presumably *different* also usually means *better.* What was life really like for today's parents, grandparents, and younger adults? Was it actually any better?

An 81-year-old woman who has lived in Newfoundland all her life helps set the stage for this recollective look at "teens past" with these succinct thoughts about life "back then":

> In the '20s and '30s Newfoundland's population was made up of people of English, Irish, and French descent. Discrimination was not common at all except between religious groups — Catholics and Protestants. Religion, prayer, and morals were taught in all schools. Parents, teachers, and clergy were very strict. Skipping school, fighting and violence were not common at all. During the "Depression," people were very poor, alcohol was scarce, gangs and drugs, except for cigarettes, were unheard of.

Here's what others had to say.

To begin with, more than half of today's adults acknowledge that **discrimination** against classmates was common when they were teenagers, with levels ranging from about 35% for grandparents to 70% for younger adults. However, **interracial dating**, according to these three generations, was fairly rare among young people until about the 1980s. One respondent in his 60s notes that such dating was "not common because there were so few people of different races."

One in four grandparents say that **skipping school** was "very common" or "fairly common" when they were teenagers. In contrast, more than two in four parents and three in four younger adults maintain the practice was prevalent during their teen years.

School fighting and violence, delinquency, and gangs are acknowledged to have been part of the lives of each generation. But their incidence, according to adults, has been increasing. About 25% of grandparents and 40% of parents say fighting at school was common when they were teenagers. Yet only 5% of grandparents and 13% of parents maintain that violence in schools was a common problem during their student days. In the case of younger adults who were in school in the '80s and '90s, 50% say fighting was widespread, and about 25% say the same about violence.

Some people, older and younger, equated and presumably continue to equate fighting with violence. Others obviously have not, perhaps because fighting at school did not involve weapons and therefore was not considered violence. One 52-year-old woman who now lives in Ottawa and works in social services recalls that fighting at school was very common when she was a teenager. But, she says, "Boys socialized by fighting. It was important. I'm not talking about bad fights but kids' fights. They weren't serious."

Such differentiation between "fighting" and "violence" does not seem to be in vogue today. Indeed, teasing and bullying increasingly have been viewed as inappropriate kinds of behaviour that can both lead to violence and in and of themselves represent aggressive and, in fact, violent acts. Students who have to live in daily fear or with daily stigma are seen by many as victims of violence.

And some want retribution. In the fall of 2000, 20-year-old Azmi Jubran made national news for asking a B.C. human rights tribunal to have the North Vancouver school district compensate him for some $100,000. He maintained he was bullied in high school to the extent he was unable to study, plan a career, or join school sports teams. He argued that the school district failed to protect him from the taunts and attacks of fellow students who thought he was gay, even though the district knew about the constant harassment.[7] Life has changed.

Table 6.1. **Recollection of Select Behaviour: Grandparents, Parents, and Younger Adults**

"Looking back to when you were a teenager (15 to 19), how common do you think the following were among young people at that time?"

% Indicating "Very Common" or "Fairly Common"

Teens in ...	ALL [1,120]	GRANDPARENTS [255] '40s & '50s	PARENTS [504] '60s & '70s	YOUNGER ADULTS [361] '80s & '90s
Discrimination against some classmates	56%	36	58	68
Dating between people of different races	29	13	21	50
Skipping school	57	23	55	82
Fighting at school	41	26	41	50
Juvenile delinquency	37	16	34	56
Gangs	21	15	18	29
Violence in schools	15	5	13	24
Suicide	8	2	8	13

As they look back to when they were teenagers, about one in seven grandparents say **juvenile delinquency** was common among their friends and acquaintances. In contrast, one in three parents and more than one in two younger adults say the same thing.

Gangs, as they remember things, were present but relatively rare during the teen years of grandparents (15%), parents (18%), and even younger adults (29%). The publicity gangs have received from the media seems to have been disproportionate to their actual prevalence.

Suicide among friends and acquaintances was almost unheard of when grandparents were teenagers and was also, as far as parents can recall, very uncommon when they were teens in the '60s and '70s. A slightly higher proportion of younger adults maintain that suicide was common when they were teens in the '80s and '90s.

It's difficult to corroborate such reports. But you readers are "walking data." You need to ask to what extent you recognize yourself in what people of various ages are saying, and, where possible, of course, we will try to compare the reports with actual "hard" data.

Kids in the mid-'60s

Vancouver Sun, Douglas Todd, June 25, 1994 — *I can still see the flames raving madly into the night sky. Halloween night, 1966: North Vancouver's Mountain Highway was on fire.*

A couple of Lynn Valley teenagers had poured gallons of gasoline onto the pavement and set it alight. Cheers rose from some in the mob of 200. Teenagers nearby threw beer bottles at passing cars. Someone I knew broke the plate-glass window of a Lynn Valley hardware store and hauled out a rifle.

I was 13 years old. I didn't throw a bottle or loot a store during the infamous North Vancouver riots. But I watched them unfold with a mixture of disgust and excitement. I didn't try to stop anyone from vandalizing. I was no hero.

The next day everyone asked: What's the matter with kids today?

Has **discrimination** against classmates been increasing? Maybe, maybe not. Certainly social awareness of discrimination has become increasingly heightened in a multicultural and zero-tolerance-oriented Canada. At the same time, the **Project Canada** national adult surveys charting intergroup attitudes from 1975 through the present have found a general pattern of growing tolerance and acceptance of racial minorities, including increases in the approval of racial intermarriage.[8] This latter finding is consistent with the greater prevalence of interracial dating reported by younger adults.

Truancy levels, fighting at schools, the presence of gangs, and even school violence are realities that have not been accompanied by particularly good record-keeping. Anecdotes, generalizations, and dogmatic declarations abound. But good reliable data are scarce. James Garbarino of Cornell University, for example, says, "When I talk with American teachers who have been in the field since the 1950s, I often ask them to identify the kinds of discipline problems they used to face." In response, "here's what they come up with: gum chewing, talking back, disorder in the halls, making a mess in the classroom, dress-code violations, and being noisy." These days, he says, when teachers are asked the same question, "their lists read like a police blotter: violence against self and others, substance abuse, robbery, and sexual victimization. Things have changed."[9]

Do his observations for the U.S., where violence rates are much higher than in Canada, apply to this country? Here you as a reader need to ask yourself to what extent you recognize yourself in what the "experts" are saying, as well as in the recollections of our adult respondents of various ages.

Our problem with charting long-term youth violence trends is that such activity, which is always extremely difficult to quantify, is almost impossible to track before the mid-'80s using existing records. Through that time, "offending" young people under the age of 16 were treated as delinquents, dating back to the *Juvenile Delinquency Act* of 1908. Delinquency encompassed not only adult crimes in the Criminal Code but a wide variety of other activities such as truancy, sexual immorality, and being uncontrollable. The *Young Offenders Act* of 1982, effective two years later, confined delinquency to federal offences and to young people 12 to 18. The changes in definitions and ages, added to the problems of what counts as an offence (being found out, being charged, or being found guilty) and who does the counting (the police, the courts, or the public through victimization surveys), make it very difficult to have confidence in existing statistical records.

That said, social historian D. Owen Carrigan of Saint Mary's University in Halifax helps to shed some light on what has been happening. In his recent book *Juvenile Delinquency in Canada: A History*, he carefully digs through the available statistics going back to the 1860s, and interprets the data in light of extensive additional qualitative information. His conclusion is consistent with what adults have been telling us: "The combination of police and court reports, special studies, observations of youth workers and teachers, and media reports can leave little doubt that youth crime has risen in recent decades." He notes that while the bulk of offences continue to be minor in nature, there is a significant increase in violence that includes females, gangs, and swarmings. School violence, Carrigan maintains, is more than the product of heightened sensitivity and zero tolerance policies. "Such views," he says "do not square with the evidence." He argues, "While it is true that much of the violence consists of the traditional schoolyard altercations, a trend to more serious confrontations is evident," complete with weapons. The president of the Nova Scotia Teachers Union, whom he interviewed in 1996, summed up the trends this way: "Our classrooms are vastly different places than they were even in the 1960s and 1970s, with our teachers and students often coping with unacceptable levels of violence." Carrigan offers this final observation:

> [T]here has been a trend towards less respect for authority and a lack of ethics and values. It appears that the cultural revolution that attacked many conventions of civility, along with the destabilizing influences of divorce and the diminution of parenting time as more parents worked or were single parents, has produced an increasing number of young people who are angry and disdainful of authority.[10]

Thanks to Statistics Canada, we do have some reliable "hard" trend data on **suicide**. Here what adults recall is very consistent with what StatsCan tells us has been taking place. There has been a noteworthy increase in suicide rates from the 1950s through the '70s to the '90s, corresponding to the approximate decades when today's grandparents, parents, and young adults respectively were teenagers. Such corroboration

The "Hard Data" on Suicide
Rates per 100,000 Youth under 18

	All	Males	Females
1950s	1.8	2.6	1.0
1970s	7.9	12.7	3.1
1990s	14.6	22.7	6.5

Source: Statistics Canada, 1951, 1971, 1991.

of what adults recall should give us reason to at least take seriously what they are reporting about the period of time when they were teenagers. They are not all reporting through the same rose-coloured glasses.

Allowing for changes in social standards, which in turn have strongly influenced social perception, there nonetheless appears to have been significant intergenerational increases in almost all of these activities we have considered so far.

Drugs, Sex, and Physical Abuse

A comparison of the recollections of their teen years by grandparents, parents, and younger adults suggests there have been across-the-board increases over time in the incidence of drug use, sexual activity, sexually transmitted diseases, sexual harassment, and physical abuse by parents. Physical abuse by teachers and principals, however, has declined.

A solid majority of parents and other adults acknowledge that **cigarette smoking** was common when they were teenagers, but the levels are higher as we move toward the present. In addition, some four in ten grandparents say their teenage friends and acquaintances commonly drank **alcohol**, compared to seven in ten parents, and eight in ten younger adults.

Only one in 25 grandparents maintain that the use of **other drugs** besides nicotine and alcohol were "very common" or "fairly common" when they were going through their teens in the '40s and '50s. In sharp contrast, one in two parent Boomers acknowledge that such drug use was common among their peers in the '60s and '70s, as do three in four Gen Xers, who were teens in the '80s and '90s. In light of the apparent increase, former prime minister Brian Mulroney was among those pressing panic buttons, proclaiming in 1986, "Drug abuse has become an epidemic which undermines our economic as well as our social fabric." His statement, made the same night former president Ronald Reagan and his wife, Nancy, launched their anti-drug crusade in the U.S., caught many experts on drugs by surprise.[11]

Another of my fast footnotes: about 60% of Boomers in the U.S. say they smoked pot at some point in their lives, a figure that drug officials in Alberta tell me is probably higher than that of Boomers in Canada, but not by much. What hopefully is *not* transferable to here?

A recent survey of teens receiving drug treatment in New York, Texas, Florida, and California found that 20% of teenagers had used drugs with their parents, and 5% were actually introduced to drugs — usually marijuana — by their own dads and moms.[12]

Generally speaking, the so-called hard data, such as are available, are fairly consistent with the drug recollections of grandparents, parents, and Gen Xers:

- Statistics Canada tells us that *smoking levels* among 15- to 19-year-olds in Canada dropped from about 35% to 25% between the late '60s and early '90s, in large part because of health concerns.[13] However, in the early '90s, smoking increased to close to 30% among both males and females, and has remained around that level ever since.[14] These patterns are consistent with what similar numbers of Boomers and Gen Xers are recalling about the prevalence of smoking when they themselves were teens. The lower level of smoking reported by grandparents is understandable; surveys document what people living in the '40s and '50s knew well — that this was still a time when smoking carried considerable stigma for women. It obviously affected the overall smoking level. With due respect to my beloved ma of 82 and some of her younger friends in their 70s, you don't see too many elderly women reaching for their cigarettes.

- *Alcohol consumption* among parents who were younger Boomer teens in the '70s was running about 75%,[15] similar to slightly lower than levels for Gen X 15- to 19-year-olds a decade or so later.[16] Again, this is consistent with what these two cohorts recalled. No, I didn't forget to check out the imbibing tendencies of grandparents when they were teens. A Gallup poll in 1950 of Canadian adults — meaning *their* grandparents, parents, and those of "them" who had reached 20 to 25 — found alcohol use at 67% for people 20 to 30, similar to the figure for adults who were older.[17] Now follow this carefully: a modest extrapolation suggests the 67% level of drinkers for people in their 20s was probably higher than the level for 15- to 19-year-olds at the time, but it wasn't any lower. That's my acrobatic way of saying that "grandparent teens" back then were not matching the 75% to 80% levels of Boomer offspring and grandchild Xers. (Not bad use of old data, eh!)

- It's generally accepted by experts in the field that **illicit drug use** in Canada accelerated in the '60s and peaked in the '70s, and then declined through the end of the '80s.[18] Mary Wiens of the Addiction Research Foundation in Toronto, in reflecting on the trends from the vantage point of 1992, assessed things bluntly: "There never was an epidemic, despite what Mulroney said."[19] However, it also is recognized that marijuana use has increased in the '90s, undoubtedly contributing to Gen Xers' feeling that drug use was common when they were in their teens. Here's my chance, with the help of another old Gallup poll, to make amends for undermining your confidence in my reasoning abilities a few lines back. Yes, they popped *the* question: in the spring of 1970, face-to-face no less, Gallup's interviewers asked Canadians, "Have you yourself ever happened to try marijuana?" Just 8% of the people of Boomer age said yes. But that was twice the national total of 4% that included their Silent Generation parents. Moreover, another 13% of the people in the Boomer cohort said they would be willing to try marijuana if a friend or acquaintance offered it to them, compared to just 8% nationally.[20] Again, these findings lend credence to the general consistency of the recollection accounts.

Table 6.2. Recollection of Drugs, Sex, and Abuse: Grandparents, Parents, and Younger Adults

"Looking back to when you were a teenager (15 to 19), how common do you think the following were among young people at that time?"

% Indicating "Very Common" or "Fairly Common"

Teens in . . .	ALL	GRANDPARENTS '40s & '50s	PARENTS '60s & '70s	YOUNGER ADULTS '80s & '90s
Cigarette smoking	86%	70	89	92
Alcohol use	67	40	71	80
Other drug use	46	4	48	73
Sexual involvement	61	21	63	85
Sexually transmitted diseases	16	4	18	21
Sexual harassment	29	18	35	27
Physical abuse by parents	28	21	33	25
Physical abuse by teachers/principals	21	23	27	12

More than 60% of the parents of today's teens recall that **sexual involvement** at the time of the sexual revolution and in the ensuing decade was common among their young peers. By way of comparison, only about 20% of older Canadians who were teenagers in the 1940s and '50s sensed that sexual involvement was common among young people at that time. Four times as many younger adults — 85% — maintain that teens in the '80s and '90s were commonly engaging in sex. In part reflecting both activity and subsequent medical responses, about two in ten Boomer parents and younger adults say STDs were fairly prevalent when they were teenagers, compared to only one in 25 grandparents.

Sound behavioural data on sexual activity are hard to come by. What we do know for sure is that some 90% of 18- to-34-year-olds approved of premarital sex in 1975, in contrast to 65% for those 35 to 54, and just under 45% for adults 55 and older. By 1995 the approval levels for the new round of these three age groups were approximately 90%, 80%, and 60%, respectively. As younger people moved into these age categories and older Canadians passed on, a general increase in the national acceptance of sex outside marriage occurred — a jump from 68% to 80% between 1975 and 1995.[21] It therefore would be expected that sexual activity also increased among teens who lived in the post-'50s. But with the sexual revolution over by the end of the '60s, behaviour, as with attitudes, would be expected to level off at a new high. That seems to be what adults are "recalling."

A related reality has been the increase in STDs among teenagers and young adults, most notably herpes and chlamydia, incidences of which escalated dramatically from the 1980s onward. Reported cases of syphilis actually peaked in 1945 and declined thereafter, while the gonorrhea levels of the late '40s were matched only by new highs in the mid-'70s and early '80s.[22] Here again the "hard data" on STDs are generally consistent with the recollections grandparents, parents, and Xers have of their teen years.

Approximately 30% of adults, led by parents and younger adults, report that **sexual harassment** was common when they were teens. But here the recollection pattern is curvilinear — low for grandparents (18%), high for parents (35%), and lower for younger adults (27%). What seems to be reflected here is a combination of awareness and response. Physical and verbal behaviour that frequently was taken for granted in earlier days came to be defined in sexual harassment terms during the '60s and thereafter, and viewed as unacceptable. By the '80s and '90s, such behaviour was seen as less common than two decades earlier.

A similar pattern of recollection is found with **physical abuse**. Reports of parental physical abuse during the teen years are higher among parents than either grandparents or younger adults. These relative differences should not obscure the fact that one in five grandparents maintain that parental abuse was common when they were teenagers in the '40s and '50s, compared to about one in three parents and one in four younger adults.

An intriguing Gallup poll released in early 1955 asked adults the question that we modified and included in our two surveys in 2000: "Looking back to when you were a teenager yourself, what kinds of punishment seem to work best on children your age who refused to behave?" No less than 30% of respondents said, "a whipping"; it was the number-one form of discipline cited. The poll release included findings for the U.S.; there "a whipping" was also the response most commonly cited, noted by 40% of Americans.[23] The Canadian poll also found that 8% of adults felt children should be spanked as long as is needed, while another 20% approved of their being spanked until the age of 16. Only 8% told interviewers that they didn't believe in spanking.[24]

But it's largely a matter of definition. Five years later, in June of 1960, eight in ten Canadians told Gallup they felt their parents had found a good balance between being too strict and too lenient with them. Just over one in ten felt they had been too strict, under one in ten that they had been too lenient. Differences in the perception of how they had been handled differed little for those under 30 and those over 50![25]

Most of us, when we think back to the physical discipline that some parents used on teens we knew, would probably interpret "abuse" by parents to refer to the use of belts, wooden paddles, and the like. Sometimes — sadly — we were aware of more vicious methods of discipline used, including kicking and punching.

The fact that reports of physical abuse by parents have declined somewhat between generations should not obscure the finding that one in four younger adults, recalling teen years as recent as the '80s and

'90s, are saying that physical abuse by parents was common among their friends and acquaintances. Perhaps such perception reflects changes in standards and tolerance; regardless, for that many people to say physical abuse of teenagers by parents was common is very disconcerting. Less troubling are the reports Gen Xers and others provide when asked, "Which of these responses did you tend to experience most when *you* were a teenager?" They had just been asked about the appropriateness and effectiveness of taking away privileges, being grounded, being "given a good talking to," physical discipline, and a discussion without discipline. Around 15% of grandparents and somewhat smaller numbers of parents and Xers say that physical discipline was dominant.

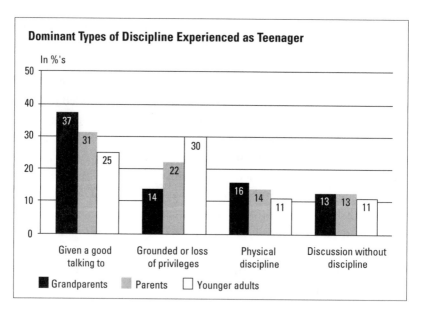

The memories of **school abuse** are a bit different. Parents (27%), followed by grandparents (23%), are *more inclined* than younger adults (12%) to report that physical abuse of young people by school personnel was common when they were teenagers. Prior to the 1980s, of course, school personnel could and often did use "the strap" to discipline students. One 81-year-old who now lives in Vancouver recalls how, as a teen growing up in England, "I used to be caned." He adds, "Our upbringing was strict but loving. Respect was ingrained in us by our parents."

The Strap

It was an event that one doesn't forget, long after it happened. Not because it hurt all that much, or was psychologically damaging. No, more than anything, at the time it was just sort of embarrassing, in part because it was so unexpected. After all, we were just laughing. And we were just kids.

Replayed through the eyes of now, I suppose it bordered on abusive behaviour. But that's not how any of us saw it back then, including my friends, my brother and sisters, my mom and dad. It was just something that was part of school life, spliced in amidst classes, recess, phys-ed, packed lunches, tests, Christmas plays, and passing. We all knew about it. When someone was sent to the principal's office, we would wonder among ourselves whether or not it would happen, and when the person came back to our home room, we'd whisper, "Did you get the . . . ?" But it was something that happened to people who acted up, the bad kids, not kids like me.

There we were, my friend and I, laughing to ourselves in class like we often did, about something so trivial it has long since disappeared from my memory bank. He was a happy funny guy who had all kinds of energy. We talked and laughed a lot that year. It made things less boring. Of course we kept it down. We had to. I don't remember much about our homeroom teacher, just that she really yelled a lot, almost every day. We never knew what she was so mad about all the time.

I remember her stopping what she was saying to everyone and, looking straight at the two of us, bellowing, "You two get down the principal's office right now!" We were startled; she usually made us stand in a corner or write lines after class. We awkwardly headed out of the portable annex into the main building and into the principal's office. He turned his swivel chair around from his desk and spoke very calmly with us, asking us what had happened, how we felt about it, and we apologized. We were relieved.

Just as we were about to leave, without saying anything, he calmly reached down, and, in full view, opened the bottom drawer of his desk, pausing as if to add to the drama. I see it vividly right now, even after all these years, brown and wide and furled neatly, as if it were taking a breather from battle. He picked it up, asked us to hold out our hands, and then he did it: he gave us both the strap — I'm not sure how many times on each hand, because I wasn't counting them up; I was just hoping the last one would be the last one. I think it was maybe three on each hand, maybe five. I was in grade two. It never happened again.

From the author's own biography

Growing up in Edmonton, I have vivid memories of the strap being used regularly on students, almost always male. In junior high, one homeroom teacher would tell a student to step into the hallway, then go over to his desk, and march out of the room, strap in hand. One student in particular that year seemed to always be summoned into the hall. I was never sure why.

A 64-year-old who also lives on the West Coast illustrates the ambiguity older Canadians have in interpreting school discipline. Asked how common physical abuse by teachers or principals was when he was a teenager, he says, "Fairly common if you are considering getting the strap physical abuse, uncommon otherwise." A 66-year-old who lives in Victoria says that physical abuse at school was not very common, adding, "A strap was used occasionally, but it was a penalty, not *abuse*." One older Boomer parent who now lives in southern Alberta says that when he was a teenager in the 1960s, "strapping was still allowed but was seldom used." The times were finally changing.

Their Perception of Teenagers

As part of our comparison of adults and young people, we asked adults for their perception of the importance today's teens place on a number of values. It should be pointed out that some, especially older respondents, indicated that they could offer only crude estimates. As one 63-year-old from Vancouver put it, "I would have to learn more and talk with teenagers to properly answer the question"; nonetheless, most offered their perceptions of teen values. Others, of course, have teenagers, and to varying degrees are also in occupations where they have considerable exposure to teenagers. For example, one 48-year-old Boomer from Saskatchewan who is both a parent of teenagers and a nurse offered the following observation:

> In my field, I see a lot of young people taking drugs, drinking an excessive amount of alcohol and trying and sometimes succeeding in committing suicide. I think the younger generation is going to have to be taught that life is hard sometimes and things do not always go your way. When they don't, you have to keeping trying — not give up or turn to drugs or alcohol.

Another Boomer, a 47-year-old daycare teacher from Toronto, who has had two teenagers of her own, commented:

> Being in the education field, I am very concerned about youth in general. I think schools, starting at the elementary level, should be more strict. Uniforms should be worn in all schools. It could be a way to control and teach discipline to teenagers.

And a third Boomer, a 49-year-old Ontario property manager, has a particularly unique background for assessing teens. She had this to say:

> I left school when I was 16 years old. I returned to regular high school in 1994–95. I saw a great change in the school system and in today's youth. Young people today have lost their will to fight for their rights or their convictions. They seem to follow the crowd and go with the flow. They do not question anything. They have not been taught respect, manners, or how to use common sense.

Pretty strong stuff. They are not, however, isolated thoughts.

When parents and grandparents think of today's teenagers, they are inclined to think that their foremost values are freedom and excitement, followed by being loved, friendship, and their appearance. Younger adults hold pretty much the same views of teens' values.

Table 6.3. How Grandparents, Parents, and Younger Adults View Teenagers
"When you think of TEENAGERS TODAY who are about 15 to 19...
HOW IMPORTANT do you think these traits tend to be TO THEM?"

% Indicating "Very Important"

	All	Grandparents (55 & older)	Parents (40–55)	Younger adults (20–39)
Freedom	80%	78	77	86
Excitement	77	73	77	80
Being loved	65	66	69	60
Friendship	65	50	66	75
Their appearance	61	39	61	77
Humour	46	35	47	53
Honesty	21	27	21	16
Cleanliness	19	22	19	17
What parents think of them	15	22	14	10
Family life	13	19	15	6
Concern for others	12	16	14	8
Politeness	9	12	10	6
Working hard	7	11	7	4
Spirituality	5	6	5	5
Religion	3	5	2	2

- Perhaps surprisingly, only about one in three grandparents and one in two parents and younger adults think humour is "very important" to teenagers.
- Only one-quarter or less think teens place high value on honesty, and a mere 10% or so see them placing a high level of importance on concern for others and politeness.
- Just 15% of adults think that family life or their parents' opinions of them are "very important" to young people.
- Less than 10% believe that young people place high value on working hard.
- Only a very small percentage of adults think teenagers regard either spirituality or religion as extremely important.

It's hard to believe that parents, grandparents, and even younger adults can be so badly out of touch with the basic values of teenagers. Then again, the national youth survey shows that teens are not exactly reading adults' values clearly, either.

A comparison of the perceived and actual importance that teens and adults place on honesty, family life, concern for others, and spirituality, for example, shows that, yes, adults dramatically underestimate the importance that teenagers place on all four traits. However, in turn, adults are inclined to value these four characteristics far more than young people think they do. The good news here is that teenagers and adults have much in common — the infamous "generation gap" has been oversold. The bad news is that most people, younger and older, aren't aware of it.

This "sneak preview" on value similarities provides a hint of what is to come.

Table 6.4. **The Values Intergenerational Gap**

% Indicating They Think These Values Are "Very Important"

| | TEENS | | ADULTS | |
	Perceived	Actual	Perceived	Actual
Honesty	21%	73	37	92
Family life	13	59	47	85
Concern for others	12	62	30	71
Spirituality	5	29	15	34

What I want to do now is take a look at how those teens of yesterday — grandparents of the '40s and '50s, Boomer parents of the '60s and '70s, and Gen Xers of the '80s and '90s — in present-day form compare with present-day teens.

Grown-Up Teens and Today's Teens

Apart from perception, how do today's teenagers actually stack up compared to those particularly sensitive and sometimes critical teenagers of the past — today's parents, grandparents, and other adults? **Put another way, how is today's emerging generation of teens turning out compared to Boomers' Parents, Boomers, and Generation X?** As I indicated earlier, we have run many of the teen items in the adult survey for 2000. I don't want to put readers to sleep by going into excessive comparative detail. What follows are some finding highlights in the main areas of life that we have been examining so far.

Values

Teens and adults differ little in the importance they give to *freedom* and *being loved.* However, **in the course of pursuing love, adults give priority to family life over friendship, whereas teens give priority to friendship over family life.** Accordingly, only about 45% of young people claim what their parents think of them is "very important." However, more than 70% of adults say what their children think of *them* carries the same weight. Among adults, more Xers than others place high value on being loved, as well as what their young children think of them.

Higher proportions of teenagers than adults endorse *a comfortable life* and especially *success.* That's hardly surprising in view of the fact that young people are still in the early stages of pursuing both goals versus having attained them or realized they are not going to attain them, and therefore being in a position to redefine their importance. The same argument would seem to account for why teens are also somewhat more inclined than adults to see *having power* as significant. Among adults, differences in the importance of these three traits are fairly small.

Similar proportions of adults and teenagers place importance on such diverse values *as concern for others, recognition,* and *spirituality.*

Table 6.5. **Valued Goals across Generations**

% Indicating "Very Important"

	ADULTS	TEENS	Grandparents	Parents	Yg adults
Freedom	89%	85	89	90	88
Family life	85	59	87	85	83
Being loved	84	77	77	83	90
Friendship	78	85	79	78	79
What children/parents think of you	72	44	68	70	79
Concern for others	71	62	72	71	70
A comfortable life	64	73	62	61	68
Success in what you do	49	71	50	50	48
Recognition	34	32	28	35	36
Spirituality	34	29	41	33	29
Excitement	29	57	19	26	43
Religion/group involvement	21	10	34	20	10
Having power	8	24	8	8	6

* In this and subsequent tables, the adult totals refer to all Canadian adults, including those older than "grandparents" in the tables (i.e., over the age of 75). Also, shaded areas indicate differences of more than 10 percentage points.

The surveys also show that 43% of adults place a high value on their *appearance*, while 39% of teens place similar value on their *looks*. Hmm, interesting, given the inclination of adults to think that teens are not particularly compassionate, are preoccupied with their looks, and are not all that interested in spirituality. . . . Adults are somewhat more likely than teens to maintain that *religion* is "very important," and considerably less likely to say the same about *excitement*. Differences between adult generations are worth noting. Xers, similar to teens, are somewhat less interested in spirituality and particularly less interested in religion than older adults. They also are quite a bit more likely than parents and grandparents to value excitement; the importance of excitement, it seems, drops off markedly with age.

Incidentally, the intergenerational importance on looks and appearance, regardless of performance, claims a wide range of victims. In 2000 one of the more interesting was star pitcher David Wells, then of the Toronto Blue Jays, who was taken to task for being too fat in an article in *Sports Illustrated*. Despite his ability, over his career he has had an array of players, trainers, managers, owners, and writers who, in the words of a *Globe and Mail* editorial writer, "have tried to make the great David Wells the great and thin David Wells, because they associate being fit and trim with being a stellar athlete." Even in sports, "the ultimate democracy, where winning supposedly is all that matters — not race, not body weight, not intelligence, not grace or gracelessness" — people are still expected to look right.[26] Anna Kournikova is not alone!

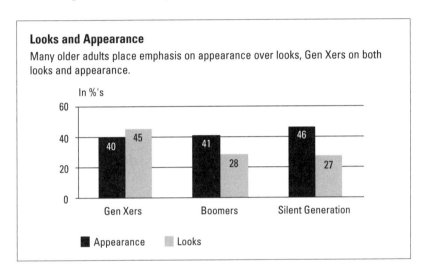

Looks and Appearance
Many older adults place emphasis on appearance over looks, Gen Xers on both looks and appearance.

The values adults seem to get particularly anxious about, as noted early in the book, are those associated with the way young people pursue what they want in life — values like honesty and hard work, along with traits that make for civility, such as politeness. Here the results are mixed:

- More than nine in ten adults say that *honesty* is "very important" to them, compared to just over seven in ten teens. *Politeness* is also regarded as particularly important by a higher proportion of adults, as is *forgiveness.*
- However, differences between adults and teens are fairly small when it comes to the importance they give such varied traits as *humour, cleanliness, working hard, intelligence, creativity,* and *generosity.*
- Differences among adults are generally minor, except for grandparents' being somewhat more likely than others to place importance on politeness and cleanliness.

Table 6.6. **Valued Means across Generations**

% Indicating "Very Important"

	ADULTS	TEENS	Grandparents	Parents	Yg adults
Honesty	92%	73	94	92	89
Politeness	76	58	82	75	73
Humour	71	73	69	75	67
Forgiveness	70	58	73	71	68
Cleanliness	67	64	73	65	63
Working hard	59	52	57	59	64
Intelligence	55	59	54	52	55
Creativity	50	42	47	50	53
Generosity	47	42	50	46	44

The differences in the importance placed on honesty and politeness by adults and teens are borne out when responses to real-life situations are posed. In the situation described earlier— where a clerk accidentally gives a person an extra $10 — adults are considerably more likely than teens to say they would go back and return the money. And even though Gen Xers and parent Boomers are just about as likely as Silent Generation grandparents to say they highly value honesty, Gen Xers in particular are less likely to indicate they would return the $10; one in seven Xers say they simply would "keep the $10 and keep

---

A Peek at Honesty in Action

"A person gives you change for what you have bought. As you walk away, you realize he/she has given you $10 more than you were supposed to receive. Do you think you would be inclined to . . ."

	ADULTS	TEENS	Grandparents	Parents	Yg adults
Go back and return the extra $10.	74%	35	88	78	57
It would depend on factors such as the size of the store, whether you expected to shop there again, and whether or not you knew the salesperson involved.	19	31	11	18	28
Keep the $10 and keep walking.	7	34	1	4	15

walking." One of the Silent Gs from B.C. who said he would give back the $10 commented, "This just happened. I don't want to be short-changed nor do I want to do it to them."

As for courtesy, adults are more likely than teenagers to endorse so-called considerate or "polite" behaviour in the situations examined earlier — parking in a stall for the handicapped, holding a door for a person, walking on a red light, saying "sorry" if accidentally bumping

Table 6.7. **Courtesy-Related Attitudes**

"Do you tend to APPROVE or DISAPPROVE of people who . . ."

		ADULTS	TEENS	Grand-parents	Parents	Younger adults
Park in a handicapped stall when not handicapped	Disapprove	97%	80	98	97	96
Go through a door and hold it for person behind them	Approve	97	89	98	97	97
Walk on a red light and make traffic wait	Disapprove	94	75	97	94	93
Say "sorry" when they accidentally bump into someone	Approve	94	86	96	94	93
Come to a four-way stop and proceed out of turn	Disapprove	91	79	93	93	88
Say "please" when order food at drive-through	Approve	87	73	92	89	78

*Options: Approve, Disapprove, Don't care either way.

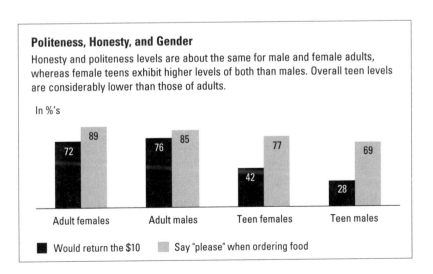

Politeness, Honesty, and Gender
Honesty and politeness levels are about the same for male and female adults, whereas female teens exhibit higher levels of both than males. Overall teen levels are considerably lower than those of adults.

In %'s

Adult females	Adult males	Teen females	Teen males
72 / 89	76 / 85	42 / 77	28 / 69

■ Would return the $10   ▨ Say "please" when ordering food

into someone, proceeding out of turn at an intersection, and saying "please" when ordering food. Younger Generation Xers are less inclined than other adults to care one way or the other about people saying "please" at a fast-food drive-through.

It's important, however, to note that it is not that adults approve of courteous behaviour in such situations and teens do not; large majorities of teenagers *also* endorse polite responses. It's just that somewhat higher proportions of adults than teens express approval of these kinds of courtesies.

Enjoyment and Activities

It's pretty safe to say that many adults and teenagers think their sources of enjoyment are pretty different. That's one of the reasons for the widespread assumption that the various generations don't have much in common. What teens, after all, really think it's possible to "live it up" with Mom or Dad, let alone Grandma or Grandpa? They might entertain the possibility, however, of being able to have a good time with someone a few years older; then again, maybe not. Surprise, kids: most parents, grandparents, and young adults feel pretty much the same.

It consequently is interesting to find that adults and teens tend to get enjoyment from the same general areas of life — notably friends, music, television, sports, and pets. That's hardly an exhaustive list, but it does include most of the primary sources of enjoyment, apart from family members and additional "significant others." All five of these sources tend to be enjoyed by somewhat higher proportions of teens than adults, but they nonetheless are important right across generations. One minor variation exists with pets: contrary to widespread stereotypes, grandparents are a bit less likely than younger generations to be reporting high levels of enjoyment from pets, perhaps in part because they frequently live in places where pets are not permitted. Among adults who actually have pets, almost 80% say they receive a high level of enjoyment from them, regardless of their ages. So much for the excessive tales about "old ladies" with houses full of cats and "old men" who live alone with their dogs. Why is it that there are all those wild stories about people with pets, anyway? Oops, there I go again. Can you tell I've had a few too many animals in my life? Back to serious business.

Table 6.8. **Enjoyment across Generations**

% Indicating Receive "A Great Deal" or "Quite a Bit" of Enjoyment

	ADULTS	TEENS	Grandparents	Parents	Yg adults
Friends	83%	94	84	82	87
Music	77	90	79	76	79
TV	56	60	58	54	55
Pets	46	51	38	50	50
Sports	39	66	36	38	45

To return to my point, adults and teens share similar areas of enjoyment. Their lack of commonality, however, obviously is tied to the different choices they typically make when it comes to the *kinds* of friends, music, television, and sports they enjoy — choices that are heavily generational in nature.

Take music, for example. As we saw earlier, the top three types for today's Millennial teens are rap/hip-hop, alternative, and pop. Generation Xers prefer rock, country, and alternative; parent Boomers like country, rock, and classical; and grandparent Pre-Boomers cite classical, country and, as a distant third, classic oldies rock. Now, as in the past, those preferences don't make for an awful lot of musical commonality. But species and even venues are not dissimilar. *Calgary Sun* writer Bill Kaufmann, writes how a 17-year-old who had attended numerous raves, asked him, "Didn't you attend raves?" Reflecting on the question, he found himself thinking, "Well sort of. They were rented community halls where garage rock bands held court and patrons danced and consumed alcohol and illicit substances. Sometimes the police would be needed at these spirited events, but they rarely made the papers." He recalls that "violence would erupt at some, as it does still at booze-fuelled house parties, but it wasn't the flavour of the month, so little note was taken."[27] From a survey participant in 1984, a 17-year-old from Saskatoon, come these pertinent thoughts:

> *Music plays an important part in my life. I'm really into heavy metal. My parents give me a rough time. Their parents didn't like Elvis or rock 'n' roll when it came out, but they listened to it anyways, and it didn't affect them. Hard rock is being put down by them now, but I don't think it will seriously affect us.*

Table 6.9. **Interest in Pro Sports across Generations**

% Indicating Follow "Very Closely" or "Fairly Closely"

	ADULTS	TEENS	Grandparents	Parents	Yg adults
NHL	30%	34	28	28	35
Figure skating	20	11	34	16	11
ML Baseball	17	17	23	18	11
CFL	15	16	17	13	15
NFL	12	21	11	12	10
NBA	8	30	6	6	11
Pro Wrestling	4	20	3	3	8

A look at interest in pro sports across generations shows that interest in the NHL is steady. Major League Baseball and CFL interest levels are similar for teens and adults, whereas teens are more likely than adults to follow the NFL, and especially the NBA and pro wrestling. Adults are more inclined than young people to be interested in figure skating. Interest in the NFL, NBA, and wrestling drops sharply beyond the teen years, while interest in figure skating and baseball is disproportionately higher among older adults.

In terms of activity, teenagers tend to differ a fair amount from adults, who in turn vary somewhat predictably by age. Two exceptions are TV viewing and computer use.

Majorities of some nine in ten teens and eight in ten adults of all ages watch TV on a daily basis. We adults, incidentally, are watching just about as much television now as our counterparts were in the mid-1970s: in 1975, 33% said they watched more than 15 hours a week, compared to 31% today; those who rarely or never watch TV is 4% now versus 3% then.

Many observers point out that computers are increasingly as familiar to schoolchildren as pencils and papers were to their parents, and frequently depict adults as bumbling and apprehensive about co-opting computer technology. The stereotype is an exaggeration.

• About four in ten of today's alleged computer-savvy Millennials are actually using a computer every day, a level above that of grandparents. But their level of overall computer use is actually below both parents and Gen Xers, while their weekly use of e-mail specifically is slightly above parents but below that of Xers. And it's interesting to note that "pre-postmodern" grandparents are far from computer illiterate: approximately three in ten claim to make daily use of computers; the same proportion use e-mail weekly or more.

- About 85% of teens, 80% of Xers, 75% of parents, and 50% of grandparents reported having access to a computer at home in the year 2000; the figure for Canadians over 75, by the way, was around 15%. Obviously these levels are going to rise. But, for the record, late in 2000 the average daily use looked like this: teens 2.1 hours, all three adult age cohorts almost exactly 1.4 hours each, people over 75 with home computers close behind at 1.3 hours. The technology is there for the taking. And people in all age categories are taking it — that is, if they can get their hands on it. In the words of one 49-year-old from Prince Albert, Saskatchewan, "I'd use the computer more if I could get it away from my son and husband."

Table 6.10. **Activities across Generations**

	ADULTS	TEENS	Grandparents	Parents	Yg adults
Daily					
Watch TV	77%	92	80	78	72
Keep up with news	66	16	85	68	46
Use a computer	46	41	29	51	59
Daily to Weekly					
Use e-mail	50	58	31	53	68
Watch videos at home	30	60	11	28	46
Read books want to read	50	33	57	50	44
Monthly or More Often					
Go to a movie	27	78	16	25	42
Attend a sports event	17	41	14	19	17
Gamble with money	10	21	11	11	6

Not everyone is enthralled with computers and the Internet. Some express alarm about the solitude it may produce. Many are worried about the information being accessed. Parents sometimes are not comfortable with what is taking place on chat lines. As one journalist recently put it, "to parents, the chat-line trend with its unconventional spellings and spicy language, is often a mystery and a little scary."[28] From Nova Scotia, a very reflective retiree of 68, a man of Scots-Irish background, has some words worth pondering regarding the Internet and virtual reality:

I follow the native (Six Nations) way of life and have respect for the land, the water and the sky and all creatures that live within these realms. Too many people are imprisoned in the "electronic village" and tend to live in cyberspace. I try to stay with reality and appreciate making friends of deer, foxes, ravens, etc. Try watching the eagle as it spirals up so far that it fades from sight and leaves your eyes watering. That's the real *thing.*

Seniors join the wired world

The Province (Vancouver), Tony Wanless, September 6, 2000 — *Move over, dot-com kids and 20-somethings, the seniors are coming.*

Recent surveys show seniors are among the largest groups of adopters on the Internet, with increases of more than 100 per cent in usage over last year. Other surveys show not only are seniors taking to the technology, they're using it more — largely because they have the time and inclination.

At Vancouver's West End seniors network, courses in computer and Internet training are routinely filled months in advance. Chief trainer Jack Paterson, who, at 80, is also a de facto computer consult for many West End seniors, notes computers have contributed greatly to his lifestyle and thinking and are doing the same for many other seniors.

While there are similarities in television and computer use between teenagers and adults, differences are also readily apparent.

- Adults of all ages are far more likely than teenagers to be keeping up with the news, suggesting that today's teens may have unprecedented opportunities for knowing what's going on in the world but are not typically utilizing resources like the Internet for that purpose. Also, more adults than teens are reading books they want to read.
- Teens are considerably more likely to be doing such things as watching videos at home, going to movies, and attending sports events. One in five of them are gambling with money at least once a month, compared to just one in ten adults. Gen Xers are not exhibiting such

gambling tendencies, suggesting it may be something most teens "grow out of"; the finding does, however, indicate that large numbers of young people are being socialized to gamble with money.

- As for variations among adults, Xers, and to a lesser extent Boomers, differ from grandparent Pre-Boomers in not being as inclined to follow the news and read books, but more commonly are watching videos at home and going to movies.

Adults worry a great deal about the prevalence of **teen smoking.** The surveys suggest, however, that the proportion of teenagers who smoke frequently is some 23%, very similar to the figures for both their Boomer parents and lower than Gen Xers. All three levels are higher than that of grandparents. In light of parental and younger adult levels, what's perhaps surprising is that adults should be expressing such concern about the smoking level of Millennials.

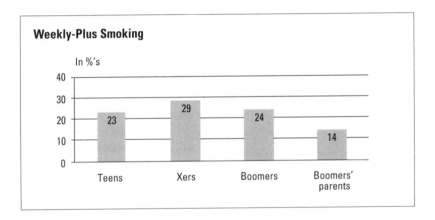

Personal Concerns

The things that tend to trouble adults also tend to trouble teenagers — but they trouble teens more. The rule of thumb is this: personal concerns are inversely related to age, being most prevalent among teenagers, followed by Generation Xers, Boomer parents, and Silent Generation grandparents.

Foremost for adults and teens alike are concerns about not having enough *time and money,* along with worries relating to one's *job* and, in the case of teens, the pressure to do well at *school.* For adults, an additional major concern is *health.*

Table 6.11. **Personal Concerns across Generations**

% Indicating Bothered "A Great Deal" or "Quite a Bit"

	ADULTS	TEENS	Grandparents	Parents	Yg adults
Never have enough time	48%	57	35	52	54
Money	47	53	32	50	57
Health	47	—	48	48	39
Your children/parents*	42	45	43	40	41
Job/school pressure	39	67	19	42	46
My looks	33	45	26	28	45
Your marriage/my parents'	31	27	25	28	39
Wondering purpose life	28	43	23	26	35
Loneliness	27	30	22	21	35
Your sex life/sex	27	26	18	28	35
Getting older	26	—	26	27	24
So many things changing	24	38	25	24	19
Depression	23	29	15	20	31
Boredom	23	42	15	18	31
Feeling not good as others	21	36	10	18	31

* "Not being understood by my parents"

- By now we all know that the *time* problem is not being resolved by technological advances; if anything it seems those advances have simply accelerated expectations and stress. Stats Canada survey data for 1998 show that Canadians are working longer hours, have less leisure time, and are feeling more stressed. One in three people between 25 and 44 describe themselves as "workaholics," and more than half feel they don't have enough time for family and friends.[29] Our current adult survey reveals 81% of Canadians feel there has been an increase in the general pace of life over the past ten years, and 69% say there has been a decrease in the time they have to do the things they want. In addition, 63% maintain they "almost never" have time on their hands that they "don't know what to do with." Even lunch hours, says Caroline Alphonso of the *Globe and Mail*, are passing into oblivion in favour of people eating at desks, if at all — except in Quebec, where people are still taking a little more time to socialize in fine-dining places. She suggests that some unobtrusive measures of such tendencies include sandwich crumbs and beverages that urgently summoned repair types come across in the course of resuscitating incapacitated keyboards, copiers, and the like.[30]

- *School pressure* is a dominant issue for teens, felt by close to seven in ten of them — quite a bit higher than the four in ten Xers and parents who express concern about issues relating to their jobs. Consistent with those findings, 67% of adults who are employed full-time say they are receiving "a great deal" or "quite a bit" of enjoyment from their jobs; just 41% of teens say they are receiving that kind of enjoyment from school.

- *Looks* trouble about the same proportion of Gen Xers as teenagers; concern drops off markedly after that. As one wisecracking 52-year-old male from Alberta put it, "I've had to give this up. Nowadays 'I yam what I yam.'"

- The level of adult concern about their *marriages* is somewhat higher among Xers than others; the adult marriage-concern level (31%) almost matches that of teens who are concerned about their parents' marriages (27%).

- Adults and teens express similar levels of concern about *loneliness, sex,* and *depression.*

- More teens than adults of any age, however, indicate they are troubled by such diverse issues as *the purpose of life, so many things changing,*

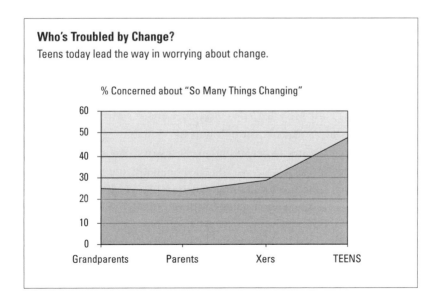

Who's Troubled by Change?
Teens today lead the way in worrying about change.

% Concerned about "So Many Things Changing"

boredom, and feelings of *inferiority*. All but the change issue would seem to reflect life stage rather than unique generational characteristics, especially since they are less prevalent among Millennials' postmodern cohort cousins, Generation Xers. The *change* finding comes as something of a surprise. The endearing words of an 86-year-old woman who lives in London, Ontario, is what the experts expect to hear: "In another fifty years I would be one hundred and thirty-six years of age. If society changes as much as it has in the past twenty, I doubt that I would want to be here." What they have not expected is our finding that she and other adults are actually outnumbered by teens who say they are troubled by so much change.

Social Attitudes

Teenagers and adults hold similar views about many things. They include such far-ranging topics as *multiculturalism*, the importance of the *CBC*, the relative value placed on *cultural heritage*, the inability of *average people* to influence government, the need for Canada to have *global concern*, acceptance of *euthanasia*, views on the legalization of *marijuana*, the perception that *lawbreakers* often are not caught, the right of everyone to *medical care*, opposition to *mandatory retirement* at 65, and support of *equal rights for homosexuals*.

    Teens and adults also have their differences.

- Young people are somewhat more inclined than adults to endorse *bilingualism*, in contrast particularly to their grandparents and, to a lesser extent, their Boomer parents. Teens were less likely than all three adult generations to applaud the performance of *President Bill Clinton* when he was in office and more likely than all three to approve of *Prime Minister Jean Chrétien*. Canada's Millennial Generation does show some occasional signs of being more pro-Canada in practice than its three generational predecessors, particularly outside Quebec. Maybe "Joe Canadian" has not been ranting in vain.

- **Teens show a consistent tendency to be less "hawkish" than all three adult generations.** They are less inclined to endorse *war*, the *death penalty*, or a toughening of the *Young Offenders Act* — although majorities nonetheless are in favour of capital punishment as well as stiffening the youth act. Gen Xers, Boomers, and Boomers' Parents differ little in their attitudes toward all three of these social issues.

Table 6.12. **Cultural and Political Attitudes across Generations**

% Agreeing

	ADULTS	TEENS	Grand-parents	Parents	Younger adults
Culture					
Canada should have TWO official languages — English and French.	60%	73	53	61	66
Canada should be a "melting pot."	28	34	40	30	16
The CBC is important to Canada.	78	68	78	77	77
Being a Canadian is "very important" to me.	58	45	69	54	51
My cultural group heritage is "very important" to me.	17	19	23	15	12
Politics at Home and Abroad					
Clinton is doing a pretty good job as U.S. president.	76	58	79	75	72
Chrétien is doing a pretty good job as Prime Minister.	50	60	47	49	55
Average Canadian does not have any influence in what the govt does.	59	66	64	57	59
War is justified when other ways of settling international disputes fail.	39	29	41	37	41
Need to worry about our own country and let rest of world take care of itself.	37	38	34	34	44

- Young people are far more likely than adults to see the social system as open. As we saw earlier, no fewer than seven in ten say they believe that "*anyone who works hard will rise to the top.*" Fewer than half of the Generation Xers, those fairly recent graduates of the teen ranks, no longer hold such a view. Their level of support for the "work hard–reach top" thesis now essentially matches that of parents and grand-parents. And they still haven't hit 40!
- **Among adults, some generational differences are worth noting.** Grandparents, in numbers similar to teens, are less likely than Boomers and Xers to subscribe to *euthanasia.* However, perhaps surprisingly, this oldest generation of Canadians is somewhat more likely than Millennials, Xers, or Boomers to say that people should

Table 6.13. Legal and Equality Attitudes across Generations

% Agreeing

	ADULTS	TEENS	Grand-parents	Parents	Younger adults
Law and Enforcement					
The *Young Offenders Act* needs to be toughened.	89%	71	90	87	90
Are some circumstances in which a doctor is justified in ending a patient's life?	75	69	67	77	81
The death penalty should sometimes be used to punish criminals.	74	59	76	75	72
The use of marijuana should be legalized.	47	50	34	49	58
People who break the law are almost always caught.	23	26	22	24	18
Equality and Personal Rights					
People who cannot afford it have a right to medical care.	96	92	96	97	96
Anyone who works hard will rise to the top.	49	71	49	51	47
A person should retire at 65, regardless of health.	30	30	34	29	25
Homosexuals are entitled to the same rights as other Canadians.	71	74	59	74	82

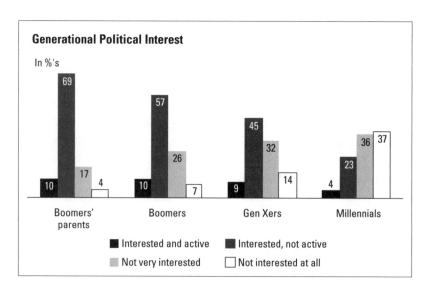

Generational Political Interest

In %'s

Boomers' parents: 10, 69, 17, 4
Boomers: 10, 57, 26, 7
Gen Xers: 9, 45, 32, 14
Millennials: 4, 23, 36, 37

■ Interested and active   ■ Interested, not active
■ Not very interested   ☐ Not interested at all

retire at 65. Gen Xers tend to be the most supportive of legalizing marijuana, as well as of homosexuals having the same rights as other Canadians — followed in order by Millennials and their Boomer parents, and then by Silent Generation grandparents.

One fairly pervasive stereotype of today's teenagers, particularly advocated by some postmodernist and generational analysts, is that Millennials are especially critical of social institutions. It's a pattern, some say, which was emerging with the first postmodern generation, the Xers. The surveys offer little support for such assertions.

Boomers, Boomers' Parents, and Gen Xers are less likely than Millennials to express confidence in *all* institutions, with the sole exception of the police. Adults of all ages are particularly critical of the television, music, and movie industries, along with the federal and provincial governments.

- It is interesting to note how uniform the lack of confidence in institutions is across adult generations. Those who are part of Generation X tend to be no more or no less critical of institutions. The most noticeable exception is religion, where Xers and Boomers are far more critical of leaders than grandparents.

Table 6.14. **Confidence in Institutions across Generations**

% Indicating Have "A Great Deal" or "Quite a Bit"

	ADULTS	TEENS	Grand-parents	Parents	Younger adults
Police	67%	62	70	64	66
Schools	47	63	47	48	43
Computer industry	45	51	46	43	46
Court system	40	52	36	40	41
Newspapers	41	60	42	37	42
Radio	41	48	42	37	41
Major business	37	48	40	35	37
Religious organizations	33	40	43	32	23
Television	29	44	30	29	28
Music industry	27	54	26	25	28
Provincial government	26	41	28	24	23
Federal government	24	41	24	21	23
Movie industry	22	60	18	22	26

- Particularly striking are the confidence gaps between teens and adults in the areas where teenagers have especially close ties — school and the entertainment industries. Young people are far more comfortable with the leadership in these areas "of theirs" than adults.

Family Attitudes

Despite the generally positive findings about the way young people seem to be turning out, adults — regardless of their generation — are inclined to want stricter discipline. To some extent, teens agree. About 85% of adults maintain that discipline in most homes is not strict enough, as do around 55% of teenagers; presumably most teens don't have themselves in mind. As a Boomer parent in Winnipeg with one teenager explains, "What's needed is not physical discipline but more careful parenting."

Table 6.15. **Family Attitudes across Generations**

% Agreeing

	ADULTS	TEENS	Grand-parents	Parents	Younger adults
Discipline in most homes today is not strict enough.	85%	56	88	82	86
It would be a good idea to have a curfew in this community for young people under 16, unless they are out with their parents.	60	29	64	63	52
Natural parents not together when I was 16/not together.	11	28	6	7	21

Further, six in ten of Canada's adults think it would be good to have a curfew for young people under 16 who are not out with their parents. Such a view is shared by only about three in ten teens. What perhaps is most striking here is that those Gen X adults who are 35 and younger now differ so little from older adults. How soon they forget! It seems that the sheer movement out of one's teens and, for many, creating a family of one's own, is accompanied by a fairly dramatic revision of one's views on how children and teenagers should be raised.

As for that discipline issue we talked about in some detail just a few pages ago, teens today say that the most appropriate and effective way for parents to respond to what they see as inappropriate behaviour is by talking to them or taking away privileges. Adults tend to concur. Young Gen X adults and parents particularly favour taking away privileges. Neither grounding nor physical discipline is seen by many teens or adults as an "appropriate" or "effective" way of responding to young people. Confinement and abuse are not exactly in touch with today's values.

Table 6.16. **Responses to Inappropriate Behaviour of Teens across Generations**

% Viewing as "The Most Appropriate and Effective" Responses

	TEENS	ADULTS	Grand-parents	Parents	Younger adults
Give them "a good talking to"	29%	23	29	21	20
Take away privileges	25	29	21	31	34
A discussion without discipline	23	16	18	17	15
Ground them	5	3	3	2	3
A discussion with discipline	5	7	3	7	10
Discipline them physically	4	1	1	1	1
Combination of responses	8	17	22	17	12
Other	1	4	3	4	5

An intriguing finding is that 56% of adults — including 57% of parents and grandparents and 55% of Gen Xers — say they "have wanted to have a home like the one I grew up in." Many are clearly troubled about the emerging generation, including their own teens. Yet no less than 71% of teens say that they "want a home like the one [they] grew up in," suggesting that, on balance, **slightly more teenagers are satisfied with their home life than their parents and grandparents were with theirs.**

It also is interesting to note that, even though grandparents grew up in an era of relative family stability, **older adults are no more likely than younger adults to say they want a home like the one they knew when they were growing up.** The finding that the proportion of adults who want to emulate their home lives is just over 50%, regardless of generational period, points to this stark reality: about half thought things were good at home and about half that things were not what they could have been, regardless of whether their parents were together. Many adults and teens hope for similar things; many hope for better things.

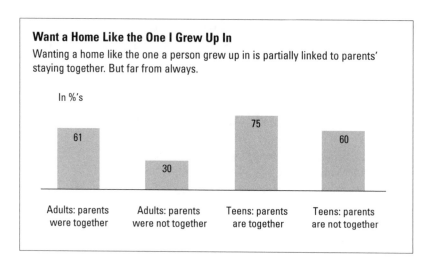

Want a Home Like the One I Grew Up In

Wanting a home like the one a person grew up in is partially linked to parents' staying together. But far from always.

In %'s

61	30	75	60
Adults: parents were together	Adults: parents were not together	Teens: parents are together	Teens: parents are not together

Moral and Sexual Attitudes

Consistent with the predictions of postmodern thinkers, today's emerging Millennials are somewhat more inclined than adults to have a personal, relativistic view of morality. Asked pointedly, *"On what do you base your views of what is right and wrong?"* greater percentages of teenagers cite personal factors over external sources, including religion. Parent Boomers and Xers base their moral views almost equally on external and personal sources, with fewer drawing on religion than do grandparents. Only a minority of teens claim to have moral criteria that resonate, for example, with that of a retired 68-year-old Protestant in Prince George, a 55-year-old CBC employee in Toronto who subscribes to no religion, and a 60-year-old Jewish salesman in Montreal — all who say their moral basis is "do unto others as you would have them do unto you."

There is little difference in the inclination of generations to assert that *everything's relative*, suggesting that relativism has become extremely pervasive in our culture; the phrase has become something of a truism. No less than 65% of teens agree with the statement, *"What's right or wrong is a matter of personal opinion."* Yet, at the same time that large numbers of young people and adults endorse relativism, more than half say values in Canada have been changing for the worse. Questionnaire comments suggest, however, that adults are more passionate than teens about the issue. A 59-year-old from a small town just north

Table 6.17. **Moral Attitudes across Generations**

	ADULTS	TEENS	Grand-parents	Parents	Younger adults
Basis of My Moral Views					
Personal factors, including values	35%	49	35	35	39
External factors	42	28	34	44	43
Religion specifically	17	16	26	16	12
Other	6	7	5	5	6
Everything's relative.	70	65	65	72	72
In general, values in Canada have been changing for the worse.	56	53	58	56	57

of Edmonton writes, "Even with all the technology and science, the world is not as great as it once was and faces extinction if great care, all kinds of caring, is not practiced. I have brought up two children hoping they will care, but I have concern for the world around them." Even more troubled is this 71-year-old woman from Regina, who also has raised two children of her own:

> There will be a greater decline of people's morals as time goes on because of their lack of interest in faith. The results are already seen in the increase of crime, broken homes, child abuse, etc. Some say crime is the result of being poor — not so. I came from a very poor home in the depression years, as did our many relatives and neighbours, but no one went out to steal or kill. We were taught to respect others as well as ourselves. We did the best we could with what we had. We were taught to fear the consequences if we disregarded the law. A man in our area had been cruel with his horses — he was put in jail for two months, and this included lashes. You can rest assured he didn't abuse his animals again.

She may be a bit dramatic, but her basic point is worth considering. Societies need norms; when people live life guided primarily by what feels good personally, social life can be difficult for everyone. We'll return to this issue later.

When adults worry about teenagers, one of the first areas they feel tense about is sex. The theme continues to make good copy. *Time* magazine ran a cover story in June of 1998 entitled "Everything your kids already know about sex" and proceeded to proclaim that "kids are in the midst of their own sexual revolution."[31]

The hype isn't warranted. Our findings show that the sexual views of teenagers differ little from those of adults as a whole. However, that generalization is also a bit misleading, since there probably is no area in the adult survey where generational differences are so pronounced. **Looked at generationally, Gen Xers and Boomers who shared in the sexual revolution of the 1960s and its aftermath hold far more liberal sexual views that both grandparents and today's teenagers.** There are two exceptions, which I'll come to in just a moment.

- A majority of Canadians, led by Generation Xers, typically followed in order by Boomers, Millennials, and Boomers' parents, approve of pre-marital sex, homosexual relations, cohabitation, unmarried couples having children, consenting adults doing whatever they want sexually, and legal abortion being available when a woman has been raped.
- About 90% of teens and 85% of adults give thumbs-down to extra-marital sex.

Table 6.18. **Sexual Attitudes across Generations**

% Approving

	ADULTS	TEENS	Grand-parents	Parents	Younger adults
Heterosexual sexual relations before marriage	84%	82	74	89	93
Homosexual sexual relations	60	54	42	64	75
Extramarital sexual relations	14	9	14	18	9
An unmarried couple living together	84	86	72	88	94
An unmarried couple having children	71	63	53	74	88
Consenting adults doing whatever they want sexually	70	61	61	71	81
Consenting teens 15 to 17 doing whatever they want sexually	23	56	11	21	37
Availability of legal abortion when rape is involved	90	84	86	89	95
Availability of legal abortion for any reason	43	55	36	46	44

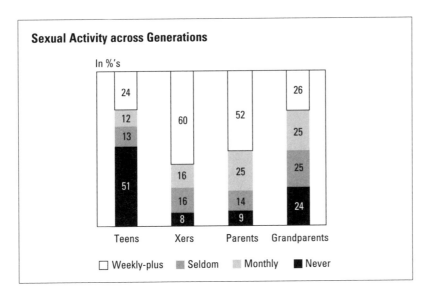

Sexual Activity across Generations

In %'s

	Teens	Xers	Parents	Grandparents
Weekly-plus	24	60	52	26
Monthly	12		25	25
Seldom	13	16		25
		16	14	
Never	51	8	9	24

☐ Weekly-plus ▨ Seldom ▨ Monthly ■ Never

The first of the two exceptions is that a slightly higher proportion of teens (55%) approve of abortion on demand; the approval levels drop to about 45% for Gen Xers and parents and 35% in the case of grandparents. The second exception to adults holding more liberal sexual views than teenagers? About one in two young people think that not only adults, but teenagers 15 to 17 as well, should be able to do whatever they want sexually. Just three in ten Xers, two in ten parents, and one in ten grandparents share such sentiments.

Beliefs, Involvement, and Spirituality

If there is any area of life where people are convinced that teens today differ from teens of the past it's religion. Ask any older person and you will get a predictable answer: "Young people today are not as interested in religion as young people were in my day."

Beyond speculation, let's take a brief look. An examination of teens' beliefs and those of the three adult generations shows **teenagers tend to embrace supernatural beliefs on levels that typically either match or exceed those of adults.**

- Majorities of people in all age categories indicate they believe in God and that God cares about them, that Jesus was divine, and in life after death. More than one in three teens think they have experienced God or a higher power. If you think that's a bit low compared to adults, remember — one in three is only the figure *so far*. Give them a few years; they're still on the other side of twenty!

- Teenagers are more likely than adults to believe in near-death experiences and astrology; they are just as likely to think they personally have experienced precognition and that we can have contact with the spirit world.

Table 6.19. **Beliefs across Generations**

"I believe . . ."	ADULTS	TEENS	Grand-Parents	Parents	Younger adults
Conventional					
God exists	81%	73	85	81	78
God or a higher power cares about you	73	68	77	72	71
Jesus was the Divine Son of God	72	65	77	71	68
In life after death	68	78	64	69	72
Have felt presence God/higher power	47	36	51	47	42
Less Conventional					
In near-death experiences	68	76	57	71	76
In ESP	66	59	59	70	67
Personally have experienced precognition	58	63	46	61	68
Can have contact with the spirit world	45	43	30	48	57
In astrology	34	57	31	34	36

- Generational differences in conventional beliefs among adults are fairly small. Generation Xers and Boomer parents, however, show an affinity for less conventional beliefs similar to Millennials' — notably near-death experiences, precognition, and communication with the spirit world. In adding such less conventional ideas to their belief smorgasbords, the three generations deviate a fair amount from Boomers' parents.

Contrary to widely held views, the levels of involvement in organized religion for teenagers closely match the overall levels of adults.

- Given that the primary source of religious commitment and involvement is the family, it should not be all that surprising that the commitment, involvement, and enjoyment levels of teens are very similar to those of parents. Identification with religious traditions, while somewhat lower than parents, is still close to 80%.

- So why, then, are leaders of organized religion in Canada constantly having to worry about declining numbers, including today? It's primarily because the latest cohort of young adults — Generation Xers — is exhibiting such low levels of participation. Most Xers continue to identify with religious groups and large numbers express a measure of religious commitment. But they are not showing up on a regular basis in very large numbers. What has to concern leaders is not just the possibility they may be unable to recruit the Xers. The danger is that, in the next decade or so, many Millennials may follow in their footsteps.

Apart from religious group involvement, we have seen that spirituality is something that is of interest to sizable numbers of teenagers. More than three in ten indicate spirituality is "very important" to them, while four in ten say the topic is of interest to their closest friends. Those figures are comparable to adult levels. Some five in ten teens openly admit that they have spiritual needs —below the seven-in-ten level of adults, but still sizable. Significantly, while there are large generational differences among adults as far as group involvement, those differences almost disappear when it comes to acknowledged spiritual needs. It is further interesting to note that, although only 8% of Gen Xers attend services weekly, more than three times that number — 29% — acknowledge spirituality is "very important" to them. One recalls the well-known lines of Douglas Coupland, the author of *Generation X,* in a subsequent book, *Life After God*:

> *My secret is that I need God — that I am sick and can no longer make it alone. I need God to help me give, because I no longer seem to be capable of giving; to help me be kind, as I no longer seem capable of kindness; to help me love, as I seem beyond being able to love.*[32]

In addition to Gen Xers, about 20% of Boomer parents are weekly service attenders, yet 33% acknowledge the importance of spirituality. That level is almost the same as that of teenagers.

A number of us have been saying a lot about teenagers and their religion. Often we've been wrong.

Table 6.20. **Involvement and Spirituality across Generations**

"I . . ."	ADULTS	TEENS	Grand-parents	Parents	Younger adults
Group Involvement					
Identify with a group	86%	76	93	86	77
Am committed to Christianity or another faith	55	48	70	56	43
Attend weekly	21	22	37	19	8
Receive high level of enjoyment from group	22	21	35	16	14
Am open to possibility of greater involvement	57	43	54	60	59
Spirituality					
Have spiritual needs	73	48	75	74	71
Have close friends interested in spirituality	42	38	52	40	38
Find spirituality very important	34	30	41	33	29
Pray privately weekly or more often	47	33	60	46	37

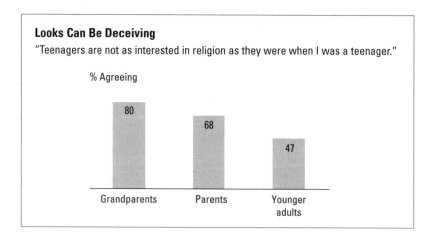

Looks Can Be Deceiving

"Teenagers are not as interested in religion as they were when I was a teenager."

% Agreeing

Grandparents	80
Parents	68
Younger adults	47

Assessment

We have looked at a considerable amount of information in this chapter. Because this material is central to our understanding youth trends, let me take a bit more space than usual to try to clarify what we have found and then offer a response.

Comparing today's teens with older and younger Gen X teen

cohorts in the '80s and '90s gave us a sense of short-term changes and continuities. To compare them with grandparents, parents, and Xers — both when those three generations were teens, as well as where they are now — is to give us "a longer look" at generational differences.

Understanding the cultural contexts adults knew as teenagers helps to clarify some of their dominant "starting point" characteristics. Most **parents** of today's teens were teenagers themselves in the '60s and '70s, when an accelerated emphasis on freedom and equality was being expressed in a variety of movements, the sexual revolution, and the expansion of choices in every area of life. Teens' **grandparents**, as teenagers in the '40s and '50s, grew up with fairly traditional values. They were frequently the offspring of parents from Britain and Western Europe, and most had childhoods that were touched directly or indirectly by the Depression and the Second World War. The 1950s were "happy days" for many, coming as a relief from times of poverty and war. **Generation Xers** were teens in the '80s and '90s, and included many who felt the fallout of the new-found freedom of Boomer Parents — dual-career parents, single parents, step-parents, and live-in parents. Marital breakdown often brought acrimony, tough economic times, and social stigma. The latchkey kids among them had to learn to fend for themselves. Xer strain was not eased by economic and unity problems in the early '90s. Their arrival coincided with the emergence of computer-based technology.

The **stories they tell** about their respective teen years reflect the characteristics of their eras. For the most part, their recollections seem a reasonable depiction of their teenage realities, as corroborated where possible by existing hard data.

Grandparents recall times of both limited discrimination at school and limited interracial dating. War and postwar days were times when energy was devoted to survival. Surveys show prejudice was high, but few seemed concerned; the status quo was taken for granted. Skipping school and fighting at school were fairly common, but juvenile delinquency and gangs were not. Things like violence in schools, suicide, and drug use were rare. Smoking was fairly pervasive and, to a lesser extent, so was drinking. Sexual activity among teens was not too widespread and STDs were uncommon, or at least kept quiet. Even today, relatively few grandparents look back on their teen years and see much sexual harassment or parental physical abuse. Maybe it's a lack of consciousness of the nature of such acts. But it also seems to be tied to a sense that standards were different back then. People weren't violating the prevailing norms.

If we use grandparents as our starting place, then the **worlds** that **Boomer parents** and **Gen Xers** recall are **progressively different.** There's an increasing sense of the prevalence both of discrimination and interracial dating, two seemingly inconsistent patterns until one realizes they reflect a society striving to know cultural and racial equality. There's also a growing sense that norms are breaking down — more truancy, fighting at school, and juvenile delinquency, in particular. To a lesser extent, violence in schools, gangs, and suicide also are seen as more common.

Smoking and drinking levels, while higher than when grandparents were teens, have levelled off. In the case of smoking, take away the increase in females smoking and things may not have changed all that much since the youthful days of grandparents. Sexual involvement, as expected, jumped among parent Boomers in the '60s and '70s, and continued to increase with Gen Xers — understandable, given the sexual socialization Xers received compared to their recently liberated parents. No significant increases in teenage sexual activity would be expected, in part because the ceiling has almost been hit. STDs are seen as having become more common, undoubtedly reflecting both greater exposure, especially in the cases of herpes and AIDS, as well as greater openness.

The perception that harassment and parental physical abuse is common has also known intergenerational increases. Along the way, the rules for acceptable behaviour were both changed and increasingly enforced. Accordingly, reports of their incidence have now begun to decline. Reports of physical abuse by school personnel, for example, have not been increasing since the days when parents were teenagers.

This is the way they remember their youth. It isn't necessarily how they themselves thought or behaved. It also isn't necessarily how they think today.

When we compare these "grown-up teens" with today's teens, some dominant patterns can be observed. The three adult cohorts give priority to family over friends, teens priority to friends over family. More teens than adults place high **value** on success, a comfortable life, and power; at this point in their lives, in the context of life as a whole, they have limited amounts of each. Young people also are more inclined to value excitement and looks, less likely to value religion. Interpersonal value levels are fairly similar. Honesty and politeness are valued by a majority of both adults and teens, but the levels are higher among adults and higher among females than males, regardless of age.

Adults and teenagers tend to get **enjoyment** from the same main areas of life, particularly friends, music, television, and, for men, sports. The specific choices and time given to specific activities are heavily generational in nature. Similarities extend to the use of computers. **Personal concerns** are similar, centring on time and money for everyone, as well as school for teens, and health and jobs for adults. However, personal concerns are expressed by higher proportions of teenagers than adults, including apprehension about so many things changing. **Social attitudes** are frequently similar. But teens shows signs of having somewhat higher levels of nationalism, being less militant about things like war, the death penalty, and the *Young Offenders Act*. They definitely are far more likely to believe hard work can lead to success. Yet, generational affinities are tricky: sometimes they exhibit commonality with Gen Xers (for example, endorsement of bilingualism); at other times they break with the other two generations in lining up with their grandparents (feeling they lack influence on government) or parents (for example, legalization of marijuana). Overall, teenagers — followed by Gen Xers — are the least interested in politics. Yet it appears to be more out of apathy than disillusionment: they exhibit more confidence in institutions, including governments, than everybody else.

Regarding **family** matters, today's Millennials, along with Gen Xers, are less likely than parents or grandparents to report that their natural parents were together when they were 16. They also are less inclined than the three adult generations to think there is a need for stricter discipline, and they break with adults particularly in opposing curfews. There is general agreement that the best form of discipline in the home involves discussions and taking away privileges. Young people are more likely than any of the three adult cohorts to indicate they want a home like the one they grew up in.

Teens today, along with Gen Xers, exhibit a highly personal and relativistic view of **morality**. Yet their views in an area like sexuality closely resemble those of their parents and tend to be somewhat more conservative than Xers. With respect to **religion and spirituality**, teens defy widely held stereotypes in exhibiting beliefs and claiming involvement levels that match those of adults, as well as being just as likely to indicate that spirituality is important to them.

I have **three** main observations. First, let's not mince words: there has been **a disturbing decline in the quality of life of many teenagers**. Everything has not remained the same. The recollection and corroborative data point to changing times. Some things have changed for the better, such as growing acceptance of racial and cultural diversity, as well as heightened sensitivity to harassment and abuse. There also is a greater respect for sexual freedom. On the negative side, teenage life over time has been characterized by a growing amount of fighting and violence at schools, increases in youth crime, a sizable jump in drug use, a slight rise in gangs, and a disturbing jump in suicides. There also has been an increase in sexually transmitted diseases.

This first point, I suspect, will be embraced and magnified, especially by observers who are negative toward teenagers, along with some people in the media who will be tempted to perpetuate "the bad news story about teens." Please read on.

Second, despite these important negative developments within the social environments in which teenagers find themselves, **the vast majority of teenagers are looking very good**. The drug situation is a good case in point. Yes, drug access has increased. Yet, generally speaking, illicit drug use since the '60s has, if anything, decreased. Violence at schools is up; yet, despite a poorer social climate, 80% of teens continue to say that they feel safe at school, and the overwhelming majority do not contribute to the violence. The same can be said for youth crime: the fact it's increased in the past fifty years should not obscure the fact such offences are still committed by only a small minority of teenagers.

The good news in all this is that most teenagers are neither contributing to these undesirable trends, nor are directly affected by them. On the contrary, our findings show that young people tend to hold values very similar to those of adults, in sharp contrast to the devastatingly negative impressions most adults have of teen values. Beyond just values, our findings on enjoyment, compassion, self-esteem, and outlook, as well as our overall comparison of teen attitudes and beliefs with the three adult generations, add up to an encouraging portrait of today's teenagers. If "the times" are making it more difficult to be a teenager, our findings indicate most are up to the challenge.

Third, one of more interesting things the intergenerational comparisons show is this: **people don't stay where they started**. If there is anything naive about some of the generational-framework assumptions, it's the idea that people differ significantly in their views and behaviour on the sole basis of the era in which they were born. Obviously we are influenced by our birth era. But we also are influenced by subsequent eras. Life is dynamic. People change. Even older people!

People born before 1950 were born before a lot of things. But they, like the rest of us, weren't and aren't imprisoned in their generational time slot. They have had a chance to access the resources that technology has made available. They have had to come to grips with lots of new ideas, including some pretty radical notions about sexuality, not to mention some "heresies" about the forms and functions of marriage. It's interesting for me to be able to inform the country that, as of 2000, 25% of teens are using the Internet daily, compared to 32% of Xers. But, it should tell us something about the reality of everyone else co-opting things from a "postmodern" world when we also learn the Internet is being used every day by 20% of parents and, yes, 12% of grandparents.

Life changes. People within age cohorts change. And guess what? **Despite our preoccupation with what today's teens look like now and our interest in comparing them to past generations, they are not going to stay the same, either.** That brings us to the third and final part of the story of Canada's teens.

Part III

Teens Tomorrow

Chapter Seven

How Today's Teenagers Are Going to Turn Out

IT'S AN OLD SCENARIO. THE SETTING IS A UNIVERSITY CONVOCATION. Mom and Dad have just changed places for the photo with the new grad when he spots some friends and excuses himself for a few moments to say hi. Mom looks at Dad and says, "It's quite the day, isn't it, given the ups and downs and those times when we wondered whether or not he would finish high school, let alone university?" "Yes," says Dad. "I just hope he can find a job."

That pretty much sums it up. **We worry about our offspring when they don't do well and we worry about them when they do.** Comedian George Carlin once said that the key characteristic of dogs is that they go through their entire lives *waiting.* Well, sometimes I think that when we become parents, we proceed through our entire lives *worrying.* The apparent "wins" at best seem momentary; we then focus on the next thing that could go wrong.

I suppose that we, as individuals and a society, see such concern as a sign of conscientiousness, something of a virtue. "Young people, after all, have been entrusted to us, haven't they? It's our responsibility to do what we can to make sure they have happy landings." Or so the thinking goes. For parents, that concern never ends. I am still on the lookout for the best interests of my three boys, who, by the way, seem awfully young to be in their 30s. It doesn't stop there. That cherished mother of 82 continues to encourage me, chastise me, applaud me, and, after all these years, still wonders out loud, I might add, if I am going to turn out OK!

Apart from our own children, many of us look out at teens today and wonder, not always silently, what kind of a world we'll have tomorrow. Among them is a 68-year-old from a small town in southern Ontario whose husband is retired. She has raised two children and chosen not to work outside the home. "I am very concerned about the future of our young people — their morals and lifetimes," she says. "I feel more thought and attention should be given to our children in their early years, 0 to 20." An older Boomer parent, 53, from rural Saskatchewan, who has raised four teens, comments, "Our young people need to have morals and convictions and with that comes responsibility. I think we as a country would have so many fewer problems if our children felt secure. Our children are our country's future and we're failing them!"

By now we have seen much data that tell us to take it easy that, as things stand, teenagers generally are going to turn out just fine by most people's standards. The vast majority of 15- to-19-year-olds are a positive presence within Canadian life right now. They'll stay that way unless they take some turn for the worse on their way to adulthood.

The asterisk attached to all this good news is that biographies are seldom simply linear. Obviously we all change. Over time the beliefs and values, attitudes and expectations we've assembled are, to varying degrees, edited, discarded, and replaced. That's life. That's why moms and dads keep worrying.

We have studied some fairly detailed footage on where Canada's teens are *today,* as well as how they look compared both to *teens yesterday,* and to those *adult "grown-up teens" of today.* That leaves us with the third and final question: what about *tomorrow?* What can we expect will happen to today's teens over the next decade or so?

When people have put me on the spot with that question, I have frequently reminded them I'm a sociologist, not a social psychic. Prophecies often fail and can leave the prophet downright humiliated. Reflecting on the first all-purpose electronic digital computer in 1946, which weighed 30 tons and was equipped with 18,000 vacuum bulbs, *Popular Mechanics* predicted, "Computers of the future may have only 1,000 vacuum tubes and perhaps weigh no more than $1\frac{1}{2}$ tons"![1] As I glance over at my tiny laptop, forgive me if I feel the need to take it a little easy with my predictions. Obviously we can't predict the future, including what teens will become as they move into their 20s, 30s, and beyond. But we do have some helpful methods and data at our disposal that can provide us with some good clues.

Some Tips on Predicting the Future

The primary way we can explore changes in teenagers as they get older is by looking at what has happened to their predecessors as they moved into their 20s and beyond. Such a method allows us, at minimum, to isolate some characteristics tied to life cycle, such as idealism, which change as teens get older. But the method also allows us to identify areas where change is not occurring, where people literally "don't grow out of it," as might be the case with lower levels of courtesy. Let me expand on this a bit.

Know What's Generational and What's Life Stage

It's easy to confuse what happens in a *life stage* **with what will happen in a** *lifetime.* The fact that teens aren't valuing parents as much as we may think they should doesn't mean things won't change when they get into their 30s and 40s. Because young people enjoy the NBA doesn't mean that basketball interest will one day rival hockey interest. Teens may well grow out of their enjoyment of the NBA as they leave their teens and rap/hip-hop music behind. Such feelings about parents and the NBA may simply be associated with being a teenager today — no more and no less, no trend and no big deal. Looking at how teens change over time can help us to see what's simply a life stage versus something more.

The reason it's so easy to confuse life-stage changes with dramatic new cultural trends is that the teen years are marked by so much *personal* change. But we all know that much of who we were then is not who we will be later. These wise words from yesteryear describe the experiences of all of us: "When I became an adult, I put away childish ways."[2] That's not a putdown. Sometimes it's for the worse. Folk wisdom and biographies are replete with adages and stories about the loss of innocence and idealism, when dreams and causes have to be abandoned in the face of the discovery of limits. Sometimes it's for the better. A number of years ago, sociologist David Matza wrote a book entitled *Delinquency and Drift.* He pointed out that most juvenile delinquents don't grow up to be adult criminals, but rather drift out of delinquency just as many of them had drifted in.[3] Sometimes it's simply different, because interests and needs change. Eric Carmen and, more recently, Céline Dion have recounted in song the difference many feel between being young and never needing anyone, when love is just for fun, versus reaching a point where one no longer wants to be "all by myself."[4]

The point here is that some things we are seeing in teens today are going to disappear with age. Therefore, before we assume on the basis of a cohort snapshot that "these teens" are destined to be different — positively or negatively — we need to look at what has been happening to their predecessors to make sure that sure that what we are observing is more than just a teen life-stage *blip*.

That's not to reduce the characteristics of this generation or previous generations to merely a life stage. As long as we see an adjacent cohort like Gen Xers becoming more polite or showing less confidence in schools as they move into their 20s and 30s, we can assume much of the change is tied to life cycle. But if their suspicion of people or their apathy about politics starts high in their teens compared to other adults and remains high when they *are* adults, then such findings suggest changes are taking place in the culture that reflect far more than people's simply getting older.

In getting a sense of the future, we don't want to fall into the trap that youth experts Neil Howe and William Strauss warn us about in their book *Millennials Rising* — of assuming "history generally moves in straight lines" and that "the next batch of youths will follow blindly along all the life-cycle trends initiated by Boomers and confirmed by Gen Xers."[5] History would be pretty dull if there were no surprises, if every new generation were simply the latest extension of the one before it, where everyone in the intergenerational photo looked exactly the same.

That said, we would expect to see some family resemblances in that shot. New generations do not drop from the skies; they are rooted in previous generations. Even cultural revolutions have some continuities with the past. Significant technological change, for example, does not mean that values, sources of enjoyment, aspirations, and institutions all undergo radical transformations, especially in only a decade or two. That's the first tip on predicting the future — knowing the difference between a characteristic that is life stage and one that is generational in nature.

Base Projections on People Patterns

The second tip is extrapolate from real people. As social scientists, we don't rely on crystal balls and tea leaves to predict what lies ahead. Our rules call us to be empiricists — to examine what we observe and to try to see if our findings point to any short-term directions. That's it.

For the sake of argument, if anyone wants to go to the other extreme of *not* basing predictions for the immediate future on current trends, what's the alternative? A psychic? Wild-eyed speculation? Grand theorizing about major historical epochs? A cyclic view of history?

Well, actually, the last two approaches characterize the thinking of postmodernists and some generational analysts respectively. By way of an example of the latter, Howe and Strauss, in *Millennials Rising*, declare, "This generation is going to rebel by behaving not worse, but *better*. Their life mission will not be to tear down old institutions that don't work, but to build up new ones that do." Moreover, the duo write, "Millennials have a solid chance to become America's next generation . . . celebrated for their collective deeds a hundred years from now." They go further: "Barring cataclysmic events, one can at least sketch out a timetable with a fair degree of confidence" of "what Millennials are likely to do, decade by decade." They proceed to do just that, telling us what will happen to those Millennial kids right through the time the last one dies around 2120![6]

Wow! If only life were like that . . .

I for one can't take it any longer and impatiently holler from the back of the room, "How the heck do you know?" Their calm response — which indicates they've heard such protests before — is that American cultural history can be summed up in terms of eighteen generations since the sixteenth century, the dominant features of which tend to repeat themselves in cyclic fashion approximately every four generations. The Millennials, for example, are similar to the G.I. Generation that preceded the grandparents of today's teens; in the U.S., the G.I. cohort included the likes of John F. Kennedy.[7] The imaginative title of Howe and Strauss's earlier book in 1991 sums up their approach: *Generations: The History of America's Future*.[8]

The problem with such a method is that rather than our engaging in an open-minded examination of the facts, we can become highly deductive — starting with a thesis and then simply documenting it. It's one thing to say some broad cultural characteristics seem to repeat themselves. It's quite another to predict dogmatically that, if no glitches take place, they *will* appear, permitting century-long prognostications. Howe and Strauss are still predicting the future based on the past, but opting for a cyclic view of history in predicting the future, and going with a cohort that's about four generations deep. I'm saying let's go with the most recent cohorts in getting our readings.

Which brings us back to our research. When it comes right down to it, either way, we are still left with having to look at the past to get a sense of the possibilities that exist in the future. There's no other choice. But don't toss out the book and turn to the psychics and prophets just yet. Our method is going to tell you more than you think.

Some Hints from the Past: Imagined

One obvious means of getting a sense of how people have changed is to ask them. Sociologists refer to this as "recollection data." Such a procedure, of course, is not without its perils. Common sense tells us that we often remember fairly selectively whether we mean to or not. Still, such information has its merits. Good surveys are just good conversations. And despite the readiness of some observers to criticize recollection data, the truth is that in everyday conversations we routinely ask people what they "used to do and used to feel" in the course of trying to understand them. "Where did you grow up?" is a recollection item. "Did you used to get down to the ocean when you lived in Vancouver?" is another. The issue is not can we remember?; of course we can. The issue is what can we remember and how do we remember it? "Did you ever get the strap at school?" might lead to a fairly straightforward response; "Did you enjoy first grade?" is considerably more subjective and vulnerable to redefinition at different points in our lives. Consequently, we can have more confidence asking people to recall some things than others.

In the **Project Canada 2000** adult survey, we asked Canadians how they think they have changed since they were 15 to 19 years old. We could hardly be exhaustive, but we did try to probe some basic values and attitudes. We kept the response options simple: "*Compared to then, would you say that over the years there has been an increase, a decrease, or no particular change?*" Frankly, I expected that most people would say they have become nicer, more mellow, more conservative, less idealistic. I was wrong.

People and Values

We asked what's been happening over the years regarding their sentiments toward Mom and Dad. **Almost six in ten adults, led by Generation Xers, maintain that their appreciation of both their parents has increased since they were teenagers.** Grandparents are more likely than other adults to indicate they appreciated their mothers and fathers then and pretty much have continued to do so since. Relatively few adults say their appreciation of parents has decreased; the rest maintain that there has been little change in their sentiments over time.

These findings suggest that the Boomers and Gen Xers of recent decades have been taking longer to appreciate their parents. Incidentally, this "delayed appreciation," sort of analogous to deferred gratification, is undoubtedly still welcomed by beleaguered parents, providing they are not too old or no longer on the planet. (Unsolicited advice to all of us: if it's true we are going to appreciate parents later if not sooner, it might be in everyone's best interests to speed up the process a little. Back now to social science. . . .)

A majority of adults acknowledge that, since their teens, they have experienced a change in how they feel about people as a whole.

- Over half, again led by Gen Xers and Boomers, say they have become more *suspicious*; it's not just your imagination that older people you don't know seem a bit friendlier than other strangers.
- Close to 40% of Xers and Boomers say they have become *more concerned about others* since their teens, as do approximately 30% of grandparents. But this is offset by the disturbing fact that some 30% of adults in all three generational cohorts acknowledge they have become *less concerned about people* over the years.
- Perhaps most surprising, about one in three adults of all ages admit they have become *less polite* and, yes, even *less honest* since they were teenagers. On the positive side, 32% of Gen Xers, 25% of Boomers, and 16% of Boomers' Parents claim that their levels of politeness and

honesty have increased. But the bottom line is not particularly good: all three generations report a net loss in honesty in their post-teen years, and grandparents and parents a net loss in politeness. In the case of Xers, as many admit they have become more polite as say they have become less polite, resulting in no net gain. In throwing this finding around with people of varied ages, the response is consistent: they feel that in order to survive they've had to "toughen up" over the years. As one grandmother put it, "I finally had to stop being such a pushover." In the case of declining honesty, one male in his 30s told me, "Aw, if I can get away with it, a lot of things are not that big a deal."

Table 7.1. **Perception of Change since Their Teen Years: People and Values**

"Looking back to when you were a teenager (15 to 19), COMPARED TO THEN, would you say that over the years there has been, AN INCREASE, A DECREASE, or NO PARTICULAR CHANGE in YOUR . . ."

	All ↑	↓	Grandparents (now 56–75) ↑	↓	Parents (now 36–55) ↑	↓	Younger adults (now 20–35) ↑	↓
Appreciation of . . .								
Your mother	59%	14	48	14	60	12	65	16
Your father	56	14	47	14	56	13	61	15
Level of . . .								
Suspicion of people	55	20	48	22	55	21	58	17
Concern for other people	36	28	32	31	37	28	38	26
Politeness	26	34	16	39	25	34	33	32
Honesty	23	30	14	32	24	27	27	32
View . . .								
Of what you could achieve in life	47	28	45	21	45	31	50	28
That most people are good people	22	37	22	30	23	36	19	44

↑ *Increase*   ↓ *Decrease*

- For many, such changes seem to be associated with a change in *how they view people*. Over time, close to 25% of Boomers and Boomers' Parents say they have been more inclined to see most people as good people; the figure is around 20% for Generation Xers. But about

30% of grandparents, 35% of parents, and a whopping 45% of Xers say they have become less inclined to see people in such positive terms. To live life, it appears, is not to become totally cynical about people. But it does seem to make one feel there are some people out there who can make life difficult.

These recollection findings are consistent with some ongoing trend research in the U.S. that might be applicable to Canada. The reputable National Opinion Research Center at the University of Chicago has found that only about 20% of today's 18- to 24-year-olds think most people are trustworthy, down from 36% in 1973. Some 32% think most people are fair, down from 43% in 1973. The Center's director, Tom Smith, says that today's young adults are more distrustful of society and more disconnected from it than their counterparts of 30 years ago. He says that lack of trust has shown up in previous surveys, but what is new is the belief that human nature is inherently more bad than good. The distrust, he notes, is not just with political leaders, but with "society in general." Commenting on the findings, Gerald Celente of Trends Research had this to say: "We are seeing precisely what the report is saying. [Young adults] have been hardened by today's realities. They have seen an acceptance of disposing of ethics and morals if that serves your needs. They see it as OK to do what you want to do as long as you meet your personal requirements."[9]

Hopes and dreams, however, appear to only increase with time, at least for many Canadians. Close to five in ten adults in each of the three generational cohorts say their sense of what they could achieve in life has increased since their teen years. Perhaps reflecting accelerated expectations, about three in ten Xers and Boomers report they have experienced a decrease in what they thought they could accomplish when they were teenagers, compared to just two in ten grandparents. The balance sheet, though, shows that adults feel that, over their lifetimes, they have accomplished more than they thought they would or could.

At first this finding appears to contradict the folk wisdom that people lose their idealism as they get older, which is consistent with our earlier finding that adults as a whole are considerably less likely than teens to think "anyone who works hard can rise to the top." What seems to be happening is that one's realization that there may be limits to upward mobility does not result in disillusionment with dreams in general. True, some dreams about reaching the top may have to be modified. But the dreams one can dream as a teenager are limited to what one is able to envision when one is under 20. **With the passage of time, many of us have been creating and realizing new dreams — some well beyond what we imagined were possible when we were younger.**

Sexual Attitudes

Adults of all ages exhibit the ability to change their attitudes over time, including attitudes about sexuality. Contrary to a widespread stereotype, older people lead the way.

- When grandparents look back to when they were teenagers, six in ten say that, since those pre-sexual revolution days of the 1940s and 1950s, there has been an increase in their approval of sex before marriage and people having children without being married, along with homo-sexuality and the availability of legal abortion. Many grandparents and parents have been confronting such realities first-hand. In some instances, the line between "approval" and "tolerance" might be a fine one. The words of an older male from near Toronto a few years back, whose unmarried daughter was expecting her first child, are probably

TABLE 7.2. **Perception of Change since Their Teen Years: Sexual and Family Attitudes**

"Looking back to when you were a teenager (15 to 19), COMPARED TO THEN, would you say that over the years there has been AN INCREASE, A DECREASE, or NO PARTICULAR CHANGE in YOUR . . ."

	All		Grandparents (now 56–75)		Parents (now 36–55)		Younger adults (now 20–35)	
	↑	↓	↑	↓	↑	↓	↑	↓
Approval of . . .								
Homosexuality	54%	7	62	9	56	10	47	3
Children without being married	53	10	63	8	56	10	42	10
Availability of legal abortion	52	9	64	7	54	9	42	9
Premarital sex	49	9	62	5	48	8	42	11

↑ *Increase*   ↓ *Decrease*

ones murmured by more than a few older parents in the course of trying to cope with change: "She's my daughter; what else can I do?"

- Boomers and Gen Xers had more liberal sexual attitudes to begin with; still, 40% to 50% also maintain that their levels of approval have increased with time. Here again, personal experience and growing awareness of the wide-ranging experiences of others undoubtedly have contributed to alterations in the views they had as teenagers.
- Among Xers, what is particularly noteworthy is the 47% who say they have become more approving of homosexuality in the relatively short time since their teens. Part of the change may be the result of

---

Love and sex in the '70s

Joan Sutton, columnist, 1979 — *Love has always been considered to be something of a miracle: the miracle of the '70s was that love survived. Never has the emotion been so assaulted. There were even attempts to euphemize it out of existence, replacing love with something called a "relationship," sometimes preceded by "one-to-one"; occasionally, "meaningful."*

Emotion was lost in the feverish attention to the clinical. Mystery died. We [responded] to a world of instant soup and instant tea with a demand for instant intimacy. Courtship was out: the meat-market atmosphere of the singles' bar was in. Where some might have thought that sexual liberation gave women the right to say no, most of its male proponents believed that liberated women should always say yes. More and more people were having more and more innovative sex, at a younger age, with more and more partners.

Venereal disease and teenage pregnancy increased and many sexual partners, waking up to a strange and nameless face in their waterbed, discovered that the aftermath of lovemaking without love was frustration, acute loneliness and alienation.

Love in the '70s: we measured it, computerized it, renamed it, psychoanalyzed it, stripped it of privacy, and rejected it, all the while longing for it, looking for it, and leaping into it.[10]

---

moving out of a teen subculture that typically has put high value on heterosexuality while stigmatizing homosexuality.

To the extent there have been *decreases* in sexual approval levels, they have been experienced fairly evenly across the three age cohorts: as people have been getting older, they have shown no greater tendency to express disapproval of these practices.

Religious Group Involvement

We also asked adults to summarize their involvement in religious groups over time. Specifically we asked them to indicate whether the level of their involvement at various points in their lives was "high," "moderate," "low," or "none."

Overall, they said there was a decline in participation during their teens and early 20s, followed by a mild increase as they moved into their late 20s and 30s, with involvement pretty much levelling off after that. There are, however, some important generational differences.

- Xers are far less likely than their parents or grandparents to have been highly involved in religious groups when they were children. This means that the pool of young people who were socialized by religious groups in their early years and are prime candidates for recruitment has decreased in recent decades. The pool characterized only some 20% of Xers versus over 40% of the two older generations.
- The practical implication is that fewer young adults can be expected to literally "return to church," since fewer were ever active in the first

Table 7.3. **Involvement in Religious Groups over Time**

% Indicating Involvement Level "High"

	All	Grandparents (now 56–75)	Parents (now 36–55)	Yg adults (now 20–35)
Prior to your teens	36%	44	43	21
During your teen years	19	31	21	8
From 18–24	10	23	8	4
From 25–29	12	20	9	10
From 30–39	15	21	13	11
From 40–49	15	21	11	—
From 50–59	17	23	11	—
From 60 onward	23	23	—	—

place. So far, that's the case. However, it's very interesting to note that the proportion of Xers who have returned is about 50%, similar to the proportion of grandparents who say they "came back" and well above the 25% figure reported by Boomer parents. This may well be signalling heightened involvement in organized religion on the part of many Gen Xers.

In short, these findings suggest religious group involvement during the teen years is *temporarily low* for some young people who once were actively involved. Some, but not most, will reappear, primarily in their late 20s and especially their 30s. This 52-year-old Boomer parent of two teenagers from Red Deer, Alberta, may or may not complete the cycle. Here is how he recalls his religious past:

> *My mother was Catholic, my father was Anglican. They received a dispensation to marry in my mother's church when Dad agreed to raise any children as Catholics. From age 7 to 12 my mother took us to church each Sunday; Dad stayed at home. From age 13 to 17 I went once a month, Mother stayed home with Dad. After age 18 we all stayed home or went out visiting and driving together.*

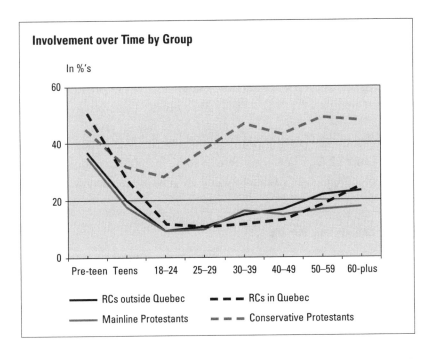

Involvement over Time by Group

In %'s

RCs outside Quebec — — RCs in Quebec
Mainline Protestants — — Conservative Protestants

The fact that Gen X young people born in the late '60s and '70s were not exposed to religious groups by their parents means that they, in turn, may "turn out" an even smaller pool of children who have been exposed to religion. This downward spiral of intergenerational religious socialization means that fewer and fewer teenagers will be coming from so-called religious homes. That includes the current emerging generation of Millennials. The asterisk lies with what we have just seen — the possible new participation of a growing number of Gen Xers.

Some Hints from the Past: Real

So far we have tried to get a sense of how today's teens will turn out by using recollection — looking at how adults perceive themselves as having changed since their teen years. **Another method is to compare what our teen cohort told us in our youth surveys with what that *same age group* is now telling us as adults.** It's like taking two photos at two different points in time of a group of high school friends, then and later in life. The method is formally known as a "cohort analysis." Young people who were 15 to 19 in the 1980s, for example, were 26 to 39 in the year 2000, since the youngest would have been 15 in 1989 and the oldest 19 in 1980. By taking "survey snapshots" of this age cohort in the 1980s and 2000, we can see what has been happening to them as they get older.

I will do just that by using the 1984 teen survey to provide us with a look at teens in the '80s — who were mostly Gen Xers with some younger Boomers thrown in — and, for the sake of consistency with our previous age cutting points, compare those 1984 teens with a camera shot of *Gen Xers* who were 26 to 35 in 2000. In addition, in an effort to extend our understanding of possible recent changes in

Two Cohorts from the '80s			
	Age in '80s	Age in 2000	Generational Label
Cohort 1	Teens	26–35	Older Xers
Cohort 2	20s	36–45	Younger Boomers

young people as they have been moving into adulthood, I want to similarly compare pictures of *Younger Boomers* when they were in their 20s in 1985 to pictures of them in their late 30s and early 40s in the year 2000.[11]

We could look at a large number of areas, but for the sake of comparison as well as keeping our overloaded heads marginally clear let's stick with the recollection zones — people, values, and dreams, along with sex and religion. As we go over this, watch how closely the actual changes in the thinking of these Gen Xers and Younger Boomers correspond with what we noted in the previous section about recollections.

Values and People

Canadians who were Gen X teenagers in the 1980s have changed little since moving into their late 20s and early 30s, with respect to the importance they place on such things as being loved, honesty, and hard work. There has been, however, a slight increase in the proportion who say that politeness is "very important" to them. These patterns have been essentially the same for Young Boomers as they have moved from their 20s into their late 30s and early 40s. The politeness shift seems to be tied more to life cycle than to social and cultural factors. In both generational instances, the change has been associated not so much with people being in their teens or their 20s during the 1980s as their simply reaching their 30s and 40s.

Two quick points here about the valuing of politeness:
- We are inquiring here about values, not behaviour. Keep in mind that when we asked Gen Xers and Boomers to recall what has happened to their levels of actual politeness since their teen years, they, along with grandparents, did not report net increases.
- Young adults may value politeness more, but they also may feel that the demands of the culture are such that they can't and don't practise politeness as readily as they did when they were teens. Ironically, some may value it more because they experience it less.

As teens of the 1980s have moved into their late 20s and early 30s, they are continuing to get a high level of enjoyment from their friends. But the level has slipped slightly, as has their enjoyment of music. Moms continue to be enjoyed by close to the same proportion of people as in the 1980s. Enjoyment from dads, however, has fallen noticeably.

The drop in enjoyment of fathers appears to be at least partially related to divorce and separation realities: 68% of young adults from intact homes say they are getting a lot of enjoyment from their fathers, compared to just 33% whose natural parents were not together when they were 16; the corresponding figures for mothers are 76% and 58%. It appears that disillusionment with fathers, who usually did not have custody in divorces, increases somewhat with age.

Table 7.4. **Values and People: Teens and Young Boomers in the 1980s and in 2000**

	1980s* Teens	2000** 26-35	1980s YB20s	2000 36-45
Importance: *Very*				
Being loved	87%	88	87	83
Honesty	85	89	96	93
Working hard	69	66	69	59
Politeness	64	73	64	74
Enjoyment Level: *Great Deal/Quite a Bit*				
Friends	96	87	94	88
Music	94	77	88	82
Your mother	79	73	84***	66
Your father	74	62		55

* *1980s teen source PTC84, sample size = 3,530; YB source PC85, sample size = 296.*
** *2000 source PC 2000; 1980s teen cohort sample size = 256, YB cohort sample size = 192.*
*** *"Parents."*

These enjoyment patterns over time are consistent with those reported by Younger Boomers. Enjoyment levels of friends and music appear to have "locked in" at around 90% and 80%, respectively, by the time people have reached about 40. However, as Younger Boomers get into their late 30s and 40s, they report receiving somewhat lower levels of enjoyment from their parents — presumably in large part tied in to the increasing attention given to their own emerging families. Putting this together with the recollection data, we can see that as they get older they may be *appreciating* them more, but that is not to say they are spending time with them and consequently actually *enjoying* them more.

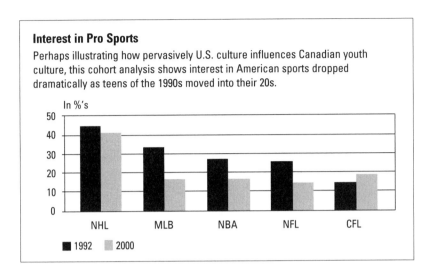

Interest in Pro Sports

Perhaps illustrating how pervasively U.S. culture influences Canadian youth culture, this cohort analysis shows interest in American sports dropped dramatically as teens of the 1990s moved into their 20s.

In %'s

1992 ☐ 2000

Attitudes and Concerns

As would be expected, some attitudes have changed very little. The views teens had in the 1980s about people having a right to *medical care* or using the *death penalty* selectively have remained pretty stable as this cohort has moved into its late 20s and early 30s. The same can be said of Younger Boomers, although these products of the capital punishment debate of the 1970s have been mellowing a bit in their support of the death penalty.

In sharp contrast to the speculation of postmodernist thinkers, some 90% of '80s teens and Younger Boomers continue to maintain that *science* will increase in influence. They obviously are impressed with the role science has played in the explosion of technological advances they have been witnessing and sharing in first-hand during their lifetimes. Some theorists might be disenchanted with science; most young people are not.

In contrast to that endorsement level, only around 15% to 20% think the influence of *traditional morality* will increase in the future, a level basically unchanged over the years. Pronounced themes of individualism and relativism leave little room for the absolutist emphases associated with traditional morality.

Consistent with the recollection data, there are signs of some significant shifts in social and sexual attitudes as young people have been getting older. Teens of the 1980s are exhibiting a more liberal attitude toward legalization of the use of *marijuana* than they did when they were teenagers. As high school students, some 70% expressed a high level of confidence in *school* leadership. Now, with more than half of them married with children, their collective confidence in the schools has dropped to about 40%. Similar patterns concerning attitudes toward marijuana and schools have also characterized Younger Boomers.

As the teens of two decades ago have moved into their late 20s and early 30s, they have become more accepting of *premarital sex* and *abortion when rape is involved*. Three times as many now indicate they approve of *homosexuality*. However, their negative attitudes toward *extramarital sex* have not changed. Younger Boomers have

Table 7.5. **Attitudes, Concerns, and Outlook:**
Teens and Younger Boomers in the 1980s and in 2000

	1980s Teens	2000 26–35	1980s YB20s	2000 36–45
Social Attitudes				
People have a right to medical care.	98%	97	96	98
Death penalty should sometimes be used.	73	69	84	70
Use of marijuana should be legalized.	28	56	40	52
Science will increase in influence.	84	90	82	87
I have a high level of confidence in schools.	69	41	58	51
Traditional morality will increase in influence.	17	21	25	16
Sexual Attitudes: *Approve of*				
Premarital sex	80	93	91	88
Homosexuality	26	77	36	68
Extramarital sex	12	11	19	16
Abortion when rape is involved	86	95	90	90
Personal Concerns and Outlook				
I never seem to have enough time.	48	50	49	57
I'm concerned about my looks.	44	42	27	26
I myself am "very happy."	25	21	27	22
I myself am "pretty happy."	63	66	66	70

likewise become more accepting of homosexuality as they have reached their late 30s and 40s; otherwise, their views have pretty much levelled off.

It would seem that cultural shifts, rather than aging, are involved in the changing attitudes of many teens and Younger Boomers toward both homosexuality and the legalization of marijuana. However, life cycle and parenthood — specifically parenthood — appear to be the key source of their decline in confidence in schools, especially in light of their retaining a high level of confidence in other areas such as science and, as we saw earlier, the police.

As they move through their 20s and 30s, people in the teen cohort from the 1980s continue to worry about both their *looks* and never seeming to have enough *time*. On balance, they are just about as *happy* with life as they were when they were teenagers, just a little less exuberant in reporting that they are "very happy" versus "pretty happy." Younger Boomers are as troubled about time as they ever were, and also are a bit less exuberant about their happiness. But for some time they have been less concerned about their looks than the '80s teen cohort. Maybe what's showing up here is what seems to be an accelerated cultural emphasis in recent years on appearance and body imaging, complete with unlimited possibilities for enhancement — a time when parents can make headlines in Britain and North America by agreeing to pay for their daughter's breast enlargements as a present for her sixteenth birthday.[12] Things do seem different.

Religion

As Gen X teens have entered their 20s and 30s, they are attending religious services less, consistent with the recollection reports. In part reflecting the tumultuous 1980s, when religious leaders were under attack for sexual and financial scandals, there also has been a significant decline in the confidence Gen Xers are expressing in religious leaders.

Yet this does not mean they think leaders should stay out of public life. On the contrary, the proportion who think ministers should "stick to religion and not concern themselves with social, economic, and political issues" has actually decreased since the '80s. But, if anything, they are even less inclined now to think that the influence of religion is going to increase in the future. Younger Boomers exhibit attitudes similar to those of Gen Xers. Consistent with the recollection reports on attendance and age, there is a slight increase, however, in their collective attendance level as they move into their late 30s and early 40s.

As for beliefs, Gen Xers express slightly lower levels of belief, both conventional and less conventional, than they did when they were teens in the '80s. That pattern also applies to concern about the meaning and purpose of life; this concern was fairly high during the teen years, but drops off and then appears to remain fairly stable from one's early 20s onward. It seems that rather than starting out with belief levels below those of adults and then, in some instances, having become "believers," things happen the other way around. Collectively, teenagers hold beliefs on a level at least as high as that of adults. Over time, a number appear — at least in the short run — to discard some of their beliefs. The data on Young Boomers suggest that such a decline continues for some people as they move into their 30s and 40s. **In short, the religious belief rule is this: they start high and decrease, rather than start low and increase.**

Table 7.6. **Organized Religion, Beliefs, and Practices: Teens and Younger Boomers in the 1980s and in 2000**

	1980s Teens	2000 26–35	1980s YB20s	2000 36–45
Organized Religion				
Attend weekly/very often	23%	9	14	18
Have confidence in religious leaders	62	27	46	29
Ministers should stick to religion	50	39	51	43
Religion will increase in influence	19	13	19	15
Beliefs and Practices				
Existence of God	85	79	80	76
Life after death	80	73	66	68
Some people have special psychic powers	69	64	71	62
Have experienced God	43	47	38	46
Communication with the dead	36	39	25	32
Concerned about meaning and purpose of life	45	37	22	25
Pray privately daily/very often	20	20	17	20

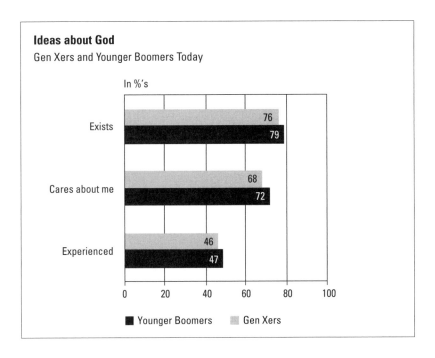

Ideas about God

Gen Xers and Younger Boomers Today

In %'s

Exists	Gen Xers: 76, Younger Boomers: 79
Cares about me	Gen Xers: 68, Younger Boomers: 72
Experienced	Gen Xers: 46, Younger Boomers: 47

0   20   40   60   80   100

■ Younger Boomers   ▨ Gen Xers

Religious experience and prayer appear to be exceptions. More Gen Xers and Young Boomers now claim they have experienced God, while private prayer levels have changed very little. Does this mean religious experience is fairly stable, that once people feel they have experienced God, for example, such a belief is not redefined and discarded later on in life?

The data here do not enable us to know, since we don't know how much overlap we have. For example, we don't know if the 47% of Xers who thought they had experienced God in 2000 includes the 43% who said the same thing as teens in the 1980s.

However, by now you should know that we attempt to have a data answer for everything! Our **Project Canada** national adult surveys spanning 1975 through 2000 have included some people who participated in the previous surveys, generating what is known as "panel data." For example, some 275 people who were part of the 2000 survey were the very same individuals who took part in the 1985 survey.[13] In response to the question, *"Do you believe you have experienced God's presence?"* 52% said "no" and 48% said "yes" in the year 2000. But when we compared their responses in 1985 with those in 2000, here's what we found.

- The 48% who said "yes" consist of 36% who *continue* to maintain, as they had in 1985, that they have experienced God, while another 12%, led by people between the ages of 40 and 54, *now* make that claim;
- The 52% who say they have *not* experienced God are made up of 45% who reported the same thing in 1985, and 7% who previously made the claim, but no longer do. The *no*'s, incidentally, include some 55% of adults under 40 versus about 40% of adults over 40.

In short, this "panel peek" suggests that as many as 85% of the people who think they have experienced God retain that belief over a considerable period of time — in this case 15 years minimum from the time we first asked. New claims of religious experience seem to be a bit higher among people in their 40s. These findings are consistent with what we have just observed for teens and Young Boomers from the 1980s, where claims of experiencing God have increased somewhat as they have moved into their late 20s, 30s, and early 40s.

Dreams

As expected, not all dreams are being realized. More than half of those Gen X teens in the '80s planned to go to university. Just over 40% did, but far fewer than that have graduated, at least so far. Most have realized their goals of having careers, with about 50% currently holding full-time jobs that provide them with "a great deal" or "quite a bit" of enjoyment. Levels for Younger Boomers are similar with slightly predictable differences given that they are a decade older — fewer having attended university, more employed as opposed to still being in school or temporarily at home raising young children, fewer reporting high levels of enjoyment from their careers.

Regarding some of the other dreams, increasing numbers of both cohorts are now married and having children — expectations that, with all due respect, are not particularly hard to fulfill. The more demanding goal is "to stay with the same partner for life," something that appears to have been the game plan of at least 90% of teenagers.[14] Some 8% of our teens from the '80s have already seen that dream disappear by the age of 35; similarly, about 6% of the Young Boomers in the '80s were divorced or separated by age 30, 12% by age 45.

As for the dream of being financially comfortable, about six in ten teens from the '80s, along with close to eight in ten Young Boomers from

Table 7.7. **Realized and Unrealized Dreams:**
Teens and Younger Boomers in the 1980s and in 2000

	1980s Teens	2000 26–35	1980s YB20s	2000 36–45
Education and Career				
Plan to go to univ/did so	54%	43	—	39
Plan to have career/ now employed full time	84	73	—	77
Expect good job/ high level enjoyment from	73	50	—	45
Other Hopes and Expectations				
Divorced/separated	—	8	6	12
High value on comfortable life/satisfied with finances	75	59	68	76
Anyone who works hard will rise to top	74	45	59	53

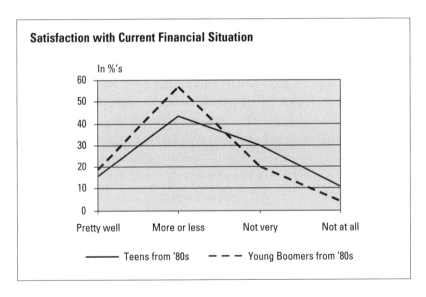

Satisfaction with Current Financial Situation

In %'s

——— Teens from '80s   – – – Young Boomers from '80s

the same decade, indicate they are either "pretty satisfied" or "more or less satisfied" with their financial situations. However, the idea that "anyone who works hard will rise to the top" is being increasingly abandoned as people move through their late 20s, 30s, and early 40s.

As we have seen, that's hardly to say they are ceasing to create new dreams and new ideals. Myrna Kostash, examining the thoughts of Canadian 25- to 35-year-olds in her recent book *The Next Canada*, concludes a pervasive theme is that Canadians "take care of each other." She writes, "It may not be true . . . it may not even be so Canadian, but they say it is. They *assert* it. It's what they want."[15] If she is correct, it sounds like an improvement on their vanishing ideal of unlimited social mobility.

Two Questions: Gender and Divorce Differences

I want to close this section on how teens are going to turn out by addressing two common and important questions. **First, do those persistent differences in values and attitudes between teenage males and females that we have been observing in the youth surveys decrease with time?** Put another and more direct way, as males grow out of their male teen subculture, do they move in the direction of being as civil and compassionate as females? **Second, given the widespread speculation about not only short-term but longer-term consequences of divorce on children, what do the national surveys actually show?**

Gender Differences

The short answer on male-female *value differences*, based on tracking teens from the 1980s who are now between the ages of 26 and 35, is that males do not appear to be changing very much.

- Slightly more young men say they are placing a high level of importance on *being loved* and *honesty* than was the case in the '80s. But male levels are still below those of females. And men are not showing any greater inclination to value *politeness*.
- Enjoyment-source changes have been fairly consistent for both males and females, *friends* becoming somewhat less important — especially for men, along with *mothers*. Enjoyment levels for *fathers* are down even more than for mothers, in part reflecting the previously noted growing disenchantment with fathers when divorce has taken place.
- There have been large declines in the confidence both men and women have in *schools*. Significantly more males now agree that *women do not have enough power* in Canadian life, but their level is still well below that of females. In both gender instances there has been a large increase in the acceptance of *homosexuality,* but here again the level for women remains appreciably higher than that of men.

Table 7.8. **Values, Enjoyment, and Attitudes by Gender:
Teens in the 1980s and in 2000**

	FEMALES		MALES	
	1980s	2000	1980s	2000
Importance: *Very*				
Being loved	93%	92	81	84
Honesty	90	91	80	86
Politeness	70	85	60	58
Enjoyment Level: *Great Deal/Quite a Bit*				
Friends	97	92	95	80
Your mother	80	74	78	71
Your father	72	61	75	63
Attitudes: *Agree*				
Have high level of confidence in schools	71	49	65	32
Women have too little power	65	73	35	52
Approve of homosexuality	31	82	21	71

With respect to *behaviour, outlook,* and *dreams,* changes are definitely taking place for both females and males over time. Some convergence is evident, yet in many instances differences between the sexes persist.

- More young women and men are drinking *alcohol* than in the mid-'80s, but *smoking* levels have reversed: more men than women are now smoking.
- The decline in *religious service attendance* has been sharper for women than for men, with the levels now essentially the same.
- Fewer females say that they are concerned about their *looks.* But further to the idea there has been an accelerated emphasis on the body, the proportion of young men expressing concern about their looks is now approximately the same as that of women. Similar proportions of females and males, as in the '80s, continue to say they are *happy,* just with a little less enthusiasm.

Expectations about success that teenagers held back in the '80s have hardly been realized by all females and males. Very significantly, women have led the way in saying goodbye to the idea that *success* is attainable for anyone who is willing to work hard. The widespread dream of attending university has come true for about 55% of females

Table 7.9. **Behaviour, Concerns, and Dreams by Gender:**
Teens in the 1980s and in 2000

| | FEMALES | | MALES | |
	1980s	2000	1980s	2000
Select Behaviour				
Drink alcohol	76%	85	77	88
Smoke cigarettes	42	32	34	42
Attend services weekly	25	9	21	9
Personal Concerns and Outlook				
I'm concerned about my looks.	52	42	38	41
I myself am "very happy."	26	22	25	19
I myself am "pretty happy."	63	67	64	66
Dreams				
Anyone who works hard will rise to top.	76	36	72	57
I plan to go to university/did so.	60	54	53	30
When I graduate, I can find a good job/enjoy current job, full time or part time.	70	53	77	61

and 30% of males. And the expectation that they could find a good job when they graduated has been partially realized, but less so for women. Some 60% of males say they are receiving "a great deal" or "quite a bit" of enjoyment from their jobs, compared to just over 50% of females.

Such ongoing gender differences raise important questions about the different ways females and males continue to be socialized in Canada, as well as the extent to which they are simply different. It may well be, as Harvard's Carol Gilligan has argued in her landmark 1982 book, *In a Different Voice*, that females are characterized by an ethic of care, a morality of "the web" that emphasizes the fulfillment of responsibilities of people who are connected to one another. They speak "in a different voice," being more caring and less competitive. For many, adolescence is a time when a major loss in self-confidence and self-esteem takes place. Male morality, says Gilligan, tends to be a morality of "the ladder," a more abstract hierarchy of rights and freedoms, resulting in an ethic of justice. Males emerge from adolescence with no such pervasive problems with self.[16]

Christina Hoff Sommers, a former philosophy professor and currently a fellow at a private American institute, has made a forceful case for ongoing differences being in large part the result of different education system emphases.[17] In her recent book, *The War Against Boys: How Misguided Feminism Is Harming Our Young Men*, Sommers maintains that schools have been creating an advantage for girls, complete with an ideology that says masculinity is bad and femininity is good. Assisted by special attention, girls are more academically successful than boys, and are also better adjusted more generally. She is highly critical of Gilligan as the person most responsible for promoting the idea that girls were in crisis and in need of special treatment. Sommers asserts that a boy's biology determines much of what he prefers and is attracted to. Aggression and competition are biologically determined male attributes. By denying the nature of boys, she says, education theorists can cause them much misery.[18] Presumably, according to Sommers, some differences between males and females are going to persist, because boys are boys and girls are girls.

Divorce Differences
Much has been said about the short-term and long-term effects of divorce on children. The September 2000 *Time* magazine cover story discussed earlier quoted retired clinical psychologist Judith Wallerstein as saying that "the harm caused by divorce" may be "graver and longer lasting than we suspected." [19] Its effects may include anxiety about abandonment and the expectation of short-lived ties, which in turn have negative consequences for enduring relationships. Children of divorce are said to be involved in greater use of drugs and alcohol during their youth, and to have fewer marriages and children and more divorces than children from intact families. Wallerstein's research is based on a comparison of about a hundred children of divorce and 45 children from intact families in the San Francisco Bay area over a 25-year period (1971 to 1996).[20] A Statistics Canada report released in June of 1999, based on tracking teenagers from 1982 to 1995, concluded that those whose parents were divorced tended to put off marriage. Once married, they were more likely to experience separation or divorce. They also tended to have lower incomes, primarily because they were starting from a home situation where their families were economically disadvantaged, making upward mobility more difficult.[21]

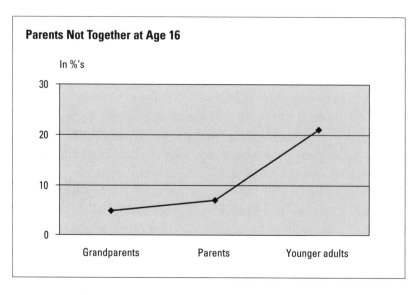

Parents Not Together at Age 16

It is obvious that a critical factor in understanding the consequences of divorce for children is financial resources, not divorce per
se. A modest amount of reflection versus rhetoric should make it abundantly clear that many of the negative consequences for children of
divorce can be traced to the lack of money and its drastic effects on
how one can live and how one can feel.[22] In the short term, lack of
resources is bound to affect young people adversely; in the long term,
that will not necessarily be the case.

In the **Project Canada 2000** national survey, we asked Canadian
adults about the marital status of their natural parents when they
themselves were 16. Some 10%, led by young adults, said they had
come from homes where their parents were divorced by that point in
their lives. These respondents tend to be disproportionately young. By
isolating those under 50, it is possible to get a brief, succinct peek at
how children of divorce have been "turning out."[23] The sample is fairly
small and the findings tentative. But the findings contribute some
information to the overall discussion of this topic.

Adults in this age grouping who are from homes where their parents divorced are so far less likely than adults from intact families to
have *married* and more apt to be *cohabiting* or *single*. However, to this
point at least, they are no more likely than others to be *divorced themselves.* Consistent with the Stats Canada findings, these adults under 50

indicate they have lower *family incomes*, in part because they are more often on their own. They are somewhat more likely to have attended *technical and business schools* rather than *university*. Their reported *health* levels are fairly similar to people who grew up in intact homes.

Table 7.10. **Social Characteristics and Divorce: Adults 18 to 49**

| | At 16, natural parents were | |
	Together [487]	Div or Sep [70]
Marital Status		
Married	58%	44
Never married	22	26
Cohabiting	11	27
Divorced/separated	8	3
Widowed	1	<1
Have been divorced	15	11
Total Family Income		
>$60,000	47	41
$30,000–60,000	37	40
<$30,000	16	19
Education		
Degree-plus	39	26
Tech-business	30	46
High school or less	31	28
Health: *Excellent or Good*	79	74

People whose parents divorced or separated are just as likely as everyone else to place high value on characteristics such as *being loved, family life, concern for others, hard work,* and *spirituality*. By the time they have reached their 20s, 30s, and 40s, they are no more likely to be *smokers* or *drinkers* — if anything, possibly less likely to drink. They are slightly more inclined to report *feelings of inferiority* but less likely to indicate they experience *depression*. Further, perhaps in part reflecting the legacy of stigma from days gone by, they are a bit less likely than people from intact families to attend *religious services* regularly.

These Canadians whose parents divorced or separated are just as likely as others to express *positive self-images* — to maintain, for example, that they are good people, well liked, and competent, if slightly less inclined to say they have lots of confidence. With respect to *resilience* over time, they, along with others, maintain that "when life has not been going well, I still have believed that things would get better." There are no significant differences in the tendency of children from divorced and separated homes and those from intact situations to claim to be "*very happy*" or "*pretty happy*," or in the level of enjoyment they

Table 7.11. **Values, Behaviour, and Divorce: Adults 18 to 49**

	At 16, natural parents were	
	Together	**Div or Sep**
Values		
Being loved	87%	83
Family life	85	91
Concern for others	70	76
Forgiveness	70	68
Working hard	63	55
Spirituality	30	34
Select Behaviour		
Drink alcohol	87	77
Smoke cigarettes	34	35
Bothered by depression	24	15
Bothered by inferiority feelings	21	30
Attend services weekly	17	13

Table 7.12. **Self-Image, Dreams, and Divorce: Adults 25 to 49, 2000**

	At 16, natural parents were	
"I . . ."	**Together**	**Div or Sep**
Self-Image		
Have a number of good qualities	99%	99
Am a good person	99	96
Am well liked	96	96
Can do most things well	90	94
Am good-looking	80	80
Have lots of confidence	77	69
Outlook and Dreams		
Have maintained hope for better things	93	91
Am "very happy"/ "pretty happy"	90	87
Have high enjoyment in my marriage/relship	78	76
Am satisfied with financial situation	71	58
Want home life I grew up in	62	30

indicate they are receiving from their *marriages and relationships*. There is, however, a slightly higher tendency for those who come from intact homes to express satisfaction with their current financial situations.

Despite all these findings of limited differences overall between people whose parents stayed together and those whose parents did not, just three in ten from homes that were not intact say they *want a home* like the one they grew up in, compared to six in ten for those whose parents were together. The message here seems clear: for the most part, adults have been able to proceed with positive living, regardless of whether their parents stayed together. But, in their own cases, they are aspiring to have marriages that last.

Assessment

We started this chapter by reminding everyone that the focus of adult concern about teenagers is not only the present but also the future. While no one can say definitively what will happen to today's teens in the next few decades, we can get some clues by looking at what's been happening to previous teen cohorts as they have moved into adulthood, keeping an eye out for life cycle versus generational characteristics.

When adults are asked pointedly for their **views about how they have changed** over time, many feel they have become more appreciative of parents but have become both more positive and more negative toward people as a whole. They acknowledge, on balance, that they themselves have tended to become less polite and honest, regardless of generation. One in two say they have expanded their views of what they could accomplish in their lifetimes. All three adult generations claim an increase in acceptance of a variety of sexual issues. The reports of all three generations, led by Gen Xers, show patterns of drop-off in religious involvement between their teens and late 20s, and some increase thereafter, but not enough to bring their cohort levels back to their preteen levels — which in turn have been shrinking inter-generationally, reducing the pools of religiously socialized children.

Two cohort examinations, of teens and Younger Boomers in the '80s versus today, reveal fairly consistent patterns as teens have moved into their late 20s and early 30s and Boomers have reached their late 30s and early 40s. There has been little change in core values pertaining to the importance of family life, being loved, friendship, and a comfortable life, except for a slight increase in the value placed on politeness. Enjoyment of friends, music, and parents has decreased somewhat as these cohorts have hit their late 20s and beyond, presumably reflecting, in part, the emergence of one's own "new" family. Social attitudes have changed little, sexual attitudes a lot — with views becoming more liberal. Religious involvement and beliefs have both decreased somewhat; experience and prayer have remained steady. Dreams relating to education, good jobs, lasting marriages, and comfortable lives have been realized for many, but to this point, at least, far from all.

We also have looked at **two controversial areas:** gender differences and divorce consequences over time. A look at teenage gender differences between 1980 and 2000 shows that variations between males and females have changed little over the past two decades. Women, however, have led the way in abandoning the idea that hard work will lead to success. A comparison of adults 18 to 49 who have come from homes where parents were together versus those who were not, reveals fairly limited differences, apart from those characteristics associated with economic disparities growing up. The home goal of the future for most people is one where partners stay together.

In keeping with all these "twos," I want to suggest **two** implications these findings have for our understanding of what may happen to teenagers as they move into their 20s, 30s, and beyond.

First, **older doesn't necessarily equal nicer.** These findings suggest that as young people get into their 20s, 30s, and beyond, many become more suspicious, more cynical, and less concerned about others. They also, on balance, become less honest and less polite. Gender differences dating back to adolescence also largely remain intact. Ironically, rather than being a period that marks the end of the problems of youth, adulthood shows signs of being a time in which some of the good things of youth disappear. The problem is not young people; it's what happens to young people when they grow up. *One important exception:* youth crime. It decreases progressively as males and females move out of their teens. Because of the publicity given youth crime, little wonder average Canadians assume teens as a whole "get better as they get older." That's true of crime. But as for attitudes and behaviour among young people more generally, the rule is this: "Some do, most don't."

Second, many of the changes that take place seem to be tied fairly predictably to **life cycle** versus **what is taking place in the culture**. Technological and cultural change, not to mention claims about unique generations and even the existence of a postmodern era, may be getting the ink. But when it comes to what people value and want, core values involving a good family life, love, friendship, and being successful and comfortable seem to persist through it all, with the "it all" including changing family structures. To the extent teens change — become more appreciative of parents, rely less on friends, parents, and music for enjoyment, become more critical of schools, even become more accepting of sexual behaviour — aging and life-cycle explanations seem to account fairly well for the shifts. The same can be said when we attempt to understand declining idealism about people and hard work, as well as declines and then modest increases in religious involvement.

Don't get me wrong. **Culture** is obviously critical to how life is being lived at its various stages. So is technology, as part of culture. In attempting to understand young people, as well as other generations, we need to have a clear reading, as we have tried to have throughout the book, of what is happening in the culture. But what's interesting to see is that, allowing for the potential impact of culture, there are so many continuities across generations with respect to what people want out of life. And when some of their values and attitudes change, these changes are inclined to be associated with the movement from one life stage to another. Culture is constantly offering us all choices. The media, friends, parents, and just about everything and everyone else bid to influence us.

But these findings suggest that these highly publicized potential sources of influence are anything but irrepressible. In the end, when people get married and have children, for example, they use the media as they see fit, frequently select new friends, and expect their parents to play new roles. The life stage determines the resources one wants and the social arrangements one expects, not the other way around. We interact with culture, including technology. Then we do what we want, based largely on where we are at that point in our lives.

We are close to "adding the findings up" and assessing what this all means for Canada's teens. Just before we do, I want to turn to some brief reflections on what we might expect of their younger brothers and sisters.

Chapter Eight

What Can Be Expected of Their Younger Brothers and Sisters

Now that we have looked at teens today, yesterday, and tomorrow, I suspect that many parents and teachers, as well as others interested in youth, will have one further question: what about the next generation? **Will the teens of tomorrow be any different from the teens of today?** What will those kids who are now in elementary school, including a fair number of their younger brothers and sisters, be like when they are teenagers?

Again, obviously we can't say for sure. But just as we got some clues about how today's teens are going to turn out by looking at what's happened to other cohorts as they've been getting older, so today's teens provide some hints as to what the next group of teenagers will look like in a decade or so.

Just who is this next cohort of teens? While age cutting points and labels are highly arbitrary, some marketing people have found it helpful to identity them as nine- to 14-year-olds, and to label them "tweens" — not quite young children, not quite older teens. Tweens and teens currently number just over two million people each, totalling about 15% of the Canadian population. In generational language, both age cohorts tend to be defined as part of the Millennial Generation, which is seen by observers such as Neil Howe and William Strauss as young people born shortly after 1980.[1] The Millennials have also been referred to by names including "Generation Y" and the "Echo Generation" (this is far from an exact science). In very rough terms — because the age cutting points are imprecise — as of the year 2004, when the

297

Size of Canadian Generations		
Birth Years	**Name**	**Size**
1985–2004	Millennials	8 million
1965–84	Xers	9 million
1945–64	Boomers	10 million
1925–44	Silent	5 million

full twenty-year complement of the Millennials will have been born, the "M's" will number about eight million, slightly fewer than the nine million Xers and fewer again than the ten million living Boomers.

Before I sketch what I see as some fairly predictable patterns, let's take a quick look at a sampling of popular views offered by the media, as well as some of the reflections of academics.

Some Views from the Media

The media have been giving a fair amount of attention to tweens, particularly their consumption habits and entertainment tastes. Much of the data are provided by market researchers. Two articles, one from Canada and one from the U.S., illustrate some of the generalizations being made about this age group.

In March of 1999 *Maclean's* gave front-cover treatment to "Gen Y," focusing on the four million older Millennials born prior to the 1990s. Writer Andrew Clark wrote that "kid culture is king," claiming that this, "by far the most racially diverse generation in Canada's history," also comprises young people who "have more money in their pockets than ever before."[2] Their influence, he said, "is everywhere — in music stores with CDs by bands ranging from the Moffats and Britney Spears to Korn and The Offspring; in clothing stores with labels such as JNCO and Snug; on TV programs such as *Dawson's Creek* and *Felicity*; and in movies such as *Cruel Intentions* and *Varsity Blues.*"

According to Clark, "never before has so much been pitched to so many who are so young." He noted that these two-million-plus tweens have been estimated to have $1.5 billion to spend, primarily via their parents. Corporate advertisers are consequently aiming their commercials directly at tweens, who in turn, wrote Clark, are exerting what experts call "pester power" or "kidfluence." As we all are well aware, companies frequently engage in "cross-referencing," uniting to promote products — toys with movies, videos with fast food.

Two points on gender and age. A YTV survey found that more boys than girls spend their allowances on video games, while girls spend more money than boys on CDs, as well as more frequently show adulation — albeit often short-lived — on rock groups such as the Spice Girls, the Backstreet Boys, and 'N Sync. Tweens are also "would-be teens." Susan Mandryk of YTV commented, "We never tell a tween that they are a tween," because they want to be teens and buy products that make them feel sophisticated — an observation backed up by Environics research showing that 12- to 14-year-olds typically want to be 18, while 15- to 19-year-olds want to be 20.

Clark also notes that young Ys are part of a Web generation: "If baby boomers were the TV generation, then their children are the Web generation who commune by the light of their computer monitors." Echo kids, he says, are accustomed to gathering information and communicating on-line, "and tweens are even more wired than their teen elders." They grew up with the Web and, thanks to the reality of tougher curfews, have more time to spend on-line.

As a data update footnote to the *Maclean's* piece, a YTV poll released in late 2000 found that 75% of tweens have a computer at home; of these, two-thirds have access to the Internet. Boys spend an average of 4.5 hours a week on-line, compared to 3.2 hours for girls. More girls use e-mail than boys; more boys than girls visit sports sites.[3] The poll also found that tweens now have some $1.8 billion at their disposal, with their allowances standing at an average of just over $9 a week. Nine- to 14-year-olds are upbeat about the future, with most of them expecting to attend college or university, own their own homes, and be better off than their parents when they grow up.[4]

South of the border, Edna Gundersen wrote an illuminating piece on the nature of younger Millennials for the September 2000 edition of *USA Today*.[5] This generation is estimated to number about 80 million people in the U.S., roughly 25% of the population, similar in size to Boomers and about twice the size of Xers. Born and raised during good economic times, they are described by Gundersen as a "rising tide of moneyed minors" who are outspending "all previous generations"

Harry Potter as a Woodstock moment

TORONTO, *Globe and Mail,* Rex Murphy, July 10, 2000 — *I don't get to deal with many books that are under embargo until a precise moment of mass release. The illustrious* Harry Potter and the Goblet of Fire *is only my second. The previous classic was* Monica's Story, *the fabled Ms. Lewinsky's swoop into sword and sorcery, White-House style.*

The marketing imagination was firing on all 32 cylinders for young Mr. Potter. It's the latest ingredient in celebrity-world-electronic-marketing's Great Stew. Harry is one now, in the news-tainment universe of Elian and Monica, Backstreet Boys and Pokémon, Leonardo DiCaprio and Star Wars — Episode I *. . . celebrity-sick dawn of the 21st-century world.*

The Harry Potter phenomenon . . . comes straight from the steaming engine room of the great glitz factory of our time. Potter is one with the weekend megamovies, pop stars, sit-coms and reality TV, and belongs to the same machine that feeds their crass, short forgettable lives. It isn't what's on the machine that counts. It is the machine itself. It merely wants to fill the air in grey hot bursts of event or pseudo-event. All the categories have melted.

"As long as it gets kids to read, it's all right, right?" Wrong. It's a megadose of fandom and faddishness . . . the need to have something now because everyone else who counts is going to have it now. Some parents in New York lined up for the 12:01 a.m. sales event so that they could FedEx the great tome tout de suite *to their kiddies at camp. They weren't buying a book; they were appeasing a monster. . . . The race for millions to buy this book is obviously more important than reading it, being part of the "event" more important than the pretext of the event.*

Once upon a time, long ago and far away, Harry Potter used to be a book. Now? Now it's in the same whirling continuum with Ricky Martin and Chicken Run, *the loudest video game and the latest CD. It's a terrible reflection, but the 7- to 11-year-olds now have their own Woodstock moment.*

and "wield unprecedented influence on the marketplace." According to market research, this cohort, she says, is "tech-savvy, coddled, optimistic, prone to abrupt shifts in tastes and tough to pigeonhole."

Gundersen writes that "Pipsqueak pop became ubiquitous with the explosion of kiddie media," noting, "Boomers relied on radio, Gen Xers got the added visuals of MTV, and Gen Y has it all — a vast Internet supply of fan Web sites and downloadable songs," along with a generous supply of cable channels.

Since the late '90s, they have been giving their adoration and entertainment dollars to groups and individuals created and groomed for what she describes as the "bubblegum market," including the Spice Girls, 'N Sync, Britney Spears, Christina Aguilera, and the Backstreet Boys. One magazine executive is quoted as saying, "This generation has a voracious appetite, and the record companies are happy to satiate it. Kids are being bombarded with more and more types of media designed for their demographic, with some marketing plans targeting 5-year-olds."

New and Old among Greatest Pop Songs

In late 2000, experts at MTV and *Rolling Stone* released a list of 100 pop songs they view as "the greatest" since 1963. Generation choices are illustrated here.

1. "Yesterday," The Beatles (1965)
2. "I Can't Get No Satisfaction," The Rolling Stones (1965)
3. "Smells Like Teen Spirit," Nirvana (1991)
4. "Like A Virgin," Madonna (1984)
5. "Billie Jean," Michael Jackson (1983)
25. "Baby, One More Time," Britney Spears (1998)
35. "Born to Run," Bruce Springsteen (1975)
45. "Tears in Heaven," Eric Clapton (1992)
55. "Bye, Bye, Bye," 'N Sync (2000)
65. "Just What I Needed," The Cars (1978)
75. "Hot Fun in the Summertime," Sly & Family Stone (1969)
85. "Surrender," Cheap Trick (1978)
90. "The Boy is Mine," Brandy & Monica (1998)
100. "Tainted Love," Soft Cell (1982)

Source: *Rolling Stone* and Associated Press, November 17, 2000.

The pervasiveness of "kiddie ditties is no surprise," says Gundersen, considering the good times. She reminds readers that Boomers were embroiled in civil rights battles, sexual liberation, and anti-war protests that launched rock music, while Generation X was mired in a depressed economy and turned to angry, brooding grunge. In contrast, "Gen Y, marinating in financial fitness, fancies peppy pop." She maintains, however, that "Cupid's arrow is fated to point elsewhere once these youngsters reach puberty," when, as one observer points out, "they get angrier and the hormones get going." Observers predict any number of scenarios — that existing entertainers like Britney Spears, the Hansons, Korn, and Limp Bizkit will grow and change with their audiences; that they simply will disappear; that there will a rise in rock 'n' roll, since the complexity and turmoil that comes with adolescence is conducive to rock; and that young Ys will eventually turn to dominant music forms, including jazz and classical.

Some Views from the Researchers

Illustrative thoughts on the next generation of teens can be seen in the work of Canadian demographer David Foot and the American duo of Neil Howe and William Strauss.

In his well-known *Boom, Bust & Echo*, written with Daniel Stoffman, Foot uses population data to make his generational observations and projections. In the process, he deviates a fair amount from the cutoff points and labels used by other generational analysts. Foot describes "Echo kids" as those born between 1980 and 1995, and maintains these offspring of Boomers currently make up "the second most important cohort group" next to the Boomers. He also adds a new category for people born between 1996 and 2010, which he calls "Millennial Busters." Our current tweens are close to what he refers to as "the back end" or youngest of his "Echo kids."[6]

Youth of the Echo generation, says Foot, have "wanted the same things that teenagers have always wanted — music and clothing their parents disapproved of and lots of unhealthy food." The big difference from the past: these kids have had more money to spend. Whereas Boomers typically had one employed parent and an average of three other siblings, their Echo offspring frequently have had dual-income parents and only one sister or brother in the household.

Saturated in television since birth, they are, according to Foot, "the most brand-conscious cohort in the history of the planet." Tweens are especially peer-oriented and brand-conscious. As for food, they are into diversity. Things once regarded as ethnic or exotic, like wraps, fajitas, and other foreign cuisines, are seen as normal daily fare for urban Echo kids. They are unique in that they've been raised with computers and the Web, making their opinions important in the family purchases of computer-related equipment.[7]

Foot sounds one negative note: to the extent teens are becoming more violent, the size of the Echo cohort means there could be an increase in youth violence as it "moves into its crime-prone years," offering "no reason for anyone to feel complacent about crime in Canada. Our police forces are going to be busy."[8]

What's the outlook for the Echo generation? Foot writes that the fact the cohort is so large is "always bad news." They crowded nurseries in the '80s and did the same thing to elementary and high schools in late '80s and '90s. Their size means those farthest back in the cohort will have a rougher ride. "Think of a cohort," he says, "as a group of people all wanting to get into the same theatre to see the same show. There is no reserved seating. So who claims the best seats? The ones who get there first." The back end "will have to scramble."[9]

American writers Neil Howe and William Strauss, as noted earlier, are buoyant about Millennials. They date them from 1982 to 2002, meaning that at the time their book, *Millennials Rising*, was published in 2000, they were speaking of young people 18 and under, including tweens, nine to 14. This is a very extensive book, in which the authors combine data, cyclical theory, extensive cultural material, and nothing short of wild imaginations to offer a comprehensive and thought-provoking look at Millennials. They describe the Millennial cohort as "more numerous, more affluent, better educated, and more ethnically diverse" than "any other youth generation in living memory." They see them as having a new focus on teamwork, achievement, modesty, and good conduct, including less involvement in crime. They identify with their parents' values and accept institutional authority. Tweens specifically are being supervised more than their predecessors of the early '80s, are conscientious students, and are growing up on computers.[10]

Messages confusing to kids

Toronto Sun, Steve Simmons, March 5, 1999 — *A group of eight-year-old boys congregated in my basement the other day and one of them loudly shouted: "What do you want?" And then everyone responded in union: "We want head!"*

This alarming piece of noise created one of those moments of parental concern. "Do you guys know what 'head' is?" I asked the youngsters, trying to be stern and hold in my laughter at precisely the same time. "Sure," one of them said boldly. "Head is Al Snow's doll. He carries the head around with him."

Al Snow, for the record, is a WWF wrestler with an act. He holds up this scruffy-looking head of a doll to the crowd whenever he works and shouts: "What do you want?" And the crowd, without failure, shouts back at him: "We want head." It's all in the name of good fun. Unless you happen to be a parent of a youngster who can't get enough of WWF wrestling. Unless you happen to be concerned about the mixed messages of sexual language, sexual stereotyping and violence that so pervades what used to pass for children's programming.

. . . My 11-year-old's favourite expression is "Suck it." He learned that from watching the WWF. He just doesn't say it any more. Time was, if you let your kids watch wrestling on television, the only thing you had to worry about was whether one of your children was going to try to put a sleeper hold on another kid in the neighbourhood. That wasn't necessarily a good thing, either. Violence was one issue. Now there are other issues. Language. Sexual stereotyping. Sexual innuendo. So many messages, so many of them confusing to kids who already are forced to grow on an unfortunate fast track.

. . . I will continue to watch the WWF from time to time, partly because I'm interested, partly because I want to see what my 11-year-old is watching. As for my eight-year-old, he's on the outside looking in and not at all happy about it. He can't understand what he's watching and I'm not prepared to explain it to him.

The American cultural context itself, say Howe and Strauss, has been becoming increasing oriented toward Millennials. Since the early 1990s, child issues have risen to the top of the nation's political agenda and youth advocacy groups have multiplied. Culturally, "anything and everything about kids" were the hottest media-growth markets of the '90s. "Even the national media now engages in wall-to-wall child absorption."[11] That extends to new kinds of gentler, more civil, and even moral emphases in mainline network programming, as well as the explosion of new programming: as of 1999, more than 1,300 kids' programs were appearing weekly on 29 channels. Top-rated kids' shows included the feel-good *Teletubbies*, and *Rugrats* — the latter about well-behaved kids, created by two Bart Simpson writers.[12]

Of considerable importance, Howe and Strauss argue that the "kid culture" is leading the way in a fairly dramatic cultural transformation. It is a Gen X to Millennial transition, where "the girl culture has moved from a risk-taking and go-it-alone survivalism to a more serious and adult-approved sweetness" — from "Buffy to Britney, from *Ally McBeal* to *Dawson's Creek*, from *Clueless* to *She's All That.*" As for males, the authors write, "The outlines of the boy transition cross a larger age divide, but are nonetheless discernible. From Eminem to Pokémon, Duke Nukem to the Legend of Zelda, Bart Simpson to Harry Potter, the boy culture is moving away from cynicism and diffuse, pragmatic violence toward . . . focused heroic violence. This X-to-Millennial break," they acknowledge, "is a fissure that has yet to appear in full beyond the younger kids."[13]

Millennials, say Howe and Strauss, constitute "America's most racially and ethnically diverse, and least-Caucasian, generation," with non-whites and Latinos now accounting for about one-third of the 18-and-under population. What's more, they maintain that non-white Millennials are not only major contributors to their generation's fresh persona but are in some ways the most important contributors. They note that African-American city children, for example, "are now the focus of a community renaissance extending through Harlem and Watts to Oakland and Chicago's South Side." Further, they assert that, with "parents even more attached to 'family values' than the white adult majority, the rapidly growing Latino and Asian youth populations are setting a distinctly Millennial tone in their schools and neighborhoods."[14]

LOS ANGELES, Reuters, November 16, 2000 — *What would happen if the Spice Girls released a record in America and no one cared? The feisty English foursome, who ruled the pop world three years ago, saw their third album,* Forever, *debut at a lowly No. 39 on the U.S. pop charts Wednesday, an omen that their* Girl Power! *war cry is losing its potency in one major part of the English-speaking world, at least.*

Rodney Jerkins, who produced much of the album, told Reuters he was "totally disappointed" by the sales, and he accused Virgin Records of not doing enough to promote the album in America. Music industry observers cite many reasons for the apparent fall of the Spice Girls in America, not the least being that every pop act since the dawn of rock 'n' roll faces a short shelf life. Few acts today predate 1990, or last more than four albums.

The Spice Girls managed to break through in America because "they had already become part of a comic soap opera by the time they got here," said music historian Dave Marsh. The pre-pubescent crowd and a few shamefaced adults all had their favourite Spice Girl. Marsh wonders if the Spice Girls were "sexually a bit too bold. The real teen idols tend to have some aura of innocence or safety about them."

Howe and Strauss emphasize they are well aware that "America has millions of kids who take drugs or have risky sex or lie or cheat or swear or are transfixed by the worst of the pop culture. Millions more live impoverished lives, with addicted or missing parents, facing life with little comfort and less hope." Still, they argue, to talk about a generation is to talk about "its social and cultural center of gravity," its direction. "Here," they say, "the Millennials are indeed special, since they are demonstrably reversing a wide array of negative youth trends."[15]

Howe and Strauss maintain that many members of this latest youth cohort are so positive about the future that they resent even being assigned a generational label such as "Y" or "Echo Boomers," feeling such names "say who we follow, but nothing at all about who we are." Surveys indicate today's youth want to be known by a word that respects their newness, "that resets the clock" around "their own timetable." Their preference? "Millennials."[16] The authors maintain this cohort has "a solid chance to become America's next great generation."[17]

Some Hints from Teens Present and Past

We've travelled through a lot of data concerning teens today and yesterday. So, on the basis of what we've learned, let's offer a few succinct and blunt expectations about what today's tweens will look like as tomorrow's teens. Just before we do, let's quickly dispel one widely perpetuated myth: **not all tweenie parents have an abundance of bucks with which to feed their consumption-minded kids' appetites.** Obviously family incomes are all over the map; no need to document that reality. But in addition, subjectively, parents who have at least one child between the ages of six and 12 (our survey's closest breakdown to pure nine- to 14- year-old tweenies) are more likely than other adults (1) to be more pressed for time, (2) to be troubled about lack of money, and (3) to not be satisfied with their current financial situation. Corporate advertisers who are relying on "pester power" are not going to win the hearts of such financially pinched parents.

Table 8.1. **Time and Finances: Adults**

	WITH AND WITHOUT TWEENS	
	Adults with tweens	Adults without tweens
Concerned *"A Great Deal or "Quite a Bit" About* . . .		
Lack of time	60%	46
Lack of money	59	45
Current Time and Finances Leave Me . . .		
Pretty well satisfied	13	23
More or less satisfied	52	49
Not very/not at all satisfied	35	28

On the basis of what we have seen, some projections about tweens who become teens are pretty straightforward. Others are not quite as obvious.

The "No Surprises" Category

1. Tweens will *value* relationships and freedom more than anything else, with success and a comfortable life not far behind. They'll continue to find their primary enjoyment in friends and music, with the only thing up for grabs the kind of music they will tend to embrace. And in the course of spending a lot of money on "being comfortable," they will be targeted relentlessly by companies of every kind, increasingly via the Internet. They will embrace technology with far less awe than adults and their teen predecessors. Interest in professional sports will continue to wane.

2. They'll continue to play down the *influence* of an array of key sources, with the exception of family and friends.

3. The primary *personal concerns* of tweens will be school and life after school, along with a sense that they have neither enough time nor enough money, despite what everybody says about their relative affluence. They'll still be arguing with parents. Their dominant *social concerns* will depend primarily on what the media convince them matters; most will be too preoccupied with personal issues to give much attention and time to addressing social problems on their own — unless the issue affects them directly.

4. **Sexual** attitudes and behaviour will change little, except for the growing acceptance of homosexuality.

5. **Drugs** will continue to be widely available, but continue to be used by only a small minority.

6. **American culture** will continue to be everywhere except in Quebec, where **Québécois language and culture** will continue to dominate.

7. Most tweens-turned-teens will continue to expect to go to **university**, pursue **careers**, and get **good jobs**, regardless of the state of the economy. Most will also expect to be **more comfortable** than their parents — regardless of the state of the economy.

8. Almost all of them will plan to **marry**, have **children**, and **stay with their partners** for life.

9. The majority will plan to **stay in Canada**, preferring to reside in either **B.C. or Ontario**.

10. **Gender differences** will persist.

The "Worth Watching" Category

1. Their older-sibling teens are showing some interest in greater involvement in the community in the future, stirring up questions about some of Howe and Strauss's notions. A question to be answered is will tweens-turned-teens place additional importance on *group life*, including family, as well as on values such as honesty and generosity?

2. Will they give back the **ten bucks**?

3. Consistent with the first question, will levels of *suspicion and distrust* subside?

4. What will be the influence of *digital technology* on teens' interaction?

5. *Violence* is a current concern. Will it continue to be? The outcome here will depend largely on (a) the extent of objective violence during the next decade and (b) how the media treat that violence.

6. Will *Quebec youth* still be divided about staying in Canada? Of course, if there's a downturn in the economy, you know what they will want to do.

7. Will *religious groups* with youth ministries continue to see an upsurge in involvement? Or, failing that, will groups continue to have large numbers of tween-teens who identify with them and anticipate having rites of passage carried out in the future ?

8. Will there be *significant variations* from the basic "good news" about teens as a whole, including the difficulties of both disadvantaged and troubled youth?

9. In the face of ongoing immigration, acculturation, and assimilation, will tweens-turned-teens be increasingly colour-blind, as many observers say people are, in their interaction with young people of different *cultural and racial groups?*

10. Will **Howe and Strauss's** radical prophecies about what Millennials are going to accomplish come to pass? The accomplishments need to be watched, at least out of one eye, just in case. If the authors are right, our culture and country are in for some interesting interaction between Millennials, Boomers, and Xers in the future.

Assessment

The two **media portrayals** of tweens that we looked at suggest that young and racially diverse Millennials are experiencing fairly prosperous economic times, are being vigorously pursued by big business, are positive about themselves and optimistic about the future, and have grown up with the Web. They look forward to getting older . . . and gender differences persist.

Using demographic data, **David Foot** looks at this burgeoning generation of Boomers' children and sees affluence, which is reflected in brand-consciousness, a large appetite for consumption, and the embracing of computer technology; he adds the cautionary note that, because of their size, they also could know a growing level of violence. For Echo kids in general and the tweenie tail-enders in particular, competition will be intense as they attempt to retain and improve on the comfortable lives to which many of them have become accustomed.

Howe and Strauss draw on varied sources and take imaginative chances in viewing younger Millennials as affluent and diverse young people who are valuing group life and good conduct, are conscientious at school, and accept institutional authority. Growing up in a culture that places increasing importance on children and young people, the tweens specifically are leading the way in a transformation of cultural values, a departure from Gen Xers that has yet to appear fully beyond younger tweens. Contrary to the expectations of some, such changes, if anything, are most evident among non-white Millennials, specifically urban African-Americans and Latino and Asian youth. Howe and Strauss concede that millions of American kids do not fit their overall depiction, yet argue that, at its social and cultural centre, "Millennials are reversing a wide array of negative youth trends."[18] They are upbeat about their future. So are the authors.

Our brief **extrapolation from our findings about teenagers present and past** suggests that, when today's tweens become teens, they will resemble their older sisters and brothers in a number of areas, including values, sources of enjoyment, personal concerns, and expectations. What is not as clear is whether they will follow in their older siblings' footsteps when it comes to such things as the value they place on group life, concern about violence, the influence of changing technology on interaction with others, intergroup relations, religious involvement, and the long-range question of what they — as part of the Millennial generation — will eventually accomplish.

Three Brief Observations

First, as I have tried to show, and everyone in a reflective moment clearly realizes, **all tweens are not affluent** because all tweens do not have affluent parents — the primary source of their money. Market researchers have a vested interest in telling corporations how they can best extract money from consumers. In their exuberance and subsequent media reports of their findings, it's easy to lose sight of the fact that large numbers of tweens can only dream of being the kind of consumers that are being so enthusiastically portrayed. The country's wealth is hardly divided evenly; "average allowances," like "average incomes," says little about the ranges involved. Of course there is much money to be spent. But the variations in tweenie consumer power need to be clearly recognized.

Second, some of the media and research reports are inclined to **confuse technological change with newness** — to equate the arrival of the Internet, for example, with transformed young people. I raised this point earlier, at the beginning of chapter 5, and it needs to be repeated in this context. Almost every observer of "tweens" speaks not only of the presence of computer technology, but assumes all kinds of things about its impact on the lives of tweens. In turn, tweens themselves can buy such a view and assume that because they have the Web, for example, they themselves are different. In a widely disseminated article on Ys entitled "Here Comes the Sunshine Generation," Vancouver writer Deborah Jones cites a grade 9 student who says, "We're totally different. We're the first to grow up with a lot of technology around us." Randy Morse, a web-site developer and head of an Edmonton educational multimedia firm, offers a blunt corrective: "At the end of the day, technology on its own changes nothing."[19]

The question, as I suggested earlier, is not what will be the impact on our young people — not to mention the rest of us — but rather, what kind of use do we want to make of the technologies that are being developed? They will keep on emerging. It's how we choose to use them that will determine what changes take place. Tweens are not changed by television; they are changed by how they and we choose to use television.

The same is true of computers or any other resource that technology devises. It's clear that, underneath all the technology/change hype, what most people value, enjoy, think, believe, and hope for go on pretty much as usual. Tweens in all likelihood will be no different.

Third, it should be obvious that the heightened consumption tendencies of tweens are not merely the result of their having more money to spend. Such inclinations are also the direct result of **corporations** in Canada — including large U.S.-based multinationals — using increasingly sophisticated methods to **target the youth market** more aggressively than ever before. Here, beyond merely attempting to identify needs and meet them, companies work hard to *create* needs and satisfy them. Some obvious areas of need creation are clothes and footwear, movies and music. But perhaps it is nowhere more evident than in the burgeoning computer industry.

Companies that manufacture and sell computers and related products are in the unique position of being able to "mystify" their products, yet insist they are things that are absolutely essential to our children and us. Just before sitting down at the keyboard, I heard a television commercial that reminded viewers we need to have optimum access to the Internet so our children can get "better grades" and everyone can get "better jobs." Really? I wouldn't have known that if they hadn't "informed" me. . . . Further, the industry produces ever-changing hardware and software that make equipment obsolete at a pace that easily outdistances the short shelf life of the fashions of our tweens and teens. Getting started and keeping up is not only essential, it is also very expensive. Such realities serve to remind us, in the words of University of Western Ontario youth researchers James Côté and Anton Allahar, that people "in the business world often have few moral misgivings about the health and well-being of their targeted market."[20]

Tweens will continue to be besieged by corporate entrepreneurs. Somewhere in the midst all of this they, along with the rest of us, need to learn to distinguish between their needs and wants and corporate sales agendas.

What's All the Fuss About?

I SUSPECT THAT IN THE DAYS FOLLOWING THE PUBLICATION OF THIS book, when people ask, "What's happening with young people today?" the primary assumption they will have is that something is wrong. Such an assumption takes us back to where we started — to that "age-old anxiety about youth." Let's address the concern with four questions and answers.

1. Q: Are there some things we should be fussing about?
    A: Yes. Violence and values.

Violence
There has been an increase in violence among young people. With every passing day, another incident seems to be reported, sometimes in schools, usually elsewhere. This manuscript has not been able to keep up with all the breaking developments. Reports have continued to come in concerning the ongoing violence among youth. And they are not going to stop.

Those who would doubt the trend of increasing violence can point all they want to declines in official rates in recent years. But they know as well as we do that those rates are imprecise and short term and say virtually nothing about intimidation, anxiety, and so on among young people. Our survey and other recent explorations of youth culture have documented the reality of these problems. The fighting isn't new; what's new is conflict in which people are getting seriously hurt and sometimes killed. The total intergenerational picture leaves no doubt that, over a period of what appears to be several decades, violence has been on the increase.

For all the anxiety adults have about being victimized by young people, *violent* acts by teens are directed primarily at one another. School violence, for example, typically involves teenage assailants and teenage victims. Obviously property offences committed by youths tend to be directed at adults. But violent crime is not.

To the extent "the teen world" has become more violent, such a situation has the potential to seriously damage the quality of life of young people. You and I can look at the finding that some 80% of males and females feel safe at school and naively conclude that all is well. But hold on a moment; since when do we look at ten kids in a class and say everything's fine simply because only two out of the ten are feeling anxious for their safety on the school site — especially if one of those two kids is ours? Go beyond numbers to people and faces, where two in ten teens wake up in the morning and feel anxiety when they think about going to school, worry when they are on their class breaks, worry when they head for home.

This is a situation that has to be addressed — and resolved.

Having sounded the alarm about youth violence, I would also rush to argue that there is need for concern, but there is no need for hysteria. Even in the so-called age of Columbine, relatively few young people are actually being killed at school or anywhere else. Canada has about two million young people between the ages of 15 and 19. From Columbine through the end of 2000, two teenagers died violently in Canadian high schools; another was killed on junior high school grounds. In Canada, some 54 youths 12 to 17, in school and otherwise, were charged with homicide in 1998, 45 in 1999, and an average of 51 during the 1990s.[1]

In the U.S., from 1993 to 1998, the rate of murders committed by youth 12 to 17 fell by 56%, with the number of teens murdered falling nearly as much; the rates are now only slightly above those of Younger Boomer teens in the late '70s. Statistics compiled by the National School Safety Center show that about one in one hundred of these homicides took place at a school. Violent deaths in schools declined from a high of 55 in the 1992–93 school year to 25 in 1998–99, with

15 — including 12 students — of these at Columbine. Of the remaining ten deaths, three were intentional homicides, two involving guns. About 20 million teenagers attend U.S. schools every day. Additional statistics for 1991–97 show that, by 1997, 30% fewer students claimed they were bringing weapons to school, 20% fewer reported they had got into fights, and 50% fewer said they feared being mugged, raped, or shot.[2]

Given such data, one cannot help but wonder why only 80% of Canadian teenagers in 2000 were saying they feel safe at school, compared to 86% of American teenagers. Further, a mere 43% of Canadian adults think "teens feel safe at school." At minimum, such perceptions contribute to suspicion and uneasiness. They also put a tremendous amount of pressure on school personnel.

In light of the wide disparity between anxiety levels and violence levels, one cannot avoid looking at the media and asking for some accountability. Manitoba youth crime researcher Paul Mallea states things bluntly: "Canadians are tending more and more to demonize our children," and "the media are to blame for focusing too much on violent crime. The public is getting a skewed picture of what is actually going on.'"[3] In covering youth violence, the media's shrill cries too frequently have been worse than only misleading: they have been socially destructive.

Values
There is also something wrong with values.

No, it's not that the bottom has fallen out of youth values. Frankly, I think it's a sad commentary on the unfair stereotypes adults have of teenagers that adults so dramatically underestimate the importance of any number of values to young people — be those values honesty, politeness, concern for others, hard work, cleanliness, spirituality, family life, or being loved. The findings show teen values look very much like adult values.

There are, however, some differences in the importance placed on two basic interpersonal traits — honesty and politeness. Politeness is highly valued by some 75% of adults and 60% of teens, with the level slightly higher for females than males in both age instances. This appears to be a short-lived difference; as teens move into their 20s and beyond, the value they place on politeness tends to increase. **But since** about 1992, we have seen a noteworthy drop, especially among young males, in the importance placed on honesty. It's a trait currently valued highly by more than 90% of adults and 80% of teenage females, but so viewed by only about 60% of their male counterparts. The trend data suggest there will be some increase in the valuing of honesty among males as they age, but not enough to match the current 90% level of adults — or young females as they get older.

The item probing the returning of the $10 raises a further important question about honesty. Among those teens who say they highly value honesty, fewer than one in two females and one in three males say they would return the money given to them by mistake. Such responses suggest that, even when teenagers do place a high value on honesty, they don't necessarily show it when they are dealing with strangers. As one teen told me, "I expect my friends to be honest with me and me with them. But it's different when I'm dealing with other people." Simply put, many teens take the position that honesty is important when relating to people in one's own circle. But outside that circle, especially when dealing with people they don't know, it can be a different story.

What seems to be happening here is that young people are increasingly interpreting values and morality in a very personal, as opposed to communal, sense. Their values tend to derive from what they've experienced personally, not from broader systems such as religion, which define what is ethical or moral in terms of the collective good. Don't think I'm being overly idealistic: a teen who is plugged into a religion-based ethical system, such as Catholicism, might not give back the ten bucks either; but at least he will feel some pangs of guilt!

If values are increasingly derived from personal experience and personal gratification, then perhaps as young people get older they will be more inclined to expand their circle of compassion. For example, if they know what it's like to have to make up a cash shortfall out of their own pockets, perhaps they will become somewhat more sympathetic to others. Then again, maybe not.

Keep in mind our finding that as adults get older, many confess it doesn't always work that way. With the passage of time, those who say they have become less honest outnumber those who have become more honest. Perhaps, at least for a few more decades, what we will see is the strange spectacle of jaded adults who are becoming less honest, and younger people who are becoming more honest, walking toward each other in the confusion of the ethical night.

Journalist Jenefer Curtis has recently written, "Our wired globalized world needs ethics. Combine globalization, pluralism, a decline in institutionalized religion and intensive individualism and you come up empty in terms of fundamental values, values needed to provide spiritual sustenance and to inform public policy."[4] At this point, it is not clear where such values and ensuing ethics will come from. What is clear is that excessive individualism and excessive relativism make group life difficult at all levels, ranging from personal relationships through organizations to the nation itself.

2. Q: Are we fussing about some things we shouldn't be fussing about?
    A: Yes. Drugs and, sex, for starters.

All things considered, nothing really changes, just different ways of looking at things.
> — a Project Canada female participant since 1975,
> now 58, teaching in Charlottetown

Drugs

I'm not exactly going to get total or enthusiastic agreement here. But the survey facts point to excessive and undue concern on the part of some people in areas that include drugs and sex.

Our surveys show that drugs have probably never been more widely available to young people. If teens want to use them, they say they can readily find them. Yet the vast majority never use illegal drugs. According to teens, the alleged use of drugs like ecstasy and crack over the years has been greatly exaggerated. Those who do tend to follow in the footsteps of many of their parents experiment with marijuana. As for alcohol and cigarettes, the levels of use have changed little over the past several decades.

This is not to say that drug abuse, when it occurs, should be taken lightly. It is also not in any sense to devalue the important proactive role that drug agencies, schools, and other organizations across the country have played in educating teens about the sources of drug use. Quite the opposite. Our findings suggest that, together, they have been highly successful. Their proactive contribution, as well their reactive role in dealing with those teens who do have drug problems, continues to be needed.

However, the findings suggest that the assumption of average adults that the majority of teens are using drugs — especially those with coloured hair or no hair, body piercings, or tattoos — is simply unfounded.

Sex

Yes, teens are obviously interested in the topic and, yes, more than one in two have been sexually involved by the time they reach nineteen. My mere presentation of such findings at a conference a few years back resulted in the high-profile spouse of a prominent politician raising her hand and exclaiming, "But that doesn't make it right!"

No, but hang on a second. I'm just the proverbial messenger here, so everybody relax. **What I'm saying is that, for all the consternation, there are lots of teens who are engaging in sex — and lots of teens who aren't.** I hope that your teens, and those you are associated with, are on the side of the line that you want. To keep things in perspective, far from being a sex-crazed bunch, on balance a smaller proportion of teenagers are having sex than their grandparents did. (The predictable response from even a sexually modest teen would invariably be "gross!" Those poor stigmatized, asexual grandparents. . . .)

The message from the findings is that most teens approve of sex outside marriage when people care about each other, and about half of teens become sexually involved. Some of the remaining 40% will have sex prior to marriage once they get into their 20s and beyond; others will wait until marriage.

However, far from being a new problem area, sexual attitudes and behaviour among teenagers have changed little over at least the past two decades and have remained fairly stable since the early 1970s. Of course, coercive sex, STDs, and teenage pregnancies are very serious matters. And there are some parts of the teenage population that are particularly at risk, where sex education generally and birth control information specifically are inadequate.

Yet, overall, as with drugs, efforts by health professionals and educators to provide improved information and care in the sexual realm have been very effective. Cases of some sexually transmitted diseases are up, but in part, it seems, because of greater openness and greater awareness. Effective health responses are also in place. AIDS rates, despite all the publicity, continue to be very, very low among heterosexuals. Teenage pregnancies, as of the late '90s, are at a ten-year low.[5]

Sex education has never been better, sexual awareness has never been higher. True, the information situation is far from perfect. Segments of the population at particular risk need to be targeted and assisted. Still, things have come a long, long way from the days of today's teens' parents, let alone their grandparents.

So reads the message. Respond as you will. But don't slay the messenger! The situation will continue well past his limited lifespan.

3. **Q: Are we *not* fussing about some things we *should* be fussing about?**

   A: Yes. One issue that stands out perhaps more than all others is the need for a new emphasis on gender equality. We need to find ways of bringing men up to the level of women.

Gender Equality

As a society, much of our attention to gender relations over the past three decades has been focused on equality issues. Much progress has been made. A higher proportion of women than men are now attending university in Canada. Women are increasingly found in a wide variety of occupations that were previously male domains. Pay inequity, while still too common, is regarded as unacceptable.

But in the understandable preoccupation with equality, what perhaps has not been as clearly recognized as it should be are the ongoing differences in the way that females and males seem to put life together. The differences are found not just among younger people; the intergenerational and cohort analyses show they are persisting over lifetimes and between generations. Some of these differences include the greater inclination of females than males to:

- value relationships, including being more inclined to associate sex with love;
- value interpersonal traits, including honesty, politeness, forgiveness, concern for others, and generosity;
- exclude prominent professional sports from their major sources of enjoyment, particularly those that are violent;

- exhibit concern about almost any person-centred social issue, from violence in schools through child abuse, suicide, and crime, to poverty;
- hold opinions on social issues such as capital punishment, rights of homosexuals, mandatory retirement, and war that reflect such traits as compassion and the valuing of equality; and
- hold higher levels of belief in almost anything of a religious, supernatural, or spiritual nature.

There are a lot of "mores" here: more relational, more honest, more civil, more gentle, more sensitive, more compassionate, more spiritual. And not too many negative qualities on the list. So are there any negatives? Well, as a matter of fact, there are. But ironically, they take the form of women taking on a number of undesirable characteristics in the course of living life in Canada with males who are exhibiting less of all of the above. Women, whether they are young or older, tend to be:

- more concerned than men about their looks;
- have less confidence;
- exhibit more fear;[6] and,
- more quickly and in larger numbers, abandon the idea that hard work will lead to success.

Recently a student in one of my classes said to me, "Why are we always talking about the need for women to become like men? Why aren't men becoming more like women?"[7] Her point is not a new one, but it's an important one that, in light of our findings, needs to be underlined. For years, people have worked hard to see that women know increasing equality, that they catch up with men. When it comes to relationships, values, outlook, attitudes, and beliefs, what we need to explore and pursue are more effective ways to enable men to catch up with women. **We need a new equality movement. It's time that, interpersonally and spiritually, males became more like females.** How does that happen? The debate is already on. Christina Hoff Sommers notes that Gloria Steinem wants us to "Raise boys like we raise girls," while Carol Gilligan suggests we need to find ways to keep boys bonded to their mothers. Sommers suggests an alternative. "The traditional approach is through character education: Develop the young man's sense of honor. Help him become a considerate, conscientious human being. Turn him into a gentleman." She adds, "This approach respects boys' masculine nature; it is time-tested and it works."[8]

As for the downside of the gender picture for women — the ongoing tendencies of young and older females to be concerned about their looks, to have less confidence than males, to exhibit fear, to discover hard work doesn't always pay off — such findings serve to remind us that gender equality is still a dream that is proving to be pretty elusive. If it is ever to be realized, it too is a goal that needs to continue to be vigorously pursued.

4. *Q*: Are there some things we should be downright enthusiastic about?
   A: Yes. Teenagers' upgrades, their resilience, and their outlook.

Teens' Upgrades

There are some areas where teens are an improvement on adults. One example is the acceptance of diversity.

Take racial and cultural differences, for example. Their grandparents frequently engaged in unconscious discrimination and normalized a fair amount of social segregation. Their parents, as teens in the '60s and '70s, thought they had advanced significantly when they championed tolerance — which often meant simply not saying the wrong things and staying out of each others' way. Today teens, especially in larger cities, are interacting as never before and are sensitive to any signs of cultural or racial discrimination. Is the intermixing and acceptance complete? Of course not. But things have come a long way over the past three generations.

They are also showing greater respect for sexual freedom. Contrary to nasty rumours, teens have personal sexual standards. They don't all have the same views about premarital sex, homosexuality, abortion, cohabitation, and children born outside marriage. But their willingness to accept other people's choices matches that of adults in all these areas. And even though they are divided on the appropriateness of homosexuality, they exceed adults in affirming that homosexuals are entitled to the same rights that other Canadians are.

Teens, led by females, also exhibit greater sensitivity and compassion in some areas. For example, they show a greater level of sensitivity to behaviour such as harassment and abuse, which devalue life and spirit. They are less hawkish about war, the death penalty, and the treatment of young offenders.

They also exhibit a fresh openness to religion, the supernatural, and spirituality. Many have not been raised in particularly devout homes. Nonetheless, the vast majority are intrigued by mystery, and a surprising one in two indicate they have spiritual needs and are receptive to religious involvement they find to be worthwhile.

These changes, I would argue, represent "area upgrades" to how adults as a whole are living out life.

Teens' Resilience
The findings on teens today, as well as what has been happening to teens yesterday, point to tremendous resilience. In the face of family problems, economic and educational disadvantages, and tough social times, teens have shown a remarkable ability both to maintain an optimistic outlook, as well as to "land on their feet."

Divorce, for example, often has immediate negative emotional and economic consequences, and can make it difficult for teens to keep up with others in the current and future education and occupation races. It also could very much dull one's feelings about marriage, along with one's prospects of having happy and lasting relationships. We find limited support for such outcomes. Teens whose parents are not together continue to get considerable emotional support from at least one and often both. It is, in my mind, quite astonishing that today's Millennial and Gen X cohorts, whose parents were far more likely than their counterparts in older generations to not be together, are nonetheless more likely as a whole than their grandparents and parents to say they want a home like one they grew up in. Further, teens who come from homes where their parents have not been together are just as likely as other young people to plan to marry, have children, and they anticipate staying with their partners forever.

Other apparent barriers can't stop them. Regardless of whether the economic times are good or not so good, teens believe they personally have bright futures. They will not only find work eventually but get the jobs they want. They not only will prosper, but do so on levels that exceed those of their parents. Family background, education, and social conditions might bring some obstacles, but they can be overcome. "Anyone who works hard will rise to the top!"

Obviously not all dreams will be fulfilled. But to the extent they are, teens of the past provide living evidence that many apparent barriers will be toppled in the process.

Teens' Outlook

Along with our findings about teen upgrades and resilience, we have to feel happy about what we have learned concerning their outlook. They want the same primary things teens have wanted since we began monitoring Canadian youth in 1984 and probably long before — friendship, freedom, being loved, success, and a comfortable life. Some express disillusionment with some institutions. Yet the fact that teens now have more confidence, for example, in government leaders than they did in 1992 suggests that disenchantment is not necessarily permanent; even institutions can be re-embraced, rather than discarded.

A sound majority of today's teens exhibit positive self-images. They believe they are well liked, have a number of good qualities, are competent, and good-looking; they also indicate they have confidence. They have high aspirations, and most indicate they are willing to work hard and pursue the kinds of education necessary to help them achieve their career and economic goals. They want good and stable family lives. Some two in three say they expect to be involved in their communities. Most value Canada and plan to pursue their economic and relational dreams here. In Quebec as well, there is good reason to believe most will continue to want to be part of Canada, as long as they find that what they want out of life they can attain as Canadians. That's not an unfair expectation.

On balance, Canadian teenagers give every indication that they are going to turn out just fine.

Final Thoughts

I don't know about you, but one of the things I like about life is that things never stay the same. They keep changing. The old block where we grew up is now a block of condominiums, the old café is now a discount store, the old A&P where we worked is now a parking lot, old friends and lovers have moved away, some relatives and other people are no longer with us. Because life and the people and things in it are constantly changing, we are not given the option of living in the past. The set keeps changing, and so must we. Change keeps life fresh.

It's certainly true of the high school years. Went back to my old high school in Edmonton a couple of years back for another one of those reunions. The school was celebrating the fortieth anniversary of its first graduating class; I finished grade 10 that first year, when everything was new and fresh and exciting. Only this was not your usual reunion. Turned out what was billed as a "reunion" was also "a celebration" of the school's closing. Good grief. My life had spanned the entire life of the school with time left over! Could I really be *that* old? Nah, the school just had a short life.

People had changed — a lot. And today's teenagers who graduate from high schools across the country over the next few years are likewise going to be changing a lot. The products that technology is wowing us with today will be the 8-tracks and rabbit ears and electric typewriters of tomorrow, only they'll be older faster. Many things about youth that trouble some people will soon be forgotten by everybody, including teens themselves. What were thought to be groundbreaking generational changes will be seen as having been the fleeting and largely inconsequential characteristics of a cohort's life stage.

Many of today's teens are going to have to modify their dreams, lower their expectations. But on the plus side, over time they will find that they are achieving far more than they ever dreamed. Older won't necessarily mean either wiser or nicer. Some will learn from life and become a bit more open to alternatives for everyone. Others will just get older. Some will become a bit more honest and a little kinder; others will limit the circle of people they care about. Some will continue to revel in the meaning and mysteries of life; others will leave the magical and mystical to their children.

In short, teenagers will eventually become pretty much like the rest of us. And at that point, they, like us, will discover a well-kept secret: adulthood, that vantage point from which we worry so much about teenagers, is not a cure for the problems of youth. In reality, once today's teens arrive there, many of the good things that started to be will now start to come undone. It's the nature of life. That's one of the main reasons we worry about youth: we are well aware they are going to have to start extra high, because we know that as life unfolds and they become more like us they are going to have to modify many of those dreams and ideals.

A previous cohort of young people on the edge of the promised land of adulthood was greeted by Robert Fulford, who was then 35. Frowning, he took a deep breath and delivered the news: "I have seen the future and it doesn't work." At 44, he greeted another fresh group of teen graduates, and delivered this amended version of his earlier announcement: "I have seen the future and it sucks."[9]

Actually, of course, life does work, or at least we have to live as if it does. When it doesn't, we hope and work for better things. Otherwise, what's the point of it all? **If we can get teens to start high — help them set life goals and develop the personal resources to pursue them — life can be good, maybe even better than everyone expected.**

Things never stay the same. The teens of today become the teens of yesterday and give way to the teens of tomorrow. That's a good thing. Even some of the worrying eventually stops.

Project Teen Canada 2000 Methodology

PROJECT TEEN CANADA 2000 WAS FUNDED BY THE LILLY ENDOW-ment. Data collection took place primarily during March, April, May, and October of 2000. The survey was carried out from the University of Lethbridge, with Reginald Bibby the Project Director and Reggie Bibby the Project Manager. The methodology used in the 1984 and 1992 **Project Teen Canada** surveys was replicated (for details regarding those surveys, see Bibby and Posterski, 1985:201–205 and 1992:32–324).

Sample Size and Frame
As in 1984 and 1992, a sample of about 3,600 teenagers was pursued, a figure that, if representatively selected, makes it possible to generalize to the overall high school adolescent population with a high level of accuracy (within about three percentage points, either way, 19 times in 20). A sample of that size also increases the accuracy of analyses involving various categories, such as region, community size, gender, and race.

Once again, since our interest was in youth on the verge of becoming adults, the sample was restricted to Canadians 15 to 19 years old in grades 10 to 12 across Canada, including CEGEP I's in Quebec. These three grades encompass about two-thirds of young people between the ages of 15 and 19. Moreover, some 65% of the remaining one-third not in high school — including, obviously, teens in post-secondary institutions — were there for one year or more. As for dropouts who on the surface have been missed, clearly some of our participants will drop out, while, according to Statistics Canada, one-quarter of the one in five students who leave will return to school and eventually graduate. Our 2000 survey has found that 4% of current students dropped out at some point in their schooling. Consequently, dropouts have not been totally omitted, just "filmed" before leaving school or after returning. To get a reading of secondary students is to get a highly comprehensive snapshot of the latest "emerging generation" as it passes through high school.

Sampling Procedures

In pursuing the sample-size goal of approximately 3,600 high school students, we again randomly selected individual high school classrooms rather than individual students because of the significant administrative advantages and minimal negative consequences for a random sample. The design involved choosing one classroom in each school selected. Based on an average class size of perhaps 25 students, this meant that the participation of some 150 schools was required (N = 3,750). Anticipating a response rate of about 75% based on our 1984 and 1992 experiences, we selected approximately 200 schools, including replacements.

The schools were chosen using multi-stage stratified and cluster sampling procedures. The country was first stratified according to the five major regions, with each region then stratified according to community size (100,000 and over, 99,000 to 10,000, less than 10,000). Each community-size category was in turn stratified according to school system (public, separate, private). Specific communities within each size stratum were then randomly selected, with the number of communities drawn from each province in the Prairie and Atlantic regions based on population. Finally, one school in each of these communities was chosen randomly. The number of schools selected in cities with over 100,000 population was proportionate to their populations in their regions. The specific grade of the classroom involved was also randomly designated.

The Administration of the Survey

After receiving board approval where required, guidance counsellors or an appropriate alternative at each school were contacted and asked to (1) choose a classroom that they viewed as representative of the requested grade and (2) personally administer the questionnaire. They were instructed to stress that participation was voluntary, and that anonymity and confidentiality would be honoured. Upon completion of the questionnaires, counsellors were asked to place them in the pre-paid postal envelope provided "in full view of the students" and to seal the envelope in their presence.

Table A1. **School Participation in the Surveys by Region**

Number of Schools

	Received	Refusals	Not received	Totals	%
2000					
B.C.	20	3	4	27	74
Prairies	31	2	5	38	82
Ontario	45	3	12	60	75
Quebec	37	1	5	43	86
Atlantic	17	1	4	22	77
Yukon–NWT–Nun	6	0	0	6	100
Totals	156	10	30	196	80
1992					
B.C.	20	0	6	26	77
Prairies	36	0	6	42	86
Ontario	58	4	12	74	78
Quebec	44	0	13	57	77
Atlantic	19	1	6	26	73
Yukon–NWT	2	0	0	2	100
Unknown	1	0	0	1	—
Totals	180	5	43	228	85

In 1992, a strategy of oversampling was used; when quotas were met, no follow-up was carried out. Thus, schools "not received" is an inflated figure. Response rates reported in Teen Trends *reflect returns against quotas and are obviously higher.*

	Received	Refusals	Not received	Totals	%
1984					
B.C.	14	5	1	20	70
Prairies	33	6	4	43	77
Ontario	46	12	6	64	72
Quebec	39	2	8	49	80
Atlantic	20	2	2	24	83
Totals	152	27	21	200	76

The Response

Questionnaires were returned from 156 of 196 schools where contact had been successful — a return rate of 80% (see Table A1). The remaining 40 schools either declined to participate (10) or did not respond to requests to do so (30). A total of 3,501 usable questionnaires were received; the 1984 and 1992 totals were 3,530 and 3,891, respectively.

Representativeness

As in the past, the sample has been weighted to ensure representativeness, with adjustments made for region, community size, and school type. In its final, weighted form, the sample is highly representative of Canadian high school students, aged 15 to 19 (see Table A2). A sample of this size and quality permits generalizations to the high school population with a very high level of accuracy. On most items in the questionnaire, the national results should come within about three percentage points of the results of other surveys probing the teenage population 19 times in 20.

Table A2. **Characteristics of the High School Teenage (15 to 19): Population and Project Teen Canada 2000 Sample**

		Population*	Sample
Region	British Columbia	13	13
	Prairies	17	17
	Ontario	38	38
	Quebec	24	24
	Atlantic	8	8
	North	<1	<1
Community Size	100,000 & over	53	53
	99,999–10,000	14	14
	under 10,000	33	33
Gender	Male	48	47
	Female	52	53
School System**	Public	79	79
	Catholic	13	13
	Private	8	8

* Population estimates derived from Statistics Canada, varied publications.
** Public includes French and English schools in Quebec; Catholic includes public Catholic schools in Ontario.

The Project Canada and Project Teen Canada 87 Surveys

This book makes extensive use of **Project Canada** adult national surveys carried out every five years since 1975. These six surveys have consisted of samples of approximately 1,500 cases each, weighted down to about 1,200 cases to minimize the use of large weight factors.

Conducted by mail with return rates of roughly 65%, they have yielded high-quality data. The samples are highly representative of the Canadian adult population and are of sufficient size to be accurate within approximately four percentage points 19 times in 20. Methodological details can be found in *The Bibby Report*, pp. 143–46. The latest survey was completed in August of 2000 and included 1,729 people; its weighted N is 1,240.

I also have made some use of the fall 1987 national survey of Canadian young people between the ages of 15 and 24 that Don Posterski

Table A3. Sample Sizes of Categories Used in Analyses, PTC 2000*

Region		Biological Mother and Father	
B.C.	455	Married to each other	2225
Prairies	595	No longer married ea other	813
Ontario	1320	Never married	107
Quebec	840	One no longer alive	82
Atlantic	280	Other	61
North	10/108**		
Gender		**Birthplace**	
Male	1583	Canada	2811
Female	1764	Outside Canada	518
Community Size		**Place of Residence**	
Over 400,000	872	Mother and father	2239
399,999–100,000	503	Mother only	386
99,999–30,000	417	Mother and stepfather	241
City/town <30,000	842	Father only	98
Rural non-farm	371	Mother and partner	65
Farm	231	Father and stepmother	48
		Father and partner	23
		Other	219

* This information is provided to give interested readers some idea of the sub-sample sizes. Further details can be obtained from the author.
** Unweighted N's are used in regional breakdown tables.

and I conducted for the Canadian Youth Foundation. Dubbed **Project Teen Canada 87** and released in 1988 (and sometimes referred to as "Project Teen Canada 88"), this survey involved face-to-face interviews with 2,033 people. The two of us constructed the interview schedule, and the data collection was carried out by the Gallup organization. The data are high quality, the sample representative of Canadian youth. The sample included about 800 high school students, 15 to 19. A complete methodological summary is found in Donald C. Posterski and Reginald W. Bibby, *Canada's Youth: Ready for Today.* Ottawa: Canadian Youth Foundation, 1988, pp. 54–55.

Notes

Introduction The Need for Some Conversations

1 Bob Harvey, "Attitude of today's youth shocking, Bishops told," *Ottawa Citizen*, October 14, 2000.

2 Jonathon S. Epstein, "Introduction: Generation X, Youth Culture, and Identity," in Jonathon S. Epstein (ed.), *Youth Culture: Identity in a Postmodern World*. Oxford: Blackwell, 1998, p. 1. Epstein notes that the sociological and cultural studies of youth have known three periods: (1) the problem-oriented approach of the University of Chicago in the early twentieth century, (2) studies of youth subcultures by the Centre for the Study of Contemporary Culture in Birmingham, England, and (3) recent cultural criticism in the U.S. by people who include Donna Gaines, Henry Giroux, Douglas Kellner, and Deena Weinstein.

3 Anthony Kerr, *Youth of Europe*. Chester Springs, PA: Dufour Editions, 1964, p. 168.

4 Gallup Canada Inc., November 28, 1991.

5 Reginald W. Bibby, *The Bibby Report*. Toronto: Stoddart, 1995, p. 103.

6 Christie Blatchford, "It's not easy being a teenager today," *National Post*, February 11, 2000.

7 Andrew Clark, "How teens got the power," *Maclean's*, March 22, 1999:44.

8 See Michael Adams, *Sex in the Snow: Canadian Social Values at the End of the Millennium*. Toronto: Viking, 1997.

9 Clark, 1999, p. 46.

Chapter One What's Important

1 Douglas Todd, "'Religion' just doesn't seem hip," *National Post*, February 6, 1999.

2 Milton Rokeach, *The Nature of Human Values*. New York: Free Press, 1973.

3 "Ditka: New generation undisciplined," Associated Press. Released by Slam Sports: NFL, May 26, 2000 (Internet).

4 Egle Procuta, "Rude and ruder," *Globe and Mail*, June 16, 2000.

5 Cited by Patrick Welsh, "Cheating devolves from 'one-size-fits-all' testing," *USA Today*, August 22, 2000.

6 Donald L. McCabe, "Academic dishonesty among high school students," *Adolescence* 34, 1999:681–87.

7   Stanley A. Miller II, "Paradise for cheaters," *Milwaukee Journal Sentinel*, June 3, 2000.

8   Jonathon S. Epstein (ed.), *Adolescents and Their Music: If It's Too Loud, You're Too Old*. New York: Garland, 1994.

9   "Even newborns seem to respond to sound of music," Associated Press, Nashville, August 1, 2000.

10 "Radio listening," *The Daily*, Statistics Canada, July 26, 2000.

11 "Sales sizzle as kids rule music," Associated Press, New York, June 4, 2000.

12 "Pop go the kids!" Canadian Press, Toronto, May 25, 2000.

13 "Beatles album fastest-selling ever," Reuters, December 6, 2000.

14 Chris Zelkovich, "CBC Sports boss in a league of her own," *Toronto Star*, July 25, 2000.

15 William Houston, *Globe and Mail*, December 13 and December 14, 2000.

16 John R. MacArthur, "Will no one rid me of this turbulent e-trash?" *Globe and Mail*, June 17, 2000.

17 Ann Oldenburg, "In a wired world, multimedia is the message," *USA Today*, August 23, 2000.

18 "BCE looks to buy into CFL: Report," Canadian Press, Toronto, October 24, 2000; "Teleglobe takeover approved," Canadian Press, Montreal, October 31, 2000.

19 "Bill Gates" in Larry King, *Future Talk*. New York: HarperCollins, 1998, p. 80.

20 "Girls just don't want to be geeks," Associated Press, Chicago, July 5, 2000.

21 Charles Horton Cooley, *Human Nature and the Social Order*. New York: Schocken Books, 1964.

22 Mark Starowicz, "A nation without memory," *Globe and Mail*, February 6, 1999.

23 Daniel Okrent, "Raising kids online," *Time*, May 10, 1999:28.

24 Alexandra Gill, "Aguilera on abuse and exes," *Globe and Mail*, July 8, 2000.

25 Alan J.C. King, William F. Boyce, and Matthew A. King, *Trends in the Health of Canadian Youth*. Ottawa: Health Canada, 1999, p. 21.

26 Quoted in Andrew Clark, "How teens got the power," *Maclean's*, March 22, 1999:43–44.

27 "Visa offers prepaid card for U.S. teens," Associated Press, New York, August 14, 2000.

28 Aliza Libman, "Wider than a rake," Canadian Press, Toronto, January 26, 1999.

29 Susan Sontag, "The double standard of aging," *Saturday Review*, September, 1972.

30 "Karrie On: Focused Webb unfazed by sex appeal slights," (GNS), *Calgary Sun*, July 4, 2000.

31 Editorial, "No nudes is good nudes," Editorial, Montreal *Gazette*, September 8, 2000.

32 Different viewpoints can be found in a variety of places. The *Calgary Herald*, for example, carried two interesting pieces on September 7, 2000, by *Herald* writer Michelle Simick — "X-country skiers bare (almost) all" — and Baltimore Sun feminist writer Susan Reimer — "Nothing nasty about nude athletes."

33 Chris Morris, "Fragile and fleeting: A teen's self-esteem can start strong but crumble fast," Canadian Press, December 9, 1999.

34 Mark S. Tremblay and J. Douglas Willms, "Secular trends in the body mass index of Canadian children," *Canadian Medical Association Journal*, 163:1429–33.

35 King, Boyce, and Matthew, 1999, pp. 44–50.

36 From "A Young Girl's Impossible Dream," in Lorraine Gllenon (ed.), *The 20th Century: An Illustrated History of Our Lives and Times.* North Dighton, MA: JG Press, 2000, p. 353.

37 William Pollack, *Real Boys: Rescuing Our Sons from the Myths of Boyhood.* New York: Henry Holt and Company, 1998, pp. 5, 7.

38 For a critique of the difficulty Americans have had in finding this balance, see Robert Bellah et al., *Habits of the Heart.* Berkeley: University of California Press, 1985. I have offered a critique of the potential excesses of both individualism and relativism in Canada in my *Mosaic Madness: Pluralism Without a Cause.* Toronto: Stoddart, 1990.

39 William F. Ogburn, *Social Change With Respect to Culture and Original Nature.* New York: B.W. Huebsch, 1922.

Chapter Two The People in Their Lives

1 William Glasser, *Reality Therapy.* New York: Harper and Row, 1965, p. 7.

2 James Gabarino, *Raising Children in a Socially Toxic Environment.* San Francisco: Jossey-Bass, 1995, p. 158.

3 Cited in Steve Sternberg, "Infants who socialize likely to avoid asthma," *USA Today*, August 24, 2000.

4 Robert D. Putnam, *Bowling Alone.* New York: Simon and Schuster, 2000, p. 326.

5 William Pollack, *Real Boys: Rescuing Our Sons from the Myths of Boyhood.* New York: Henry Holt and Company, 1998, p. 18.

6 Jimmy Long, *Generating Hope.* Downers Grove, IL: IV Press, 1997, p. 50.

7 Putnam, 2000, pp. 31–180.

8 Sharon Begley, "A World of their own," *Newsweek*, May 8, 2000:54.

9 "Time spent with children," *The Daily*, Statistics Canada, June 13, 2000.

10 Associated Press release, Los Angeles, October 7, 2000.

11 "Grandparenting today requires extra effort," Canadian Press, Calgary, July 15, 2000.

12 "School 'grandparents' bridge gap between young, old," Canadian Press, Vancouver, June 19, 2000.

13 Walter Kirn, "Should you stay together for the kids?" *Time*, September 25, 2000:43–48.

14 Bogdan Kipling, "Divorce in America: stats paint bleak picture," in *Lethbridge Herald*, June 19, 2000.

15 Personal interview reported in *Context*, July 1992, vol 2:3. Published by World Vision Canada, Mississauga, ON.

16 Philip F. Rice, *The Adolescent*, third edition. Boston: Allyn and Bacon, p. 41.

17 Reginald W. Bibby and Don Posterski, *The Emerging Generation*. Toronto: Irwin, 1985, p. 113.

18 *Youth and Road Crashes*. Toronto: Traffic Injury Research Foundation, 1999.

19 Cathy Drixler, Harvey Krahn, and Robert Wood, "Teenage Drinking and Driving in Rural Alberta, *Youth & Society*, 2001.

20 Corinne Robertshaw, "Injustice for children," *Globe and Mail*, July 7, 2000.

21 Editorial, "Punishment and crime," *Globe and Mail*, July 7, 2000.

22 "Canadian youths push for repeal of spanking law," Canadian Press, Ottawa, July 13, 2000.

23 "Mother guilty of assault after paddling boy," Canadian Press, Leamington, ON, November 28, 2000.

24 Peggy Burch, "The spanking debate," Scripps Howard News Service, Memphis, TN, October 5, 2000.

25 Theresa Boyle, "Now parents must pay for children's crime," *Toronto Star*, August 14, 2000.

26 "Dress code takes studs out of students," Canadian Press, Hamilton, ON, September 3, 2000.

27 "Study suggests Mondays trigger migraines in kids," Canadian Press, Montreal, June 24, 2000.

Chapter Three Five Areas of Particular Concern

1 See, for example, the *National Post* story of April 21, 2000, "Threats of violence abound in schools since Taber, Columbine" by Ian MacLeod.

2 "Teens pleads guilty to making hit list of students," Canadian Press, Toronto, November 28, 2000.

3　Robert Remington and Chris Wattie, "$30 debt seen as motive in killing," *National Post*, November 21, 2000.

4　Jane Christmas, "A parent's dilemma in the age of Columbine," *National Post*, April 21, 2000.

5　For a summary article on the sentencing of one of Virk's assailants, see Rod Mickleburgh, "Virk's killer gets minimum sentence," *Globe and Mail*, April 21, 2000.

6　"Virk's killer off to prison," Canadian Press, Vancouver, April 20, 2000.

7　Details are provided by Jim Rankin and Michelle Shephard in their article, "Teen beaten to death didn't defend himself," in *Toronto Star*, November 17, 1999.

8　See Michelle Shephard, "Four teens charged with torturing girl, 14," *Toronto Star*, November 18, 1999.

9　Ian Williams, "Teens charged with murder after boy's death," *Edmonton Journal*, November 17, 2000.

10　"Kid says he used dad's gun to 'scare' man he shot," Canadian Press, Lytton, Quebec, November 27, 2000.

11　Alan J.C. King, William F. Boyce, and Matthew A. King, *Trends in the Health of Canadian Youth*. Ottawa: Health Canada, 1999:23.

12　Siu Kwong Wong, "Acculturation, peer relations, and delinquent behavior of Chinese-Canadian youth," *Adolescence* 34, 1999:107–19.

13　"Advisory group recommended to reduce youth crime," Canadian Press, Toronto, June 22, 2000.

14　"Junior high violence shocks officials," Canadian Press, Calgary, May 8, 2000. For a summary of a parallel earlier study in Calgary, see Joanne J. Paetsch and Lorne D. Bertrand, "Victimization and delinquency among Canadian youth," *Adolescence* 34, 1999:351–67.

15　*The Daily*, Statistics Canada, December 19, 1995.

16　*The Daily*, Statistics Canada, November 2, 2000.

17　"Crime rate drops to 20-year low," Canadian Press, Ottawa, July 18, 2000.

18　"British statistics show jump in violent crime," Reuters, London, July 18, 2000.

19　"Sentencing of young offenders," *The Daily*, August 1, 2000.

20　"Teens given more jail time than adults for same crime," Canadian Press, Vancouver, August 1, 2000.

21　Janine Ecklund, "Schools safe, say police," *Lethbridge Herald*, December 1, 2000.

22　"Ottawa, provinces disagree on youth crime," Canadian Press, Hamilton, ON, October 4, 1999.

23 "The Perception Gap," *Time*, April 24, 2000:40–41.

24 "The Sex Files on Discovery pushing the envelope," Canadian Press, Toronto, October 4, 2000.

25 See, for example, Vanessa Lu and Richard Brennan, "No-prescription test for morning-after pill," *Toronto Star*, September 8, 2000.

26 "Injectable birth control approved in U.S.," Associated Press, New York, October 6, 2000.

27 Tanya Talaga, "American women get approval to use abortion pill RU-486," *Toronto Star*, September 29, 2000.

28 Graeme Smith, "Doctors to test French abortion pill here," *Toronto Star*, July 7, 2000.

29 Editorial, "The consequences of sex," *Globe and Mail*, December 1, 1999.

30 "Multiple-risk behaviour in teenagers and young adults," *The Daily*, Statistics Canada, October 29, 1998.

31 "Tobacco use," *The Daily*, Statistics Canada, January 20, 2000.

32 "Pot possession law ruled unconstitutional," Canadian Press, Toronto, July 31, 2000.

33 "Ontario NDP wants marijuana decriminalized," Canadian Press, Toronto, August 2, 2000.

34 Susan Oh, "Rave fever," *Maclean's*, April 24, 2000:39–43.

35 "Inquest urges steps for safer raves," Canadian Press, Toronto, June 1, 2000.

36 "Ecstasy seized in major drug bust," *Globe and Mail*, August 22, 2000.

37 Cited in Susan Oh, "Rave fever," *Maclean's*, April 24, 2000:41.

38 Christopher John Farley, "Rave new world," *Time*, June 5, 2000:42–44.

39 Kevin Michael Grace, "Spontaneous congestion," *The Report*, July 24, 2000:47.

40 "Safe to rave? Putting a price on partying," *Vancouver Sun*, December 10, 1999.

41 Bill Kaufmann, "Rave hysteria amusing," *Calgary Sun*, June 5, 2000.

42 Tracy Ford, "Regulating the rave: Keeping ravers safe in Toronto," *Developments*, AADAC, Oct/Nov 2000.

43 Mark Starowicz, "A nation without memory," *Globe and Mail*, February 6, 1999.

44 Quoted in "Ottawa failing on bilingualism, watchdog says," Canadian Press, Ottawa, October 6, 2000.

45 "Whitfield strikes gold for Canada in triathlon," Canadian Press, Sydney, September 16, 2000.

46 Robert Kiener, "What teens really think," *Reader's Digest*, June 2000:52.

47 See, for example, Bruce Kidd, "How do we find our own voices in the 'New World Order?' A commentary on Americanization." *Sociology of Sport Journal* 8, 1991:178–84.

48 "Frank Lowe" in Larry King, *Future Talk*. New York: HarperCollins, 1998, p. 141.

49 "D'Oh! Bart and family back for 12th season," Reuters, November 2, 2000.

50 "Rocket's rare personality will endure time," Canadian Press, Montreal, May 30, 2000.

51 Reginald W. Bibby, *The Bibby Report*. Toronto: Stoddart, 1995, p. 50.

52 "Canadians enjoy long and healthy lives," *Globe and Mail*, June 5, 2000.

53 M. Wolfson and B. Murphy, "Income inequality in North America: Does the 49th parallel still matter?" *Canadian Economic Observer*, August 2000.

54 David Suzuki, "Comparing 'Quality of life' between Canada and the U.S." Science Matters column, in the *Lethbridge Herald*, August 20, 2000.

55 "1995 graduates who moved to the United States," *The Daily*, Statistics Canada, August 27, 1999.

56 "Brain drain and brain gain: The migration of knowledge workers into and out of Canada," *The Daily*, Statistics Canada, May 24, 2000.

57 The case for the resilience of religion is made in Reginald W. Bibby, *Restless Gods: The Renaissance of Religion in Canada*. The book will be published by Stoddart (Toronto) in the spring of 2002.

58 See, for example, Reginald W. Bibby, *Unknown Gods*. Toronto: Stoddart, 1993, pp. 29–46.

59 Harvey Cox, foreword to Tom Beaudoin, *Virtual Faith*. San Francisco: Jossey-Bass, 1998, p. ix.

60 Tom Beaudoin, *Virtual Faith*, p. ix.

61 Cox, 1998, p. xi.

62 Church of the Rock meets in a school auditorium. Dave Overholt can be contacted at revdave@river.netrover.com.

63 For an extensive discussion of the nature and significance of ongoing identification, see Bibby, 1993, pp. 152–68.

64 From *Commonweal*, December 17, 1999; cited in Martin Marty (ed.), *Context*. Mississauga, ON: World Vision Canada, May 1, 2000, p. 4.

65 Thomas Moore, *Care of the Soul*. New York: HarperCollins, 1992.

66 James Redfield, *The Celestine Prophecy*. New York: Warner Books, 1994.

67 John Naisbitt and Patricia Aburdene, *Megatrends 2000*. New York: Warner Books, 1990.

68 Ron Graham, *God's Dominion: A Skeptic's Quest*. Toronto: McClelland & Stewart, 1990.

69 *Entertainment Weekly*, October 7, 1994.

70 Reginald W. Bibby, "Who will teach our children shared values?" *Globe and Mail*, February 3, 1994.

71 Douglas Todd, "'Religion' just doesn't seem hip," *National Post*, February 6, 1999.

72 For a detailed critique of multiculturalism, complete with an array of thoughts on how diversity might be better tapped, I invite readers to look at my book *Mosaic Madness: Pluralism Without a Cause*. Toronto: Stoddart, 1990.

73 A higher prevalence of firearms at schools, for example, appears to reflect a higher prevalence of concern about violent neighbourhoods; see David C. May, "Scared kids, unattached kids, or peer pressure: Why do students carry firearms to school?" *Youth & Society* 31, 1999:100–127.

Chapter Four Their Hopes . . . and Expectations

1 1996 Census *Nation* tables. Ottawa: Statistics Canada.

2 Labour Force Survey, June 2000. Ottawa: Statistics Canada.

3 "Baby boomers a prosperous lot," Associated Press, Washington, D.C., August 3, 2000.

4 "Generation Xers will do better than their parents, study says," Canadian Press, Toronto, November 20, 1999.

5 "The Labour Force," *Canada Year Book 1999*. Ottawa: Statistics Canada.

6 "The Economy," *Canada Year Book 1999*. Ottawa: Statistics Canada.

7 "Education," *Canada Year Book 1999*. Ottawa: Statistics Canada.

8 Karen Kelly, Linda Howatson-Leo, and Warren Clark, "I Feel Over-qualified for My Job," *Canadian Social Trends*, vol. 3. Toronto: Thompson, 2000, pp. 182–87.

9 "Survey of labour and income dynamics: the wage gap between men and women." *The Daily*, Statistics Canada, December 20, 1999.

10 "Report says gender barriers exist at top executive levels in business," Canadian Press, Ottawa, June 14, 2000.

11 Warren Clark, "Search for success: Finding work after graduation," *Canadian Social Trends*, vol. 3. Toronto: Thompson, 2000:174–79.

12 Al Beeber, "An interview with Bryan Adams," *Lethbridge Herald*, November 11, 2000.

13 *Time*, August 28, 2000.

14 David Popenoe and Barbara Dafoe Whitehead, *Sex Without Strings, Relationships Without Rings*. New Brunswick, N.J.: Rutgers University. See also Reuters, New York, September 1, 2000, story on the release of the report.

15 For documentation of these diverse patterns, see, for example, "Household and family life," *Canada Year Book 1999*, Ottawa: Statistics Canada.

16 Linda Williamson, "Of Ms. and men," *Ottawa Sun*, September 7, 2000.

17 "Household and family life," *Canada Year Book 1999*. Ottawa: Statistics Canada.

18 Allan Bloom, *The Closing of the American Mind*. New York: Simon and Schuster, 1987, p. 128.

19 "Mom or dad at home is best," *USA Today*, August 2, 2000.

20 "More men may take parental leave," Canadian Press, Toronto, June 23, 2000.

21 Cindy Starr, "Dads quit day jobs to be CEOs at home," Scripps Howard News Service, August 17, 2000.

22 "Employment after childbirth," *The Daily*, Statistics Canada, September 1, 1999.

23 Finn-Aage Esbensen, Elizabeth Piper Deschenes, and L. Thomas Winfree Jr., "Differences between gang girls and gang boys." *Youth & Society* 31, 1999:27–53.

24 Janine Ecklund, "Kids remarkably resilient, counsellor tells convention," *Lethbridge Herald*, February 26, 2000.

25 "Bad behaviour, not bad kids," Canadian Press, Toronto, September 28, 2000.

26 Janine Ecklund, "Teachers must examine their own attitudes, says expert," *Lethbridge Herald*, February 26, 2000.

27 Neil Howe and William Strauss, *Millennials Rising*. New York: Vintage Books, 2000, pp. 4, 8.

28 Similar findings are reported in the U.S., where teens may view the world as grim but nonetheless have high personal hopes. See, for example, Jeffrey Jensen Arnett, "High hopes in a grim world," *Youth & Society* 31, 2000:267–86.

Chapter Five What Teens Were Like in the Early '80s and '90s

1 The knowledge and computer power illustrations are drawn from J. David Hester, "Address to Memphis Theological Seminary Alumni," Louisville, June 18, 1997.

2 My word. Similar to the idea of ethnocentric, only applies to the lack of historical perspective.

3 Don Tapscott, *Growing Up Digital*. New York: McGraw-Hill, 1998, pp. 85–157.

4 William A. Stahl, *God and the Chip: Religion and the Culture of Technology*. Waterloo, ON: Wilfrid Laurier Press, 1999.

5 Ecclesiastes 1:9, New Revised Standard Version.

6 Daniel J. Adams, "Toward a theological understanding of postmodernism," *Cross Currents 2000*, vol. 47, issue 4, Winter 1997–98:7.

7 Jean-François Lyotard, *The Postmodern Condition*. English publication: Minneapolis: University of Minnesota Press, 1984.

8 See, for example, Michel Foucault, *The Order of Things*. New York: Pantheon, 1970, and *The Archaeology of Knowledge*. New York: Harper and Row, 1976.

9 See, for example, Jean Baudrillard, *The Mirror of Production*. Trans. by M. Poster. St. Louis: Telos Press, and *Simulacra and Simulation*. Trans. by S. Farua Blaser. Ann Arbor: University of Michigan Press, 1994.

10 Alexandr Solzhenitsyn, "A world split apart," commencement address at Harvard University, June 8, 1978. Cited in Jimmy Long, *Generating Hope*. Downer's Grove, IL: InterVarsity Press, 1997, p. 69.

11 Kenneth Allan and Jonathan H. Turner, "A formalization of postmodern theory," *Sociological Perspectives* 43, 2000:363–85.

12 Daniel J. Adams, 1997–98:2.

13 Ben Agger, "Critical theory, poststructuralism, postmodernism: Their sociological relevance," *Annual Review of Sociology*, vol.17, 1991:105–31. This quote comes from p. 116. Palo Alto, CA: Annual Reviews, Inc.

14 Agger, 1991:114.

15 Adams, 1997–98:3–7.

16 Agger, 1991:117.

17 Sylvia M. Hale, *Controversies in Sociology*, second edition. Toronto: Copp Clark, 1995, p. 504.

18 Kenneth Allan and Jonathan H. Turner, "A formalization of postmodern theory," p. 379. For the whole article see pp. 363–385.

19 Hale, 1995:505–6.

20 Walt Mueller, *Understanding Today's Youth*. Audiotape. Elizabethtown, PA: Center for Parent/Youth Understanding, 2000.

21 See, for example, Jimmy Long, *Generating Hope*. Downers Grove, IL: InterVarsity Press, 1997, p. 69.

22 See, for example, *Webster's New Compact Format Dictionary*, New York: Leisure Entertainment, 1992.

23 Neil Howe and William Strauss, *Generations: The History of America's Future, 1584 to 2069*. New York: Quill, 1991.

24 Noted by a number of observers, including Tim Celek and Dieter Zander, *Inside the Soul of a New Generation*. Grand Rapids, MI: Zondervan, 1996, p. 31. For an example of major media attention given Xers, see *Time*, July 7, 1997.

25 Front-page treatment of American "Millennials" is available in *Newsweek*, May 8, 2000; see also Neil Howe and William Strauss, *Millennials Rising: The Next Great Generation*. New York: Vintage Books, 2000.

26 Dawson McAllister with Pat Springle, *Saving the Millennial Generation*. Nashville: Thomas Nelson, 1999, p. 7.

27 David K. Foot with Daniel Stoffman, *Boom, Bust, & Echo*. Toronto: Macfarlane Walter and Ross, 1996.

28 Michael Adams, *Sex in the Snow: Canadian Social Values at the End of the Millennium*. Toronto: Viking, 1997.

29 Robert Barnard, Dave Cosgrove, and Jennifer Welsh, *Chips & Pop: Decoding the Nexus Generation*. Toronto: Malcolm Lester Books, 1998.

30 See, for example, Long, 1997:11ff.

31 Two additional items that may be familiar to readers of the two earlier teen books, "your stereo" and "your own room," have not been included in this section. The importance of stereos seems to be encompassed in the item about music. Our 1992 and 2000 surveys documented the importance, especially among females, of their own rooms; we suspect that remains largely unchanged since 1984. Unfortunately we didn't include the item in the 1984 survey, and cannot show 1984-to-2000 comparisons. We don't think the rank-order of the existing items would be seriously altered.

32 Chris Zelkovich, "Baseball ratings drop across North America," *Toronto Star*, October 13, 2000.

33 Steve Simmons, "The last word," *Toronto Sun*, October 22, 2000.

34 "Young people pragmatic about future, says demographer," Canadian Press, January 2, 2000.

35 Sharon Begley, "A world of their own," *Newsweek*, May 8, 2000:56.

36 Reginald W. Bibby, *The Bibby Report*. Toronto: Stoddart, 1995, p. 95.

37 Cited in James Garbarino, *Raising Children in a Socially Toxic Environment*. San Francisco: Jossey-Bass, 1995, p. 38.

38 Long, 1997:45.

39 C. Wright Mills, *The Sociological Imagination*. New York: Oxford University Press, 1959.

40 Michael Adams, 1997.

41 See Wade Clark Roof, *A Generation of Seekers*. San Francisco: HarperCollins, 1993, and *Spiritual Marketplace: Baby Boomers and the Remaking of American Religion*. Princeton, N.J.: Princeton University Press, 1999.

42 Daniel J. Adams, 2000.

43 Arthur Levine, *When Dreams and Heroes Died*. San Francisco: Jossey-Bass, 1980, p. 105.

Chapter Six What Their Parents and Grandparents Were Like as Teenagers

1 See, for example, William Strauss and Neil Howe, *Generations*. New York: Quill, 1991.

2 James Garbarino, *Raising Children in a Socially Toxic Environment*. San Francisco, Jossey-Bass, 1995, p. 43.

3 Phil Lind, "The Cable TV Explosion," in Anna Porter and Marjorie Harris (eds.), *Farewell to the 70s*. Toronto: Thomas Nelson & Sons, 1979.

4 Strauss and Howe, 1991.

5 Garbarino, 1995, p. 1.

6 Adapted from J. David Hester, "Address to Alumni", Cumberland Presbyterian Church, Louisville, June 18, 1997. Hester's source is vague: in a magazine, "Household tips by Earlene" addressing, "Were you born before 1945?"

7 "Victim of bullying wants compensation," Canadian Press, Vancouver, September 12, 2000.

8 Reginald W. Bibby, *The Bibby Report*. Toronto: Stoddart, 1995, pp. 152–18.

9 Garbarino, 1995, p. 1.

10 D. Owen Carrigan, *Juvenile Delinquency in Canada: A History*. Toronto: Irwin, 1998, pp. 163–212.

12 Donna Leinwand, "20% say they used drugs with their mom or dad," *USA Today*, August 24, 2000.

13 Marc Eliany, "Alcohol and drug consumption among Canadian youth," *Canadian Social Trends*. Toronto: Thompson, 1994, pp. 385–88.

14 "Report on smoking prevalence," *The Daily*. Ottawa: Statistics Canada, February 16, 2000.

15 Canadian Health Survey, 1979, cited in Paul Whitehead, *Young Drinkers: A Review of Recent Canadian Studies*. Ottawa: Health Promotion Directorate, Health and Welfare, 1984.

16 Eliany, 1994, p. 386.

17 Gallup Canada, release of February 4, 1950.

18 Trend estimate provided by an AADAC official in conversation with the author, November 14, 2000.

19 "Recreational drug use down," Canadian Press, Toronto, August 8, 1992.

20 Gallup Canada, release of April 8, 1970.

21 See Bibby, 1995, pp. 69–70.

22 Carol Strike, "The incidence of sexually transmitted disease in Canada," *Canadian Social Trends*, 1990:79–82.

23 Gallup Canada, release of April 6, 1955.

24 Gallup Canada, release of March 30, 1955.

25 Gallup Canada, release of June 15, 1960.

26 Editorial, "Weighing in on David Wells," *Globe and Mail*, July 7, 2000.

27 Bill Kaufmann, "Rave hysteria amusing," *Calgary Sun*, June 5, 2000.

28 "Chat lines given teens a place to vent," Canadian Press, Halifax, January 4, 2001.

29 "General Social Survey: Time use," *The Daily*. Ottawa: Statistics Canada, November 8, 1999.

30 See, for example, Caroline Alphonso, "The death of the lunch hour." *Globe and Mail*, August 11, 2000.

31 Ron Stodghill II, "Where'd you learn that?" *Time*, June 15, 1998:38–45.

32 Douglas Coupland, *Life After God*. New York: Pocket Books, 1994, p. 359.

Chapter Seven How Today's Teenagers Are Going to Turn Out

1 Cited in Lorraine Gllenon (ed.), *The 20th Century: An Illustrated History of Our Lives and Times*. North Dighton, MA: JG Press, 2000, p. 345.

2 1 Corinthians 13:11, New Revised Standard Version.

3 David Matza, *Delinquency and Drift*. New York: John Wiley, 1964.

4 "All by Myself," Island Music Ltd., 1974.

5 Neil Howe and William Strauss, *Millennials Rising*. New York: Vintage Books, 2000, p. 6.

6 Howe and Strauss, 2000, pp. 7, 5, 307ff.

7 Howe and Strauss, 2000, p. 327.

8 Neil Howe and William Strauss, *The History of America's Future, 1584–2064*. New York: Morrow-Quill, 1991.

9 Karen S. Peterson, "Pessimism gives rise to generation vexed," *USA Today*, October 18, 2000.

10 Excerpted from Joan Sutton, "Love," in Anna Porter and Marjorie Harris (eds.), *Farewell to the '70s*. Toronto: Nelson, pp. 107–9.

11 In chapter 6, following the lead of many but certainly not all, I have pegged Xers as being born between 1965 and 1984 — literally 1965 to 1980 if referring, as I was in that context, to non-teen adults. Boomers are being seen as born between 1945 and 1964; consequently, a dividing point for "Younger Boomers" is around 1955, meaning they would have been approximately 21 to 30 in 1985 — essentially in their 20s.

12 "Breast implant gift sparks debate," Associated Press, London, January 4, 2001.

13 This is a preliminary figure. We are spending the early part of 2001 checking and cleaning panel matches.

14 We didn't ask the question in 1984 or in the adult survey in 1985; however, the special Project Teen Canada survey in 1987 found that 98% of young people 15 to 24 felt it was "very likely" (69%) or "fairly likely" (29%) they would "stay married or keep committed to the same person for life."

15 Myrna Kostash, *The Next Canada*. Toronto: McClelland & Stewart, 2000, p. 327.

16 Carol Gilligan, *In a Different Voice*. Cambridge, MA: Harvard University Press, 1982.

17 Sandra Martin, "Boys' own feminist crusader," *Globe and Mail*, June 17, 2000.

18 Christina Hoff Sommers. *The War Against Boys: How Misguided Feminism Is Harming Our Young Men*. New York: Simon & Schuster, 2000.

19 Walter Kirn, "Should you stay together for the kids?" *Time*, September 25, 2000:43–48.

20 Judith Wallerstein, Julia Lewis, and Sandra Balakeslee, *The Unexpected Legacy of Divorce: A 25 Year Landmark Study*. New York: Hyperion, 2000.

21 "Impact of parental divorce on adolescents," *The Daily*, Statistics Canada, June 9, 1999.

22 See, for example, S. Duncan, "Economic impact of divorce on childhood development," *Journal of Clinical Psychology* 23, 1994:444–57.

23 The sample of people from homes where parents were not together at 16 has also been weighted for age and gender to facilitate comparisons with the rest of the population.

Chapter Eight What Can Be Expected of Their Younger Brothers and Sisters

1 Neil Howe and William Strauss, *Millennials Rising*. New York: Vintage Books, 2000.

2 Andrew Clark, "How teens got the power." *Maclean's*, March 22, 1999:42–46.

3 *YTV Kid & Tween Report 2000*, Canadian Press, Toronto, October 25, 2000.

4 *YTV Kid & Tween Report 2000*, Canadian Press, Toronto, November 18, 2000.

5 Edna Gundersen, "Where will teen tastes land next?" *USA Today*, September 22, 2000.

6 David K. Foot with Daniel Stoffman, *Boom, Bust & Echo 2000*. Toronto: Macfarlane Walter & Ross, 1998, pp. 3, 30–31.

7 Foot and Stoffman, 1998, p. 122.

8 Foot and Stoffman, 1998, p. 195.

9 Foot and Stoffman, 1998, pp. 30–31.

10 Howe and Strauss, 2000, pp. 4, 8.

11 Howe and Strauss, 2000, p. 13.

12 Howe and Strauss, 2000, p. 250.

13 Howe and Strauss, 2000, p. 260.

14 Howe and Strauss, 2000, p. 16.

15 Howe and Strauss, 2000, p. 17.

16 Howe and Strauss, 2000, p. 12.

17 Howe and Strauss, 2000, p. 5.

18 Howe and Strauss, 2000, p. 17.

19 Deborah Jones, "Here comes the Sunshine Generation." *Globe and Mail*, May 10, 1997.

20 James E. Côté and Anton Allahar, *Generation on Hold*. New York: New York University Press, 1996, p. 119.

Conclusion What's All the Fuss About?

1 "Crime statistics," *The Daily*. Ottawa: Statistics Canada, July 18, 2000, p. 5.

2 Data cited in Howe and Strauss, 2000, pp. 206–9.

3 Quoted in "Youth not so bad, study says," Canadian Press, Brandon, Manitoba, November 18, 1999.

4 Jenefer Curtis, "The business of ethics," *Globe and Mail*, August 21, 1999.

5 "Teenage pregnancy," *The Daily*. Ottawa: Statistics Canada, October 20, 2000.

6 In the Project Canada 2000 survey, about 55% of women indicated there is an area within a kilometre of their homes where they would be afraid to walk alone at night; just 18% of men indicated similar apprehension. Those levels have remained almost unchanged from those found in the first Project Canada survey in 1975 (women 60%, men 21%).

7 Thanks to Kelly Cardwell of the University of Lethbridge for her input.

8 Christina Hoff Sommers, *The War Against Boys: How Misguided Feminism Is Harming Our Young Men*. New York: Simon & Schuster, 2000.

9 Robert Fulford, *Toronto Star*, January 25, 1967. This and the second quote are both cited in John Robert Colombo, *New Canadian Quotations*, Edmonton: Hurtig, 1987, p. 144.

Index

Copyright Acknowledgements

THE AUTHOR EXPRESSES HIS GRATITUDE TO THE FOLLOWING FOR permission to reprint previously published material. Every effort has been made to obtain applicable copyright information. Please notify the publisher of any errors or omissions. All rights reserved.

"An aberration or a peek at the future?" by Doug Saunders and "Values, music and the Internet" by Matthew Ingram reprinted with permission of *The Globe and Mail.*

"Beavis and Butthead: No Future for Postmodern Youth," by Stephen Best and Douglas Kellner, in Jonathon S. Epstein (ed.), *Youth Culture: Identity in a Postmodern World* reprinted with permission of Blackwell Publishers.

"'Brady Bunch' ideal simply unrealistic," "Canadians celebrate from coast to coast," "Canadians literally sick of unity squabble," "Children are scared of nuclear war," "Dale Lang prays for peace," "The demolition of an orphanage," "Jackson clears air on sexuality," "Jobless rate at seven-year high," "A much rarer story," "Rapper beats rap," and "Young Roman Catholics in the millions" reprinted with permission of the Canadian Press.

"The cable TV explosion of the '70s" by Phil Lind reprinted with his permission.